lewis green

THE GOLD HUST

A. N. C. Treadgold, age 86, en route to the Law Courts, London, in June 1950 for his action against The Yukon Consolidated Gold Corporation Limited. Since 1898 he had schemed to consolidate Klondike gold mining under his control, eventually succeeding, only to lose everything in an involved court action.

KEYSTONE PRESS AGENCY, INC.

LERS

ALASKA NORTHWEST PUBLISHING COMPANY
Anchorage, Alaska

Library of Congress cataloging in publication data:

Green, Lewis, 1925-
    The gold hustlers.
    Bibliography: p.
    Includes index.
    1. Klondike gold fields.   2. Treadgold, Arthur
Newton Christian, 1863-1951.   3. Mining engineers—
Yukon Territory—Biography.   4. Yukon Territory—
Biography.   I. Title.
F1095.K5G73   971.9'1'020924 [B]   77-7341
ISBN 0-88240-088-6

Design by Hilber Nelson

Alaska Northwest Publishing Company
Box 4-EEE, Anchorage, Alaska 99509
Printed in U.S.A.

To the Klondikers
and their dreams

Contents

Preface

As the summer visitor approaches Dawson on the gravel road from Whitehorse, little is seen of placer mining until the road passes onto the dredge tailings near the mouth of Hunker Creek, about 10 miles east of Dawson. Unexpectedly, an open wooded valley with scattered bright green fields turns into a wasteland, covered with crescent-shaped mounds of coarse river gravels. Closer to Dawson there are glimpses of workings on the hillsides, several hundred feet above the valley floor, and huge fans of white tailings spreading below them. Later, the visitor who stays long enough to visit the creeks will see many miles of dredge tailings, more gravel fans, abandoned dredges and company camps and here and there a small mining operation. To those preoccupied with the preservation of the environment much of what they see is a glaring example of the damage man is capable of inflicting on a primeval landscape. That may be true, but the present day observer should realize that much of the preparatory work, including moving the material for the dredges to the construction sites, was done using little more than the muscles of men and horses. What was accomplished, considering the simple machinery available, the distance from the factories, the uncertainties of transportation and the never-ending struggle against the underlying permafrost, is a monument to man's ingenuity.

There are colossal engineering works that the casual visitor will not see. They include a seventy-mile ditch and pipeline—used to bring water for mining from the Tombstone Range about thirty miles northeast of Dawson—two hydroelectric power plants, a thermal power plant and hundreds of miles of hand-cleared line, cut for the powerlines that lead to the many dredges and pumping plants. The water system and the power plants are now abandoned.

In Dawson, stories are still told of the Guggenheims ("Guggs"), Joe Boyle and A.N.C. Treadgold and of the legal battles as each attempted to build his own placer empire. The main mining in the Klondike took seventy years, from 16 August 1896, the

day gold was discovered on Bonanza Creek, to 15
November 1966, the day the last gold dredge shut down.

The Klondike story has two parts. The first is
the gold rush itself, culminating in the summer of 1898
when close to 30,000 stampeders reached the Klondike
and gold production was increasing at an incredible
rate. Much has been written of the struggle to reach the
Klondike and of Dawson where miners went through
their pokes with the help of the girls and the gamblers.

The second part of the story is the battle of
businessmen for control of the Klondike. It began
during the rush as some individuals, sensing that the
richer ground would be mined out in a few years,
schemed to acquire larger blocks of ground for the
second phase of the mining certain to follow. At the
time, they had not even determined the form that the
large-scale mining would take. Hydraulic mining was
one possibility, but it would require an extensive scheme
to bring in the needed water. Dredging was another
possibility; the technique had been developed in New
Zealand a few years before, but it was still relatively
primitive.

The story I have attempted to reconstruct is
this second part of the story, the battle for control. In it,
two contrasting groups of men played a part. First were
the promoters, who were responsible for consolidating
the huge blocks of ground needed for large-scale
mining; later came the engineers, who attempted to turn
the promoters' dream into a workable operation. Each
group made its contribution, and the story can only be
told with reference to both.

A.N.C. Treadgold, an Oxford-educated
Englishman, was the principal promoter, involved in
attempts to corner the Klondike gold field from 1898
until his death in 1951. Successful at times, his schemes
were doomed by his insistence on managing the
operations personally. After each defeat, Treadgold,
apparently undaunted, would raise more money and
begin to build anew. The apparent ease with which he
did it is difficult to understand. Physically, he was
unimpressive, but one who knew him well claimed that

on hearing Treadgold's voice carrying from another room he could visualize a speaker eight feet tall. Others, less charitable, suggest that he succeeded through sheer persistence. Whatever his secret, it seldom failed him. Even when his backers closed in on him, demanding an accounting, he could put them off and, at times, even wheedle more money from them. His contribution, using others' money, was to put together the ground needed and to build the North Fork power plant, both vital to later mining operations. The losers were his English backers, left with little to show for their money.

Joe Boyle (Joseph Whiteside Boyle), the second promoter, is more readily understood. Popular, physically powerful and unafraid of anything on earth, he parlayed a government concession in the Klondike River valley into a placer empire that included four dredges (three of them among the largest in the world at the time) and an efficient power plant to run them. Much of the money—and the power plant itself—came from Granville Mining, an English company promoted by Treadgold. But Boyle was in full control of his operation; he ran the enterprise as his own, and it would be ten years until there was a final accounting. Treadgold, already well aware of the difficulties of dealing with Boyle, had been outmaneuvered in his plan to control the Klondike.

The engineers, in contrast to the promoters, worked quietly in their attempts to build a profitable operation. Most were young Americans brought in when the Guggenheims took over Treadgold's consolidation on Bonanza and Eldorado creeks in 1906. Years later, one of these engineers, W.H.S. McFarland, returned to build a profitable enterprise that encompassed the entire Klondike and lasted from 1934 until dredging ended in 1966.

Dawson and the Klondike began a long period of decline soon after gold production peaked in 1900. As world-wide interest in the Klondike waned, the shrinking community turned inward, living in the past, and became increasingly indifferent to events Outside, as the rest of the world was known. The isolation was always there. Communications were slow until an all-weather road reached Dawson in the early 1950s and a telephone line about ten years later. Attempts to float new Klondike enterprises were greeted with increasing condescension. Granted many of the schemes were totally impractical, and, besides, no Outsider could be expected to understand the problems of operating in the Klondike. A disgruntled correspondent tried to explain this to the backer of a faltering company:

"And in so far as the question of mismanagement is concerned . . . you can be absolutely certain of this. That so long as Home authorities continue to supply their managers from the London end, just so long will they continue to suffer in a similar degree to mismanagement. The reason is obvious. Dawson people and Yukon conditions in every respect are so vastly different from what are to be found in any other part of the world, that one coming direct from the old country does not awake to a full realization of the situation until he has resided here for at least a year or more—or in other words until it is too late. "[1]

Much of the mining history is drawn from the Dawson newspapers, fortunately preserved and now available on microfilm, and from the many technical and semitechnical articles on company operations. In addition, there is an intriguing oral history, full of humor, for the period from about 1910 on. Over the past twenty years I have heard many of the stories, often second-hand; now, with the help of written sources, I am able to confirm some of them and fit them into the mosaic. Some are recorded in the newspapers, but others are one person's recollection of an incident.

At one point I telephoned a former Dawson resident who had been involved with the Klondike dredging for more than sixty years. At first he was reluctant to talk, saying that it was all in the past and of little interest to anyone still alive. But gradually he warmed to the subject, and, near the end of a long conversation over some of the dealings, he exploded with: *"Scalawags! Scalawags! Should have been in jail! Scalawags! Scalawags!"* He was speaking figuratively, but still it is true that many fortunes were lost and countless bills were left unpaid. Those responsible were the promoters, men who were oblivious of the standards that most men either attempt (or are forced) to follow in their business dealings. Entranced by their dreams as moths are by a light, they were convinced that personal success lay just ahead. Once it was attained there would be plenty for all, but, until then, why wreck everything for want of a few dollars? After all, no one had forced their backers to support them. Quite the opposite. The backers had glimpsed the promoters' dreams and built their own dreams on it.

One must appreciate the intoxication that a handful of placer nuggets can induce. Under such an influence, who can hope to sort out truth, misrepresentation and falsehood?

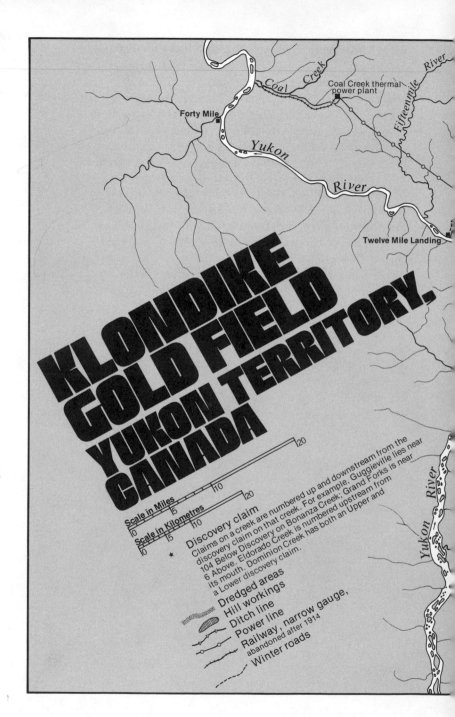

Coal Creek

Coal Creek thermal
power plant

Forty Mile

Fifteenmile River

Yukon

River

Twelve Mile Landing

KLONDIKE
GOLD FIELD
YUKON TERRITORY,
CANADA

Yukon River

Scale in Miles
0 5 10 20

Scale in Kilometres
0 5 10

Discovery claim
Claims on a creek are numbered up and downstream from the
discovery claim on that creek. For example, Guggieville lies near
104 Below Discovery on Bonanza Creek; Grand Forks is near
6 Above. Eldorado Creek is numbered upstream from
its mouth. Dominion Creek has both an Upper and
a Lower discovery claim.

Dredged areas
Hill workings
Ditch line
Power line
Railway, narrow gauge,
abandoned after 1914
Winter roads

xiv

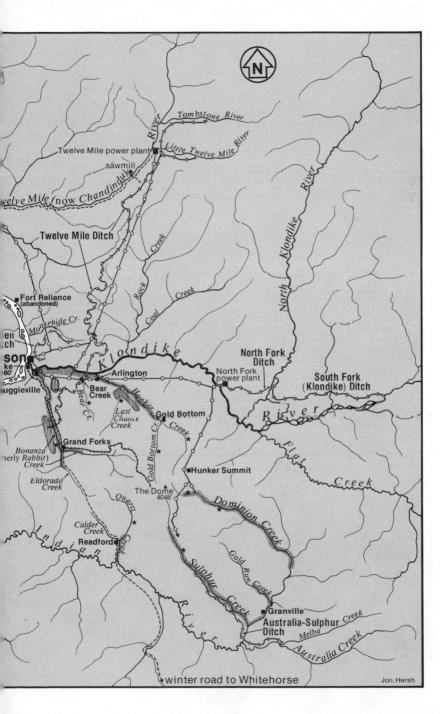

N

Tombstone River

River

Little Twelve Mile River

Twelve Mile power plant

sawmill

Twelve Mile (now Chandindu)

Twelve Mile Ditch

North Klondike River

Creek

Rock

Coal

Creek

Fort Reliance
(abandoned)

Moosehide Cr.

en
.ch

son
ke
80'

Klondike

Arlington

North Fork
power plant

North Fork
Ditch

South Fork
(Klondike) Ditch

uggieville

Bear Cr.

Bear
Creek

Hunker

Last
Chance
Creek

Gold Bottom

River

Gold Bottom Cr.

Creek

Grand Forks

Bonanza
merly Rabbit)
Creek

Hunker Summit

Flat

Eldorado
Creek

Quartz

The Dome
4048'

Dominion Creek

Creek

Indian

Calder
Creek

Readford

Sulphur Creek

Gold Run Creek

Granville

Australia-Sulphur Creek
Ditch

Melba

River

Australia Creek

winter road to Whitehorse

Jon.Hersh

xv

The Klondike discovery could have come many years before 16 August 1896, the day George Carmack's party found coarse gold in the gravels of Rabbit Creek. For more than twenty years, restless men advancing from northern British Columbia and the lower Yukon River area had been testing the creeks of Yukon and Alaska for placer gold. In late August 1874, Jack McQuesten had established a trading post at Fort Reliance,[1] about seven miles downstream from the mouth of the Klondike or Trundeck River as he knew it. The post became the reference point for this part of the Yukon River and many tributary streams such as the Fortymile and Sixtymile rivers were named from the approximate distances down- and upstream, respectively. Working from Fort Reliance, McQuesten and his partners, Arthur Harper and Al Mayo, had prospected and found traces of gold in a vast area that included the Fortymile and Sixtymile gold fields. Somehow, the Klondike had been missed although McQuesten had tested the creeks behind Fort Reliance where, "I found colors but did not find anything that would pay to work."[2]

1

In 1885, fine gold was discovered on the bars of the Stewart River;[3] about $100,000 was taken from them in 1885 and 1886 but the bars were deserted the following year after discovery of coarse gold on the Fortymile River. In 1887 and 1888, between 100 and 350 miners were at work on the Fortymile; production was about $100,000 in 1887, falling to $20,000 in 1888 because of continued high water throughout the summer. The town of Forty Mile grew at the mouth of the river, supplied by sternwheelers operating from St. Michael on Norton Sound, a distance of about 1,600 miles away on the lower Yukon River. Later, more promising discoveries were made upstream on the Fortymile, on the Alaska side, and, in 1892, the Sixtymile gold field was rediscovered by prospectors who crossed the divide between the two watersheds.[4] Gold production increased slowly and there was always the hope that richer deposits, as yet undiscovered, lay somewhere in the area.

When George Carmack and his party reached Forty Mile about 21 August 1896,[5] those who saw the gold he shook from a brass Winchester cartridge case knew from its appearance that it was not from any of the placer diggings they were familiar with. Some scoffed, but others stampeded to the new discovery, hoping that this was the El Dorado they had been waiting for. Gold, if it was there in paying quantities, would lie on bedrock beneath a cover of permanently frozen black muck and gravel, probably ten feet or more thick, and testing would have to wait until winter when the surface water had frozen. However, if Carmack, no miner, could find coarse gold in the stream gravel there was almost certain to be pay on bedrock.

Events were moving swiftly. On 22 August 1896, before the Forty Mile stampeders arrived, twenty-five men (some of whom had staked before learning of Carmack's discovery) held a miners' meeting on the new creek.[6] At it, they resolved, among other things, that henceforth the name should be Bonanza Creek, a more fitting name than Rabbit Creek. One of the last in the area to learn of the new find was Robert Henderson, whose earlier discovery on Gold Bottom Creek, some ten miles to the east, had brought many of those at the miners' meeting to the Klondike. Late in July, Henderson, en route to his ground, had stopped in at the camp at the mouth of the Klondike River, told Carmack of his find and invited him to stake. Carmack arrived at Henderson's camp on Gold Bottom a few weeks later with two Indians,

Skookum Jim and Tagish Charlie. They were completely out of tobacco and nearly out of grub; Henderson, perhaps because of his dislike of Indians, refused to sell them any. The group left soon after without bothering to stake. Their new find was made on their return journey, close by the spot where Skookum Jim had shot a moose. No one took the news to Henderson, although it was his understanding that Carmack had promised to let him know if they found anything better than his Gold Bottom ground. By now, there was no ground left for Henderson to stake on Bonanza and, if that were not enough, Andy Hunker had already been granted a claim on the other fork of his creek, now officially named Hunker Creek. At Forty Mile, Henderson was allowed to record a single claim, close to Hunker's discovery claim. Years later, the Canadian government would award Henderson a pension of $200 a month for his part in the discovery of the Klondike. Until the early 1920s, however, he was still searching the Yukon creeks and hills for the bonanza that would forever elude him. [7]

During the winter of 1896-1897, many of those lucky enough to hold claims were at work testing their ground. Shafts were sunk; the permanently frozen muck and gravel were heated by fires lighted at the bottom of the shaft; and the thawed material was hoisted by hand-operated windlass ("Armstrong hoist") after the smoke had cleared. Once the lightly-timbered shafts reached bedrock, tunnels were driven beneath the main channel of the creek by the same method. Some claims proved rich almost from the beginning, but many others were given up or sold after preliminary work proved discouraging. Once a paystreak was located, about four feet of gravel and broken bedrock, carrying the bulk of the gold, was hoisted to a dump on surface for sluicing once water was available in the spring. Values in the hoisted material were checked by constant test-panning, and the more fortunate claim-holders marvelled at the wealth in their growing dumps. By now, those in the Klondike knew that the richest field of all had been found in the search that had led north from California in the 1840s, the Cariboo in the 1860s, and the Omineca and the Cassiar in the 1870s. Perhaps there were other discoveries to be made but would they lie close to the Klondike or somewhere else in the vast, poorly-explored, area that surrounded them?

In September 1896, the Canadian government was

3

Underground mining at 16 Eldorado Creek. The paydirt, consisting of the lower gravel and broken bedrock, was thawed by fires or steam points and then hoisted to the surface for sluicing.

represented in the Yukon by the North-West Mounted Police detachment stationed at Fort Constantine, across the river from Forty Mile, and by William Ogilvie, a government surveyor. Ogilvie, first in the Yukon in 1887-1888, had returned in the summer of 1895 to fix the location of the international boundary at the point where it crossed the Yukon River about ninety miles downstream from Dawson. The task was completed in mid-April 1896 but his departure had been delayed by conflicting orders and later by weather. Early in January 1897, Ogilvie laid out the new townsite of Dawson, staked by Joe Ladue in September 1896. Later, on a petition from the claim owners, Ogilvie surveyed the claims on Bonanza and Eldorado creeks. All was confusion on Bonanza Creek after the miners' meeting on 22 August 1896 had agreed to adjust the claim boundaries. The adjusters, using a piece of rope about fifty feet long as their measure, had covered fifty claims in an afternoon, removing and defacing the original posts as they went. The result was that no one was certain where their ground lay and eventually, despite some wild and woolly talk,[8] all agreed to accept Ogilvie's survey based on the original staking.

Increasingly aware of the potential of the Klondike, Ogilvie had done his best to send word of the strike to the Outside. In November 1896, he sent out a short report, giving the limited information then available, with Captain Moore, who was

4

en route to Juneau. Later, in January 1897, he was able to send word with two separate parties attempting the difficult trip that "The new camp gave much promise of being the greatest yet established in the territory and probably would prove world-startling."⁹ The next opportunity to send word came in mid-June 1897, when he met two men travelling light who waited while Ogilvie sat on the river bank and wrote a brief letter to the Minister of the Interior, informing him that the camp had lived up to expectations and that output for the season would be about $2½ million. Others had sent word Outside as well. Ogilvie had been in Dawson on 16 May 1897, the day the river opened, and an estimated 200 boats reached Dawson.

Despite earlier reports, the main Klondike excitement began soon after two ships, the *Excelsior* and the *Portland,* made their way south from St. Michael in the summer of 1897. The *Excelsior* reached San Francisco in mid-July and the *Portland* was in Seattle two days later. Both carried returning Klondikers bringing the gold they had washed that spring, and a press report that the *Portland* had a ton of gold aboard electrified the world.

The news came at a time of crippling depression. This might be the opportunity to start again, and men flocked from all over the world to the new El Dorado. Many were Americans, and the cities of San Francisco and Seattle were crowded with men impatient to head north. In Canada, others left from Victoria and the new city of Vancouver (incorporated in 1886). Few in the rush had any idea of the equipment and food required; various guidebooks, some accurate and useful, others misleading and irrelevant, flooded the market. Men started north with horses, dogs and even goats, reasoning that the latter could be used as meat at the end of the long journey. Most would travel over the Chilkoot or White passes at the head of Lynn Canal but there were many other routes, both by water and overland, and each had its boosters. Many of the boosters were concerned only with the business that a host of stampeders could bring to their community.

By early 1898 each man crossing the divide into Canadian territory was required to bring a year's supplies with him,¹⁰ and all through the winter unending lines of men were relaying their supplies to the North-West Mounted Police posts at the passes. There the supplies would be checked and customs duties paid before the stampeders were given permission to

5

proceed. Once across the pass, supplies were relayed to Lake Lindeman or Lake Bennett, where boats and rafts were built in readiness for the opening of the Yukon River. On 8 June 1898, boats of the main rush began arriving in Dawson.

Although most of the stampeders dreamt of mining gold from their own claim in the Klondike, the horde also included merchants, professional people and government personnel, together with the hangers-on who were parasitic on the rest. A city was already growing at Dawson. During the summer of 1898 it had a population of 25,000,[11] larger than anything west of Winnipeg. In the winter, fires were a constant threat, but after each one the buildings would be quickly rebuilt using local green lumber. The townsite was underlain by permafrost; in summer the streets were a morass of mud. The new community required transportation and communications with the rest of the world, and there was a new rush to supply them.

Boats were needed on the Yukon River. Many were built on the West Coast and either towed or travelled under their own steam on the long ocean trip to the mouth of the Yukon River. In Seattle, the Moran shipyard built twelve "by the mile and cut them off when necessary";[12] all but one reached the Yukon River safely, paying for themselves on their first voyage. Other boats were assembled at Bennett and Lake Lindeman after parts and machinery had been worried over the passes. At Skagway in May 1898, work began on the narrow-gauge White Pass railroad. The steel reached Lake Bennett, head of navigation on the Yukon River system, in June 1899. By the end of July 1900 the railroad was completed to Whitehorse. Here, below the Whitehorse Rapids, the last serious obstacle to river navigation, the trains made contact with the growing river fleets of the White Pass's own BYN Company and the independents. In 1902, a winter road was completed between Whitehorse and Dawson, about 333 miles;[13] horse-drawn sleighs, operating between roadhouses about twenty miles apart, made the trip in five days.

Communications with the Outside were slow and difficult, but this was partially overcome when a government telegraph line, about 600 miles long, was completed on 29 September 1899 from Dawson to Bennett on the White Pass railroad.[14] The line followed the Yukon River and was completed in 133 days; it consisted of a single strand of iron wire strung mainly between insulators on trees. Now messages could be sent to Skagway and thence carried by ship to Vancouver or Seattle for transmission to their destination. Later, on 24 September 1901, about 1,200 miles of land line, running through the mountains east of the Alaskan panhandle, was completed;[15] thus, was the Yukon system joined to the Canadian Pacific Railway's telegraph line at Ashcroft in southern British Columbia.

Newspapers thrived in the new community. First to appear was the *Klondike Nugget* on 29 May 1898. For the moment it was a typed copy; Gene Allen, the publisher, had left his press behind in the rush to beat the rival *Yukon Sun.* Later, as the community shrank, both papers and a number of later ones would go to the wall, leaving only the *Dawson Daily News;* the *Daily News* was first published on 31 July 1899 and continued until 1954. Other communities, including Atlin, Bennett, Dyea, Skagway and Whitehorse, also had their own newspapers, most for only a brief period during the early years. Initially, all carried local news plus weeks-old Outside news gleaned from any source available. Later generous amounts of both telegraphed news and boilerplate were added to their offerings.

In June 1898, the Yukon Territory was established under the control of the Department of the Interior of the federal government in Ottawa. All ties to the Northwest Territories and its government at Regina were severed. The first of the new government representatives, Thomas Fawcett, Gold Commissioner and Land Agent, arrived in Dawson in mid-June 1897,[16] about a month before Ogilvie's departure. Fawcett did his best to cope with the rush and, as the excitement grew, plans were made to send in more personnel. Major Walsh, formerly with the North-West Mounted Police, was appointed Commissioner of the Yukon Territory; he and his staff came in over the Chilkoot Pass in the fall of 1897. Clifford Sifton, the all-powerful Minister of the Interior, anxious to see the country for himself, accompanied the government party as far as Tagish Post in southern Yukon. Most of the party reached Dawson early in 1898 but Walsh, perhaps overwhelmed by the task ahead of him, wintered along the route and did not reach Dawson until 21 May 1898, by which time he had already decided to resign. Following Walsh's resignation, William Ogilvie was appointed Commissioner and returned to Dawson in September 1898. By now the community was in a ferment over staking on Dominion Creek and charges that many of the new government officials had profited through

The winter stage from Dawson to Whitehorse. Operating between roadhouses about twenty miles apart, the stage took five days or more to make the trip, depending on the weather and snow conditions.

their positions. Early in 1899, an ineffectual investigation of the charges by Ogilvie simply added to the discontent.[17]

Mining had increased rapidly during the winter of 1897-1898, and sluicing in the coming spring would see gold production jump to an estimated $10 million, four times that of 1897. Surprisingly, the next major find was not on some distant creek but on the hillsides above Bonanza, Eldorado and Hunker creeks. Claim owners, busy working their ground, had ignored the cheechakos, or newcomers, who, left with nowhere else to prospect, had been grubbing on the hillsides since the autumn of 1897. Suddenly, after four separate discoveries had been made, it was realized that a rich paystreak lay at the base of gravel deposits that were found on the hillsides 150 to 300 feet above the creek bottoms. At some earlier time, the White Channel Gravels, as they were known—up to 150 feet thick and composed mainly of boulders and pebbles of white vein quartz cemented by a matrix of white mica and tiny quartz grains—had filled the valleys.[18] Later, perhaps a million or more years ago, the entire region had been uplifted and the creeks had eroded through the White Channel Gravels to a new base level far beneath them. Remnants of the

YUKON ARCHIVES, MARTHA L. BLACK COLLECTION

White Channel Gravels perched on the west side of Hunker Creek and on the west side of Eldorado and Bonanza creeks to about 44 Below; near the mouth of Bonanza Creek, they formed much of the ridge between that creek and the Klondike River valley. The best pay on the creek claims was found where the White Channel Gravels had been eroded, and it was soon realized that most of the values found in the present-day creeks had come from the reworking of the eroded White Channel paystreak. New mining claims blanketed the hillsides months before the stampeders reached Dawson in 1898.

Most would-be miners dreamt only of owning a single rich claim, but others had more ambitious plans. Originally each miner was permitted to stake one claim per creek but there was no restriction on acquiring additional claims either by purchase or after abandonment. Soon entrepreneurs were buying claims to work either as a block or on a lay basis. In the latter, the layman would mine the claim and the gold return would be divided with the owner on an agreed basis. Most spectacular of these was Big Alex McDonald who at one time held many claims. In addition he had branched out into many other ventures all of which seemed to promise instant success. But early in 1909, his fortune gone, he died of a heart attack while sawing wood in front of a miner's cabin, miles from the main creeks of the Klondike.[19] Others were successful; some of the larger operations had crews of one hundred men or more. In addition, mining schemes had been touted throughout the world but, in most cases, the hapless shareholders, far from the Klondike, received nothing but glowing reports right up to the moment they were forced to step in and salvage what little they could from the wreckage of their company.

Mining methods were changing. It was soon realized that claims where the bedrock lay within fifteen feet of the surface could best be mined by open cut methods. Underground mining had been improved by the accidental discovery of steam thawing in the winter of 1898-1899.[20] The technique was discovered when a leaking hose and pipe used to steam clean boiler flues were left lying on the ground outside a boiler room. The discovery led to the development of the steam point, a heavy, hammer-driven steel pipe six to eight feet long with two steam outlets at the tip; steam was fed in through a rubber hose connected to a nipple on the side of the driving head. Another important innovation was the steam-operated self-dumper, designed so that a bucket holding three wheelbarrow loads could be hoisted from the shaft, carried laterally and tripped automatically onto a dump where it would be ready for sluicing. For surface mining, the self-dumper replaced the hand-operated windlass and wheelbarrows, but underground mining still required a brutal physical effort.

A crew of six miners would tunnel out seventy-five feet from the bottom of a shaft. Working stooped over, each miner was required to deliver a wheelbarrow load of gravel and broken bedrock to the shaft every six minutes, ten hours a day, seven days a week throughout the operating season. A crew of twelve men working with steam points, a self-dumper and a steam-driven pump to deliver water to the sluice boxes could thaw, mine, hoist and sluice fifteen cubic yards of pay-dirt in a ten-hour shift.[21] With wages for each man about one dollar an hour, only rich ground could be handled by this method.

The bench and hillside workings presented different problems. Little water was available at higher elevations, and attempts to pump water from the main creeks had failed due to high operating costs. Even where water was available, it was necessary to build extensive log cribs to stop the tailings from encroaching on the creek claims below. As work on the high level deposits increased, the disputes and legal problems over water and dumping rights rose in proportion.

Some of the larger creeks tributary to Bonanza Creek carried heavy runoffs in the spring. If this water could be impounded towards the headwaters, ditch and flume systems could bring it to the workings in the White Channel Gravels at sufficient head for hydraulicking. Before long, a number of companies were attempting to consolidate the ground needed to make such an installation economically feasible. Operators who were unable to obtain water rights, often used tramways to carry the pay-dirt down to the main creeks where water was available for sluicing.

The first gold dredge in the Yukon had been installed on Cassiar Bar on the Yukon River, about seventy-five miles north of Whitehorse, in September 1899 by McPherson and Hines, operating as the Lewes River Mining and Dredging Company.[22] The steam-driven dredge, built by the Risdon Iron Works of San Francisco, had buckets with a capacity of $3\frac{1}{4}$ cubic feet. Results during the summer of 1900 were disappointing, and in June 1901 the dredge was brought downriver to Dawson with the intention of either selling it or returning it to the builders. J. Moore Elmer, manager since 1899, arranged for the dredge to be moved to 42 Below on Bonanza Creek where it was operated on a lay basis, with half the gold recovered going to the claim owners. Two years later, in 1903, it was moved to the Discovery group of claims, now held by the dredge owners. Though of primitive design, it proved that dredging was practical in the Klondike and was the forerunner of the fleets of dredges that would systematically tear up the main creeks of the Klondike in the years to come.

Dawson, once the town where wealthy miners caroused and legends were made, was disappearing, gradually replaced by the Golden Metropolis of the North, an incorporated city for a few years. Gold was still pouring in from the creeks; no one will ever know the exact amount since there was a royalty to be evaded if possible, but the Gold Commissioner estimated the output at $10 million in 1898,[23] increasing to $24 million in 1900 and then beginning a gradual decline as the rich ground on Bonanza and Eldorado creeks was mined out. The $24 million was a huge sum in a year when Canada's federal budget was well under $60

Top—Rocking on Gold Hill, across from Grand Forks, in 1899. Rockers were used rather than sluices because water was scarce then, and with rockers most of the water could be saved and recirculated.

Bottom—Mining using a self-dumper. The steam-operated device replaced the hand-operated windlass, called "the Armstrong Hoist."

Top—Shovelling-in. Paydirt mined during the winter was sluiced as soon as water was available in the spring.

Bottom—The first dredge in the Klondike, operating on the Discovery claims on Bonanza Creek, about 1905. Built on Cassiar Bar near Whitehorse in 1899, the dredge was moved to the Klondike during the summer of 1901. Steam-operated, she burned three cords of wood per day. The cribbing in the background restrains tailings from hydraulic mining of the White Channel Gravels on Cheechako Hill.

Left—A timber-cribbed mine shaft used in early deep mining on a Dominion Creek bench. The shaft, buried for many years, was exposed in 1963 during a test, carried out by Ballarat Mines, Limited, of the use of irrigation sprinklers for stripping muck.

Right—Cold water thawing in advance of dredging. Point drivers have driven the hydraulic points to bedrock; a point doctor has taken over to ensure that the thaw is complete. By kinking the rubber hose supplying the point and listening to the sound, the point doctor can determine whether the point is operating properly.

million. The change brought a veneer of respectability that would soon see gambling prohibited, the dancehalls closed and the prostitutes and their cribs relocated across the Klondike River in Klondike City, better known as Lousetown. The population soon fell to about 10,000, less than half that of the summer of 1898, but many, for the moment at least, considered themselves permanent residents; others waited impatiently to join the next big rush. By late 1899, the cheechakos had taken over; moccasins and flannel shirts were out and a Vigilance Committee of six women, who seemed to know everything about everybody, ruled on the suitability of applicants for tickets to the St. Andrew's ball.[24] By now, most of Dawson's early buildings were gone, either replaced or lost in disastrous fires, the worst of which took 117 buildings on 26 April 1899.[25] New, more substantial wooden buildings replaced them, including the government's post office, administration building, court house and commissioner's residence. But, in one way, even the new buildings were temporary, betrayed by the permanently frozen black muck with ice wedges that underlies most of Dawson. The permafrost was too thick to penetrate, and most of the buildings rested on mud sills of heavy timber set in the frozen ground. Every few years, each building would have to be levelled using jacks, wedges and blocks as the ground beneath thawed unevenly. If neglected, the building would soon be leaning drunkenly, often damaged beyond repair.

In those first years, many in the Klondike had acquired great wealth, but many more had seen their dreams fail to materialize. A few had dreamt of controlling the heart of the Klondike but none would come so close to achieving it as a diminutive Englishman, A.N.C. Treadgold. Beginning in 1898, Treadgold had come to the Klondike each summer, preparing to make his move once the present claim owners had finished mining and were ready to sell out or abandon their ground. His main interest was in the mines in the high-level White Channel Gravels. Many of these had been worked underground and the pay-dirt trammed to the creek bottom where water was available for sluicing. No matter how carefully the mining had been done, gold was certain to remain in the pillars of frozen gravel left to support the workings and in sections too low-grade to be mined undergound. If he controlled most of the properties, water could be brought to the hillsides under pressure and the White Channel Gravels, often up to 150 feet thick, washed down by hydraulic monitors. There were also the creek claims. Some of the richer ones had already been mined three times, once by underground methods and twice by open cuts, but some gold still remained, either missed during the earlier mining or in lower grade sections beyond the open cuts. Treadgold was never seen in the saloons where most of the miners did their business.[26] Instead, he worked quietly behind the scenes. He had already secured the three main elements for his scheme: financial backing in England, the blessing of Clifford Sifton, Minister of the Interior, and possession of the key claims needed to hold the huge fans of tailings that would build up once hydraulicking of the White Channel Gravels was underway.

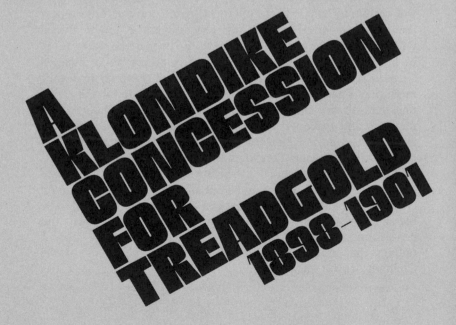

Even before the Carmack party made their discovery on Bonanza Creek (16 August 1896), there had been regulations governing the staking of placer claims. True, there had been problems, but most had arisen when the regulations were set aside—when an area was withdrawn from staking and later reopened.[1] In contrast, little, if anything, had been done in preparation for handling the applications for licences, franchises and concessions for enterprises such as utilities, railways, bridges and other services that would be needed in the growing mining camp. For the moment, decisions on such matters were made in the offices of the Department of the Interior in Ottawa, many by Clifford Sifton himself. No guidelines had been given to the government employees in the Yukon, and many were involved, either directly or as silent partners, in the blizzard of requests to Ottawa.

One request, made by Robert Anderson of London, differed in that it dealt with a lease, rather than a claim, on placer ground. Anderson wrote to Gold Commissioner Fawcett on 2

September 1897, asking to lease about 2½ miles of ground on Hunker Creek between Last Chance Creek and the mouth, stating that the ground in question was too wide to search for a pay streak and that he proposed to mine it using hydraulic methods. Impressed by the proposal, Fawcett had written a covering letter to Sifton endorsing the request and had given both letters to Anderson to take to Ottawa. Then, acting on his own initiative, Fawcett had closed the ground to staking. Two years later, the *Klondike Nugget* had published what it claimed was a letter to a miner who had tried to stake a claim covering 250 feet of the ground in question:

"Dawson, 5th Dec. '97

"Sir: The ground you are applying for was staked by Mr. Anderson in Aug. last—he having first obtained my permission, which permission was not granted until I had talked the matter over with miners who knew the country and assured me it was not a locality suitable for mining by the ordinary methods of drifting and could only be worked to advantage by the aid of machinery. His application was taken to Ottawa by himself, together with my recommendation to the Minister of the Interior—also of my intention to hold the ground until such time as a decision had been arrived at in regard to the problem at issue—which is—as to whether the Mining Regulations will be amended so as to admit of claims being acquired direct from the gov't or whether it will remain as at present—& capitalists . . . will have to gather a number of loafers take them to the ground practically useless for gumboot mining— . . . and acquire the ground in that irregular manner. The ground Mr. Anderson has staked is not open for staking by anybody else etc. etc.

"I am respectfully yours,
"Thos. Fawcett,
"Gold Commi'r"[2]

Clifford Sifton was impressed by Anderson's proposal. Large-scale mining using machinery might help to break the cycle of boom and bust that had been the history of most placer camps. There was little delay; the Order in Council granting the Anderson

18

Treadgold in 1903 at the Britton Commission inquiry into his dealings in the Klondike. The cartoon, by Buel, appeared in the *Yukon Sun* of 18 August 1903.

Concession, Lease Number 1, was approved on 12 January 1898.[3] These were its terms: 1—Rental was $500 per year. 2—A twenty-year lease was to be issued on receipt of an approved survey of the ground. 3—Hydraulic machinery was to be in operation on the ground within one year and each year after. 4—Existing mining claims were protected. 5—A 10-percent royalty was to be charged after output exceeded $20,000.

At the time the lease was granted, dredging was still in its infancy. The hydraulic mining envisaged by Anderson may have involved construction of a bedrock drain and the use of water brought to the ground by either a canal system or a wooden flume. If the water system had sufficient elevation above the workings, monitors (essentially large nozzles) could be installed and the resulting streams of water used to sweep the gravels into sluiceboxes located at the head of the bedrock drain. If slopes were suitable, the tailings, or washed gravels, could be carried away in the drain; otherwise, some means would have to be found to lift them to a dump on previously mined ground.

Similar leases, commonly referred to as hydraulic concessions, followed, and ultimately forty were granted.[4] Some were on ground "useless for gumboot mining" but others blanketed the main creeks in the Klondike. There seemed to be little concern over the condition that the ground be "not suitable to be worked under the regulations governing placer mining."[5] If the prize were rich enough there was always an engineer willing to state that the ground was "not suitable," and, in some cases at least, the commissioner and the gold commissioner seemed only too willing to provide the supporting statements required of them.

But the most enterprising scheme to obtain placer ground was that of Arthur Newton Christian Treadgold—"Mr. Treadgold" he was always called in the Klondike. The scheme (it evolved from three years of negotiations with Sifton on the one side and Treadgold's English backers on the other) would tie up the heart of the Klondike after the gumboot miners had finished high-grading their placer claims. Treadgold was promising a vast scheme that would bring in the water needed to mine the huge volumes of lower grade gravels certain to be left on the benches and the hills, but, to make it profitable, he would have to control most of the ground. For Sifton, it offered an opportunity to ensure continued mining in the Klondike and, if he were interested, a chance for personal profit.

Treadgold was an unlikely candidate for King of the Klondike. An Oxford graduate, he had been a master at Bath College, a private school, before resigning and returning to live in Oxford in 1897.[6] That autumn he met Grace Henderson, a Canadian student who was a sister-in-law of Inspector Constantine, who had established the North-West Mounted Police post near Forty Mile in 1895. Through letters that Grace Henderson received from Mrs. Constantine, Treadgold learned details of the Klondike strike. Unknown to many of his friends, Treadgold took a course in geology and arranged to visit the Klondike as a special correspondent for both *The Mining Journal* and *The Manchester Guardian.* In addition, he had promises of financial support. If the opportunities were there, it would be a simple matter to change from a mere observer to an active participant in the Klondike mining scene. On 2 January 1898 he sailed from England aboard the *Etruria,* bound for New York.

Treadgold did not leave for the Klondike immediately; he waited to make the trip in May and early June. Others going over the passes in mid-winter might have their boats and scows ready sooner, but, even so, they would be unable to reach Dawson until the ice on the rivers and lakes of the Yukon River system had broken, probably in early June. The Anderson Concession had already been granted, and Treadgold, sensing the potential value of the concessions to a larger mining enterprise, began negotiations for an interest in the Anderson and other concessions.[7] It was all new, and the fate of the concession applications would hinge on decisions by Clifford Sifton, Minister of the Interior. Busy behind the scenes, Treadgold did not approach Sifton until 9 May 1898 when he wrote identifying himself as a special correspondent of *The Mining Journal* and requesting an interview.[8] The interview appears to have been granted, and Treadgold left Ottawa soon after, bound for the Klondike.

Treadgold's trip to the Klondike differed little from that of many others caught up in the Gold Rush. His dispatches describe Skagway (then ruled by Soapy Smith), the climb over the Chilkoot Pass, boat building at Bennett and the river trip to Dawson, which he reached in late June 1898.[9] A keen observer, he included lengthy descriptions of the country he was travelling through in addition to those of the rush itself. Once in the Klondike he began to size up the opportunities certain to follow the hand mining. His dispatches in early August 1898, about the time of his departure from Dawson, describe the creeks and mining activity and his river trip to Dawson. Apparently satisfied with what he had seen, and in no hurry to return to Ottawa, Treadgold joined a Geological Survey of Canada party led by J. B. Tyrrell for the remainder of the season. Possibly he was waiting until his dispatches were published in England, or he may have hoped that a new gold field lay in the territory the party would be exploring. Treadgold had met Tyrrell when Tyrrell and R. G. McConnell of the Geological Survey had made a hurried visit to verify the Klondike strike in late July and early August 1898.[10] Returning to Tyrrell's camp at the mouth of the Nordenskiold River, near the present-day Carmacks, the party set out to reconnoitre the area to the west. It was a difficult trip; Tyrrell lacked experience working in the mountains and the party's horses were in poor condition. It was late August and the poplar leaves were beginning to fall when they reached the mouth of the Nisling River, about 100 miles west of their starting point, and Tyrrell decided to turn back, worried that the Chilkat Pass would soon be plugged with snow. Only three of the fourteen horses the party had started the summer with survived the trip and Tyrrell later wrote: "We had spared them all summer as much as possible, by carrying just what was absolutely necessary for the work in hand, and by walking almost all the time ourselves, but the change in their conditions of life from southern British Columbia to the Yukon district, had proved too much for them, and they dropped off one by one."[11]

Luckily, the party had been able to borrow six horses on the trip out. They reached Pyramid Harbor, near Haines, Alaska, on 25 September 1898.

Tyrrell and his party, together with Treadgold, were passengers on *Manauense,* an ocean steamer chartered for the gold rush trade, when she arrived in Vancouver on 6 October 1898. A reporter from the *Vancouver World* was on hand to meet the boat: "There was another passenger a Mr. Treadgold, who admitted to having seen some exciting times up North."

" 'How are things at Dawson?' was the everyday question that was asked him.

" 'Oh, Dawson,' replied the gentleman, 'that's not far away. I've been away north of Dawson,' but he would not give any further particulars of his trip."

Treadgold's opinions on the Klondike were reported by a fellow correspondent in *The Mining Journal* article datelined Vancouver, 14 October 1898:

"The writer has meanwhile had the pleasure of meeting your Special Correspondent from the Yukon, who seems to have made excellent use of his time there by engaging himself— amongst other good experimental tests—as an actual worker on placer claims, respecting 'good,' bad and middle-grade. He takes a very different view of the Yukon position in certain regards from that adopted by most others, but gives apparently good reasons for his opinions. Thus he declares that the chief difficulty affecting Klondyke hydraulicking is the cost of obtaining adequate water supplies, and not the obstacle of a severe winter climate. This latter can, he asserts, be largely obviated by making full use of between four and five months of summer—when nights are frequently quite light enough for placer mine working—and putting on double shifts of ten hours each, thus making the summer period practically equivalent to nearly twice its actual length in ordinary working days. But there must be union of claims under sufficient capitalisation, and specially skilled and careful management to justify large expenditures in hydraulic appliances in the case of some of the most likely creeks, to which a sufficient water supply for hydraulic purposes must be brought from a considerable distance. On this point, . . . so too, on the probability of much larger use as a miner's aid of the power of a strong summer sun, your Special Correspondent in the Yukon has apparently very noteworthy revelations to make."[12]

For more than fifty years, Treadgold's actions would be based on opinions formed in his first, brief trip to the Klondike.

From North Bend, a small town in southern British Columbia, Treadgold had telegraphed James Smart, Sifton's Deputy Minister, asking to meet with him on 24 October 1898.[13] Unexpectedly, as a member of the English press, Treadgold was becoming important.

Miss Flora Shaw, Colonial Editor of *The Times* of London had also travelled to the Klondike in the summer of 1898. In a report printed 28 September 1898, she stated:

"It is deplorable to have to admit, but it is idle to ignore, the fact that the administration of the Klondike district and the relations which exist between the representatives of the Government and the public leave almost everything to be desired. The population remains, on the whole, orderly and law abiding, but it is in an open and emphatically expressed anticipation of changes which, to give satisfaction, must include within their operation both the system and the *personnel.* To put the position as plainly as it is daily and hourly stated in the mining fields and in the streets of Dawson, there is a widely prevalent conviction not only that the laws are bad, but that the officers through which they are administered are corrupt. It is hard on innocent and upright individuals whose administrative duties may be performed with scrupulous integrity to be associated in the sweeping charge which is made against the whole official body, but there is no disguising the universal dissatisfaction, and innocent and guilty stand at present condemned together. It is impossible to talk for five minutes on business with any one on the mines or in the streets without some allusion occurring to the subject, and it is a painful experience for Englishmen proud of the purity of the British system of government to be compelled to listen to the plain-spoken comments of Americans and foreigners."

Even worse, *The Times* had supported her in a strongly worded editorial comment. Across Canada, the antigovernment press took up the cry while papers supporting the government sniffed that there was nothing specific in the charges. In the words of the editor of the *Yukon Sun,* then on a visit to Toronto: "She was there for a few weeks and is a pretty smart woman but she was guided by loose street talk."[14]

Sifton and his colleagues, inured to hostile comment in the Canadian and American press, were stung by the criticism. It may have been the last straw. On 7 October 1898, William Ogilvie, now the newly appointed Commissioner of the Yukon, was chosen to head a commission to investigate complaints registered in a miners' petition of 25 August 1898.[15] A more favorable English comment would do much to negate Miss Shaw's remarks, Treadgold provided it. In a letter printed in *The Manchester Guardian* of 20 September 1898, he said:

"Those men in a long line over yonder, quite 40 yards long, have been waiting hours to get into the post office to get the mail, which is worse distributed in Dawson than in any important town on earth. It is a hard task to be sure for the officials, but it could be better done than it is. . . . When we come to the several blocks of Government buildings we find another long line of men at the Gold Commissioner's office. There, too, there is more business to do than the staff can cope with and many a miner has had to wait many hours with the thermometer many degrees

Miners waiting to register claims at the Gold Commissioner's office at Dawson in 1898.

below zero. . . . All these Government offices are hopelessly undermanned and, I fear, underpaid, with resulting dangers to business. I think, too, that the Gold Commissioner has had far too many things thrust on him. . . . Dawson has had to emerge through very rough times, but she is emerging—the marvel is that things work at all and they would not have but for the very orderly character of the Klondike mine owners and miners. I have never seen such patience, such willingness to help the authorities as up here."

Treadgold saw Sifton in Ottawa and, in late 1898, Treadgold, now back in London, wrote him over the use of bedrock drains in mining large blocks of ground, one of the points discussed at their meeting. In his letter he pointed out that gradients on most of the better placer creeks were low, and he doubted that the drains could be used in the large-scale mining operations certain to follow the initial high-grading of individual placer claims. He continued with his opinion on concessions:

"We were talking about the *size* of concessions. I am very glad to see you have given 5 miles. I am sure you are right; there is a marked disposition over here to take up such concessions; but men want to be sure of an amount of gravel that will last some time. . . .

"I do not see how you can decide *by law* what should be given in big grants; save through your own inspectors on the spot. . . . Roughly speaking all applications for gravels on the *big* streams and at *the lower end of the big creeks* and up the hills above the 400 foot level deserve encouraging; they will not hurt the 'free miner'. . . . All applications for gulches and lower sidehills of creeks and ordinary parts of creeks should, I think, be viewed with suspicion. . . .

"I need hardly tell you that all my notes and drawings are entirely at your service all the winter. I was absolutely independent up in the Yukon, working hard to get to know the conditions for myself and my friends. I hope to come back in March to use my knowledge. With a man whom you know well I am trying to bring about a very strong combination for the Yukon. His name later."[16]

25

Treadgold returned to Ottawa about the beginning of May 1899 and there were more discussions of a scheme. Later, en route to Vancouver, he wrote to Sifton, trying (not too successfully) to keep his hand steady despite the swaying of the railway car:

> "I will be very careful to find out the *essential* requirements of the big scheme; it only wants a little deft handling now in *the Klondike itself.* I will be careful. Your letter will be all I want to help me to get at the ground and see what we really want of it and the possibility of a howl. I will see to that. We do not need to talk about our scheme. Other schemes will drop, failing active support from you. When the time comes we can make others talk about ours and *for* it, I have no doubt."[17]

At last, Treadgold was prepared to reveal his backers, and the names of eight are given in a footnote.

By now, Treadgold was lobbying for a grand scheme that would give him complete control of the water supply and hydroelectric power in the heart of the Klondike. With this the holders could bring water to the high-level gravel deposits at sufficient head for hydraulicking and sluicing, and the resulting large-scale operation would stabilize production at an acceptable level. Two alternatives, neither one attractive, were to have the government install a water and power scheme or to simply do nothing and hope for the best.

Events were moving swiftly, and Treadgold, encouraged by Sifton's interest, brought in a consulting engineer, Sir Thomas Tancred. Sir Thomas, together with Captain Draper, an engineer for J. J. Healy's North American Transportation and Trading Company, spent most of July and August 1899 studying the scheme. Treadgold reported the results to Sifton in mid-September:

> "I was glad, you may be sure, when both the Engineers after due consideration reported to me that my idea about the power for the pumping was sound. I believe we are going to tame that tough north country. Then the hardest placer diggings ever known will be the

first to be kept alive right along from the start! We can get water by the end of next summer and I know there can be no break in the development of the Klondike if we get water in.''

Treadgold too had been busy in the Klondike:

"I found considerable difficulty likely to occur on the question of dumping grounds because nearly every one of the gulches on the left side of Hunker and Bonanza had turned out rich for at least three claims from the mouth. I set to work and, in other names, bought creek claims at convenient intervals. I have invested 219,000 dollars in this way and when I have got three more claims on Lower Bonanza there will be no need of expropriation and no chance for blackmailers. My friends were very nice indeed about it; they had not the least idea what I wanted so much [money] for."[18]

Treadgold was back in Ottawa in early September 1899, and negotiations for the concession continued, but now they were with Walter Barwick, a Toronto lawyer and business associate of Sifton. With this switch, probably not even Treadgold could be certain of Sifton's part in later developments. In October 1899, shortly before Treadgold returned to England, Barwick reported to Sifton:

"I do not know what his programme would be if he actually had a concession in his hand, and I am satisfied that he does not know himself what he intends doing were he to go home merely with the satisfactory assurance that the concession would be granted but there are a great many preliminaries still to settle, for no preliminary agreements have been entered into, in fact they have hardly been discussed, and I am not sure yet as to the form which I would like the concession to take when it is granted."[19]

Treadgold, back in Ottawa in early February 1900, wrote a more direct letter to Sifton:

"I managed to keep this business absolutely clear and today I owe no man except yourself any kind of duty with regard to it. I did not consider it possible to serve you properly in this enterprise unless I kept *everybody* out of it until the time should come when you could say to me 'now you can let them come in'. I made my personal friends give me £40,000 with which to buy good ground and I was able to exempt the water business specially from my agreement with them while at the same time using their money to buy a safe basis of good ground on which to build this enterprise in due time. So I am in a splendid financial position with entire control of everything at which I have worked. *You* have kept me free for this enterprise and we have no need to make a single mistake in our men. Keep me free and strong and the enterprise is the gainer. That is why I want the concession made out to mere nominees of my own: the enterprise is still in the stage at which *orders* must come only from you (and will be for some time still and the longer the better, you will say and so I.

"Yours faithfully,
"A.N.C.Treadgold"[20]

Once again, Treadgold spent the summer in the Klondike, working quietly behind the scenes, getting everything ready for his big scheme. There was no publicity; other entrepreneurs, such as Big Alex McDonald, and the budding politicians held the spotlight at the moment. In mid-July 1900, Treadgold wrote Sifton:

"The output is safe to be more than maintained this year and maintained next, but I think that by the end of 1901 you may reduce your royalty (and your expenses too, eh?) for the Klondike, because by then the Yankees on Eldorado and Upper Bonanza will have cleared out and the lowgrade gravels can begin to be treated, if we get the water going all right."[21]

In August, Barwick submitted a draft Order in Council to Sifton. In late September, James Sutherland, Acting Minister of the Interior, reported to Sifton:

"Treadgold arrived from the Yukon a few
days ago and he and Barwick have started the water
right matter again. If they can arrange, I will see that it
is put through."[22]

There were delays. An Order in Council had been
passed on 9 October 1900, but Treadgold's backers had balked at
the terms and it had not been implemented.[23] Finally, on 12 June
1901, after more than three years of lobbying, Order in Council
Number 1293-1901 granting Treadgold the concession he had
dreamt of was finally approved. The order, only a page long,
deals in generalities:

"Whereas the mining now carried on in the
Klondike District is, because of the inadequate supply
of water necessarily confined to the washing of the
richest gravel only, comparatively small in area, thus
leaving large tracts of gold bearing gravels unworked;
and from the information obtained from the Gold
Commissioner of the Yukon Territory and others it is
believed that the riches of the Klondike District can only
be properly utilized by such a water supply as that which
the before mentioned applicants are prepared to
establish;
"Therefore the Governor General in Council
is pleased to order. . . that the said application by the
said Malcolm H. Orr Ewing, A.N.C. Treadgold and
Walter Barwick, bearing the date the 31st May 1901, a
copy of which is hereto annexed, and which is hereby
made a part of this Order in Council . . . is hereby
accepted; and that the said parties . . . are hereby
granted all and every of the powers, privileges, rights
and franchises asked for. . . ."

The accompanying letter, five pages long, is specific.
There are 13 sections each beginning with the phrase: "The
right," occasionally strengthened by the adjectives "sole,"
"prior" and "exclusive." Basically, with the exception of existing
claims and water rights, the Treadgold Concession, as it would
soon be known, gave Treadgold control of the portion of the gold
field lying in the Klondike River watershed. It included all of

29

Bonanza, Eldorado, Bear and Hunker creeks—it was the heart of the Klondike! Within this district the holders had the exclusive right to construct water systems, cross any ground with either water or electrical schemes, take any timber required. They would have rights to any mineral deposits found in their operations and could take over and work any abandoned placer claims. The rights were conferred for a period of thirty years, following which the works were to remain the property of the concession holders. In return for the concession, the holders undertook to spend $250,000 prior to the end of 1902 and to deliver a flow of 1,000 miner's inches (about 1,500 cubic feet per minute) of water to the district not later than 1 July 1905.

Clearly, Orr Ewing, Treadgold and Barwick had written their letter of application with their own interests in mind, and little protection was offered to the ordinary miners. True, they undertook to distribute up to one-half of the water to other claim owners but at a rate not to exceed one dollar per miner's inch per hour. If they charged the full rate this would mean an unconscionable fifty dollars per hour to operate a standard sluice-box adequate for four men shovelling in! If water supplies to the district were inadequate, the holders were prepared to supply up to 500 miner's inches more—provided 1) that they were given two years' notice and 2) that they had earned a *net profit* of at least 10 percent per annum upon the capital stock of the company for the three previous years!

But it was still not enough to satisfy Treadgold's English backers, and he had cabled:

LONDON, JUNE 19, 1901
HON. CLIFFORD SIFTON
OTTAWA

WILL YOU CONSENT TO EXPRESS WHAT I
BELIVE TO BE YOUR INTENTION IN
CONDITION THREE, BY CHANGING THE WORDS
NET PROFIT INTO DIVIDEND AND INSERTING
ALL BEFORE THE CAPITAL ERASING STOCK
AND IN REGULATION E, FIRST PARAGRAPH,
BY INSERTING OBLIGATORY QUANTITIES OF
BETWEEN THE AND WATER? BOTH CHANGES
VITAL TO ME HERE. REPLY TREADGOLD,
TOM TOM, LONDON [24]

The proposed changes would ensure that there would be no forced expansion of the scheme until it was profitable and that the concession holders would never be required to deliver more than 750 miner's inches to other claim owners within the district. A new Order in Council granting the requested changes was passed on 29 June 1901, a scant seventeen days after the original. At last, Treadgold had everything!

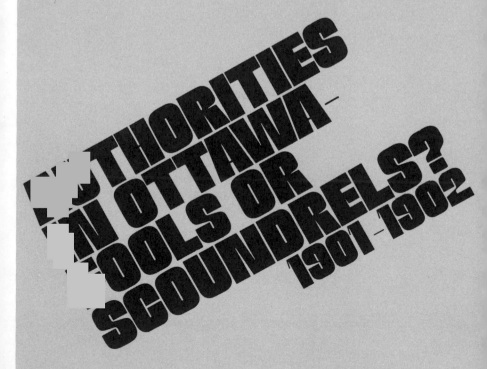
AUTHORITIES IN OTTAWA—FOOLS OR SCOUNDRELS? 1901-1902

A copy of the Order in Council granting the Treadgold Concession reached Dawson on 15 July 1901 and was posted in the gold commissioner's office the following day. It was also printed in full in the *Klondike Nugget* but, surprisingly, there was little immediate reaction.

A protest meeting was called for Tuesday evening, 30 July 1901, by Colonel Donald McGregor, a '98er who had been involved in public affairs since his arrival in the Klondike. Perhaps to ensure support from all three Dawson newspapers, who were at war with one another, the Treadgold Concession was only one of the items for consideration, the others being exorbitant freight charges to Dawson (the *Klondike Nugget's* current cause) and the future municipal government of Dawson. The *Nugget* reported it had been a "small" meeting with an indefinite "few score" in attendance but did acknowledge that there had been strong attacks on the Treadgold Concession by several speakers. One attack was by C. M. Woodworth, a Dawson lawyer; eyes blazing with indignation, he charged that the authorities in Ottawa who had granted the concession were either fools or scoundrels and compared their actions to the government of Spain at the time of the Inquisition. Others attacked the rate of one dollar a miner's inch per hour for water, stating that some operators were already putting water on the benches at eighteen cents per miner's inch using electricity from the wood-fired Dawson thermal plant. As for the 1,000 inches, there was enough gravel on the benches and hillsides of Bonanza to employ 5,000 inches for over 100 years. The meeting passed a resolution calling for the repeal of the Treadgold Concession, and a special committee of three was chosen to continue the fight.

Gold Commissioner Senkler, probably as surprised as anyone by Sifton's decree, had an immediate problem with one section of the Treadgold Order in Council:

Commissioner J. H. Ross speaking at the 24th of May celebration at Dawson in 1901. The holiday marked the birthday of Queen Victoria, who had died in January of that year.

"10. The right, subject to no payment except the royalty prescribed upon output, to enter upon, make entry for and work all mining locations now or hereafter abandoned on Bonanza, Bear and Hunker Creeks and their tributaries."

Did this mean that any claim reverting to the Crown should be reserved for Treadgold? Uncertain what to do, he refused to issue the grants to relocators of such claims and wrote to Ottawa for guidance. [1] Here was an issue that all the newspapers could speculate on and attack!

Newly-appointed Commissioner Ross, away on a short trip to Whitehorse to meet his family, had returned to Dawson a

few days after the protest meeting. He was unable to see that the Order in Council gave unusual privileges; under Section 10 Treadgold would only escape fees, and as for the water rate of one dollar per miner's inch per hour, that was a maximum, although it might be preferable if there was a clause to permit the rate to be set by Governor in Council. He concluded: "I may say that everything has been done to see that the rights of the people on these creeks have been thoroughly protected and I may say further that I think it is largely in the interests of the whole territory that these large schemes for development of resources should be fostered and encouraged."[2]

By now, the campaign against the concession was beginning to build. Gold Commissioner Senkler had written for a ruling two weeks earlier but his letter was probably still en route and there would be a long wait for the answer. Unfortunately, the new telegraph line to Ashcroft in southern British Columbia was still not completed, so the message would have to go the slower route: by telegraph to Skagway, boat to Vancouver and then telegraph to Ottawa.

DAWSON, Y.T., AUGUST 6, 1901

HON. CLIFFORD SIFTON
MINISTER OF THE INTERIOR
OTTAWA

DOES CLAUSE 10, TREADGOLD WATER
CONCESSION, GIVE ABSOLUTE GRANT OF
RELOCATED CLAIMS, AND MUST GRANTEE
ENTER UPON OR MAKE ENTRY FOR IN
COMPETITION WITH FREE MINERS? OPINION
OF LEGAL ADVISER AND MY OWN THAT
SECTION DOES NOT GIVE EXCLUSIVE RIGHT.
ANSWER

E. C. SENKLER

DEPARTMENT OF THE INTERIOR
OTTAWA, AUGUST 14, 1901

E. C. SENKLER
GOLD COMMISSIONER
DAWSON, Y.T.

ABANDONED LOCATIONS ON BONANZA, BEAR

AND HUNKER TO BE HELD PENDING
TREADGOLD COMPANY'S COMPLIANCE WITH
PROVISIONS OF ORDER IN COUNCIL
                    PERLEY G. KEYES

But a few weeks later Sifton had second thoughts after
an appeal from Commissioner Ross:

                    DEPARTMENT OF THE INTERIOR
                    OTTAWA, SEPTEMBER 6, 1901
E. C. SENKLER, ESQ.
GOLD COMMISSIONER
DAWSON, Y.T.

RESPECTING CLAUSE 10, EWING-TREADGOLD
ORDER IN COUNCIL, COURSE TO BE
FOLLOWED IS AS FOLLOWS: GROUND IS TO BE
OPEN FOR ENTRY BY ORDINARY MINERS AS IF
NO SUCH ORDER WERE PASSED; ENTRIES TO
BE GRANTED TO APPLICANTS IN THE USUAL
WAY; NO RESERVE MADE OR AUTHORIZED BY
SUCH ORDER. CLAUSE 10 ONLY CONFERS ON
GRANTEES A RIGHT TO STAKE AND ENTER
FOR THE ABANDONED CLAIMS IN SAME WAY
AS ANY OTHER FREE MINER. IF EWING-
TREADGOLD COMPANY APPLY TO BE
REGISTERED FOR ANY OF THESE ABANDONED
CLAIMS, YOU WILL REQUIRE THEM TO LOCATE,
STAKE AND COMPLY WITH ALL FORMALITIES
IN EACH INDIVIDUAL CASE OF EACH
INDIVIDUAL CLAIM, EXCEPT PAYMENT OF
ENTRY FEE. ADVISE PUBLIC OF THESE
INSTRUCTIONS AT ONCE TO AVOID
MISUNDERSTANDING; ALSO LET IT BE KNOWN
THAT PROVISIONS OF THIS ORDER IN COUNCIL
DO NOT TAKE AWAY FROM THE RIGHTS OF
MINERS AND MINING COMPANIES TO SECURE
WATER RIGHTS UNDER WATER REGULATIONS
                    CLIFFORD SIFTON [3]

Sifton's telegram would allay the immediate problem. But it was a compromise and the step marked the beginning of a long struggle. Publicly, Sifton would be pressured by the Klondikers to cancel the concession and, behind the scenes, by Treadgold to keep the concession unchanged for fear of losing his backers. Caught in the middle, Sifton's officials carried out their duties without public comment, although Sifton was warned privately of the growing opposition to the concession. For the moment at least, Treadgold would have to stake claims like any other miner. But as the *Nugget* pointed out, there were still differences in that there was no limit to the number of claims Treadgold could stake, there were no fees, and there was no work requirement of $200 a claim to be met each year.[4]

Treadgold was in the Klondike for a brief period late in the summer of 1901, but, in an interview with him, a *Nugget* reporter had been able to learn little more than that the concession holders intended to meet the work commitment of $250,000 required prior to 31 December 1902.[5] A young man representing Treadgold had been at work in the Gold Commissioner's office for a month compiling lists of claims and the date they would expire if the required representation work was not performed. There was nothing illegal in this activity but the *Nugget* warned would-be miners to do the same thing and to get their ground before everything was taken up by the concessionaires.

On 12 February 1902, minutes after noon, a new Order in Council amending the terms of the concession was posted in the Gold Commissioner's office.[6] The order, dated 7 December 1901, had been received in the mail that day, and there had been no advance warning from Ottawa. Virtually all of the changes won the previous autumn had been lost and, as of 1 January 1902, all abandoned claims went to Treadgold! This time the entire community, including the three newspapers, united in the attack.

The contested Section 10 now read:

"The right, subject to no payment except the royalty prescribed upon output, to obtain entry for and work all mining locations now or hereafter abandoned on Bonanza, Bear and Hunker Creeks and their tributaries.
"All such locations shall be deemed to be vested in the grantees on the first day of January, 1902, but the grantees shall not receive the entry for any of

such locations until they have expended the sum of
$250,000 as herein provided, nor shall they work any of
the said locations until the provisions of condition 2,
respecting the delivery of two thousand (2000) miner's
inches of water, have been fulfilled. In default of the
delivery . . . of water as provided in conditon 2, the
right of the grantees to the said locations shall forthwith
cease and determine."[7]

**The last boat of the 1901 season arriving in Dawson on 8 November. The
Nora was caught in ice floes several times on the trip from Whitehorse,
and she lost one of her barges. The *Oro,* also of the Klondike
Corporation, was the last boat to make the trip upstream, leaving Dawson
on 24, October 1901.**

Other changes included the change of Condition 2,
Section 13, to require the grantees to deliver not later than 1 July
1905 a flow of water of 2,000 miner's inches for distribution along
the line of a conduit constructed from the mouth of Bonanza
Valley to Grand Forks, at such an elevation above Bonanza Creek
as to afford an effective head of 300 feet at any point along the
conduit. Under Regulation F, the maximum charge for water had
dropped to twenty-five cents a miner's inch per hour from the

previous one dollar. A new Regulation G restricted the amount of water the grantees could divert from a creek that was being worked downstream from their intake. Next, a brief final paragraph had been added: "The plans of the grantees' works shall be submitted to and approved by the Governor General in Council before the works are actually proceeded with."

Indignation over the changes in the concession spread through the Klondike and a few days later the *Nugget* spluttered: "There never in the history of the civilized world was a greater, more malignant or more unpardonable outrage heaped upon the heads of a long-suffering public than this same Treadgold concession and it may be safely stated that the people of Dawson and the Yukon territory at large are a unit in denouncing it as the blackest act of infamy that ever blotted the history of the country."[8]

The Liberal Association called a meeting for Saturday evening, February 15th, to discuss the question. It was chaired by F. T. Congdon, formerly Legal Adviser to the Yukon Council, now in private practice in Dawson. About 150 persons attended, and the discussion was animated. A few speakers thought the water scheme itself might be of value but deplored the giving of the abandoned claims to Treadgold. One impassioned speaker raged: "I have been a Liberal all my life, but I would not stay with any party that has acted like the present government. My interests are in the Yukon, and that's the part I am wanting protected."[9] The meeting appointed a committee to collect additional information on the concession and its probable effect on the Klondike and passed a resolution to be telegraphed to Commissioner Ross, who was en route to Ottawa:

"Whereas, the Liberal Association of Dawson has summoned this meeting of the association to discuss the Treadgold Concession, and to make such representations in respect thereto to the government as might be deemed necessary, and has invited all Liberals, whether members of the association or not, to attend this meeting; and

"Whereas, this meeting has the greatest confidence in the judgment and ability of the Commissioner, . . . and in his desire and determination to guard the interests of the people of this territory; and

"Whereas, in the opinion of this meeting their confidence in the Commissioner is shared by the people of the territory at large; therefore be it

"Resolved, that this meeting requests the Commissioner to undertake the presentation to the government of the representations which it is desired to make in regard to such concession, and that this meeting urges the Commissioner to use all his great influence to secure a cancellation of the obnoxious features of the recent Order in Council, and the other Order in Council relating to such concession, and to relieve this territory from the disastrous consequences certain to ensue if such Order in Council is allowed to stand in full; and be it further

"Resolved, that the Commissioner's attention be called to the fact . . . that, in the opinion of this meeting, the insertion of such features in the Orders in Council could only have been procured by the grossest misrepresentation and fraudulent concealment; that it never could have been represented to the minister who proposed said orders, or to the Governor in Council, that the orders were an interference with and abrogation of vested rights; that it was retroactive in operation and most far-reaching and uncertain in effect; that it was certain to produce distrust and lack of confidence among the mining communities of this territory, and prove fatal to the progress of the territory; not could it have been presented and made apparent that the only consideration promised for the enormous interests granted was a monopoly to supply water at an exorbitant and prohibitive price."[10]

A mass meeting was held the following Monday at the A. B. (Arctic Brotherhood) Hall. Colonel McGregor called the meeting to order, prophesying, according to the *Nugget,* that "If the meeting did not take some forceful action the Moosehide Indians would in a very short while be occupying the palatial apartments now occupied by the minions of Mr. Sifton."[11] Mayor Macaulay of Dawson was then chosen chairman and George Black, a Dawson lawyer, secretary. As at the earlier Liberal meeting, interest centered on Section 10, but attention was given to other schemes, including a government water system. Even the Assistant Gold Commissioner, Dufferin Pattullo, later destined to become Premier of British Columbia, risked his job to speak against Section 10. The meeting decided to pool their efforts with those of other groups and a committee of 20 was chosen to carry on the action.

Another meeting held at Grand Forks two days later favored a more direct approach, and Walter Woodburn, unofficial mayor of the community, telegraphed Prime Minister Laurier:

> DELAY PROCEEDINGS TREADGOLD
> CONCESSION UNTIL DELEGATION WHICH WILL
> BE SENT ARRIVES. THAT MATTER REFERRED TO
> SIFTON IS UNSATISFACTORY. WE LOOK TO
> YOU FOR PROTECTION [12]

Later in the week, Commissioner Ross was interviewed in Vancouver, en route to Ottawa, and commented that he had not seen a copy of the amended Treadgold concession as yet, and could not discuss it until he had, but, "All I can see concerning the discussion of the matter at Dawson seems chiefly hot air." [13]

The committee of 20 met on Saturday, 22 February 1902, and considered the report of a subcommittee of five, chaired by F. T. Congdon, reporting on the objectionable features of the Treadgold Concession:

"It is easy to understand how intelligent gentlemen at the capital could be misled, both as to the value of the water supply contemplated by the Treadgold Concession, as to the size of the capital proposed to be used by him and as to the value of the concessions made to him, but in the opinion of your committee no one in possession of the information that your committee has been enabled to obtain by search at the Gold Commissioner's office, by numerous interviews with miners, engineers and men practically acquainted with conditions of this territory and every source available, can doubt that the supply of water contemplated by the scheme of the applicants for a concession is a mere stalking horse under cover of which they may obtain absolute possession of enormous mining tracts practically embracing the richest known mining ground in the territory.

"It seems to your committee that while from a logical or scientific point of view the instruments containing the Treadgold Concessions are of a most imperfect and inartistic kind they are from the point of view to Treadgold and his associates framed with clever adroitness. They are complex, involved and obscure, and as a consequence difficult to readily understand and appear to have been purposely framed in that way to deceive into the belief that the Treadgold people were conferring an enormous benefit on the country and receiving small return, whereas they are in effect giving little or nothing and receiving vast benefits."[14]

But the initial impetus was slackening. The full committee adopted the report, later rescinded their adoption of it, and, after much discussion, adopted it again. Finally, early on Sunday morning, the meeting ended in confusion over the selection and number of delegates to be sent to Ottawa. Another mass meeting on Monday night did no better and concluded by passing all the resolutions and amendments before it, no matter how contradictory. Subscription lists had been out around Dawson but as the *Nugget* noted, "No casualties have been reported from people falling over each other in a mad rush to get to the lists."[15] Finances settled the question, and two delegates were selected: Arthur Wilson, representing and financed by miners on the creeks, and Barney Sugrue from Dawson. At month-end they were away on the long trip to Ottawa.[16] By now, the feud between the newspapers had broken out again with the *Nugget* blaming *News* overplay for reports in the Outside press about the economic disaster that had befallen the Klondike through the granting of the Treadgold Concession.[17] In fact, there had been only limited comment in the Outside press. The Klondike was far away and, in eastern Canada at least, other more exciting and contentious events were taking place much closer to home.

Ottawa was little concerned. Commissioner Ross had brief meetings with Clifford Sifton after his arrival in the city at the end of February, but two days later Sifton left for White Sulphur Springs, Virginia, where he planned to spend a few weeks "in search of health." Meanwhile, Treadgold and his consultant, Barwell, a Dawson engineer, were in Ottawa meeting with Ross. Ross followed Sifton to Virginia, the two returning to Ottawa a few days before delegates Wilson and Sugrue arrived on 24 March 1902. A meeting with Sifton was arranged for the following day.[18] Little news of the negotiations reached Dawson during the following three weeks but, finally, Sifton telegraphed his decision to Gold Commissioner Senkler:

OTTAWA, APRIL 17, 1902

THROW OPEN FOR ENTRY AT ONCE ALL THE
LAPSED AND ABANDONED CLAIMS WITHHELD
FROM ENTRY BY REASON OF TREADGOLD
ORDER IN COUNCIL
                       CLIFFORD SIFTON
                       PER G.U.R.[19]

In Dawson, the telegram reached Gold Commissioner Senkler shortly after 4:00 that day, and the notice was typed and posted in his office by 4:30 p.m.[20] The Assistant Gold Commissioner estimated that some 3,500 claims might be involved. The rush was on. Would-be claim owners raced to the claims they had their hearts set on. One such hopeful, Frank Slavin, a heavyweight boxer, appeared at the Recorder's wicket just after noon the following day.[21] Busy training for a fight with Burley about a week away, he had taken time out to stake a hillside claim near the mouth of Last Chance Creek, a tributary of Hunker, and had made the round trip of thirty-two miles in about 6¼ hours. Next day, there was a line of about fifty stampeders waiting to record claims, reminiscent of lines in the initial days of the gold rush. Dawson and the creeks were jubilant.

A partial text of the Order in Council of 21 April 1902 revising the Treadgold Concession arrived a few days later.[22] This time it was sent by telegraph and there were no retroactive features. Section 10 was still there, but it now read:

"The right, subject to no payment except the royalty prescribed upon output, to make entry for and work any abandoned mining claim or claims on Bonanza, Bear and Hunker Creeks, such right to be exercisable only when the grantees by the construction of works in pursuance of this franchise are in a position to deliver water upon such claim or claims for the working thereof."

There were other, more subtle changes. The grantees

44

had six years in which to exercise their rights, free of any spelled-out work or financial commitments. Their properties would be exempt from the requirement that each claim had to have $200 worth of representation work done on it every year. They had the right to sell water but all references as to the amount of water to be supplied, any obligation to sell a certain portion, or sale price had disappeared. The new scheme appeared to be intended to assist Treadgold and his associates to work their holdings; there was little in the order that could either benefit or hinder the individual miner in the working of his claim.

Sensing victory, those opposed to the Treadgold Concession now extended their attack to include the hydraulic concessions. About 350 were present at a meeting called by C. M. Woodworth for 21 April 1902,[23] even though sluicing had begun on King Solomon Hill the day before and would soon be in full swing throughout the Klondike. Woodworth was the main speaker. He and the others concentrated their attacks on eight of the concessions: the Anderson, Milne, Boyle, Bronson and Ray, Doyle, Matson, Slavin and Gates, and Miller Creek.

Woodworth described how persons requesting a concession would do some perfunctory prospecting and declare the ground worthless for placer mining, totally ignoring the many claims being worked on it. Commissioner Ogilvie and Gold Commissioner Senkler would then agree with the declaration, and the Department of the Interior in Ottawa would grant the concession. Woodworth said that some of the concession holders had close ties with the Minister of Interior, Clifford Sifton, and that Sifton himself had once been a part owner of the Anderson Concession. Concessions already covered large portions of the main creeks in the Klondike! The boundaries of some concessions appeared to have been shifted to accommodate requests from the holders. In the one area covered by the Matson and Doyle Concessions, there were provisions for incorporating lapsed or abandoned claims.

Woodworth had collected much of his information from public documents at the Gold Commissioner's Office in Dawson and at the Department of the Interior in Ottawa. At the close of the meeting, a resolution was passed calling for an enquiry as to whether the concessions had been acquired through fraud or misrepresentation. A resolution was also passed calling for cancellation of the concessions.

Another mass meeting was held on Wednesday evening, the 30th of April, to hear the report of the committee, now twenty-four strong, appointed by the earlier meeting. The *Sun,* losing interest in the cause, reported: "That the people are getting tired of the professional agitator was proven last evening when . . . about 200 people gathered in the Arctic Brotherhood hall which has a seating capacity for over 1,000."[24] Both other papers reported the hall "comfortably filled." The committee had little to report other than the partial text of the latest Order in Council and a statement from the delegates in Ottawa that was telegraphed to the *News* by their Ottawa correspondent:

"We interviewed Sir Wilfred Laurier and Hon. Clifford Sifton March 27th. Our objections were noted and favorably received. The matter was under consideration until April 16, inclusive. The sale of water has been cut out. The right to impound water, etc., on the creeks has been cut out. The right of entry is given on abandoned ground when they can place water thereon. The onus of proof rests on Treadgold. Such right of entry does not interfere with the private right to locate. Treadgold has received the exclusive right to create power on the Klondike River. He may sell such right at prices regulated by governor in council. This right only refers to power for sale."[25] Signed Arthur Wilson and John F. Sugrue.

In reply to this statement the committee had already telegraphed:

EFFORTS SATISFACTORY, RESULTS
DISAPPOINTING. PEOPLE DEMAND COMPLETE
ABROGATION. REPLY[26]

There had been no answer. With the limited information available the meeting was soon in a quandary, unable to resolve possible ambiguities over abandoned claims and unable to determine whether Treadgold had sole rights to the Klondike River water and any power developed from it. Frustrated, the meeting passed a resolution to be telegraphed to the delegates:

"Resolved that the Anderson, Boyle, Philp,
Bronson and Ray, Doyle and Matson concessions
within the Treadgold Concession be cancelled together
with the Treadgold Concession itself and that failing

46

this the sole rights and exclusive privileges in the latter
be clearly defined and ambiguities eliminated."[27]

Further action would have to wait until the return of
Commissioner Ross and the delegates. Travel over the winter road
had ended for the season and, with the exception of the telegraph
service, Dawson would be isolated from the Outside until the ice
broke on the Yukon River and the first steamers arrived.

Concrete evidence of at least a partial victory over the
Treadgold Concession came the following week when the Gold
Commissioner's office issued grants for some 200 claims staked in
the rush that followed Sifton's telegram throwing the concession
open.[28]

By Saturday, 17 May 1902, it was obvious that the
winter isolation would soon be over. The river in front of Dawson
was open and running ice, and telegraphed reports from upriver
said that the main jams had broken and that the river was clear
with the exception of a heavy flow of ice past Ogilvie. Boats that
had wintered at the lower end of Lake Laberge had already passed
Five Finger Rapids and were expected in Dawson within the next
two days.

At five Sunday afternoon, smoke was sighted upriver,
and in less than five minutes the waterfront was lined with people
from one end of town to the other. The *Seattle No. 3* lead the
procession, passing the foot of Queen Street at 5:15, and followed
by the *Will H. Isom* at 5:17. The *Seattle No. 3* had to pass down
the waterfront to her dock and while she was doing so the *Isom*
made a brilliant turn in her own length and got a line ashore first.
Then followed the *Susie* at 5:22, the *Sarah* at 5:23, the *T. C.
Powers* at 5:25½, the *Sybil* at 5:29, the *Prospector* at 6:15 and the
Sifton about 8:30.

"Of the nine, five are lower river boats that have
wintered at Stewart and four are upper river boats from the foot
of Laberge, loaded with cattle, eggs, lemons, potatoes, oranges,
condensed cream and everything that is scarce and high in the
Dawson markets, and much that is not scarce. Last but not least is
the mail, the first in three weeks, and which was followed to the
post office as by a triumphal procession. Postmaster Hartman
was prepared to receive it with a large force of clerks, and the
nearly a hundred sacks were all distributed long before
midnight."[29]

The Commissioner's Residence in Dawson, one of the many new public buildings completed just after the turn of the century.

In early June, Commissioner Ross received a triumphal welcome on his return to Dawson. The N. C. Company donated the steamer *Susie,* and a crowd of 500 paid ten dollars each to make the trip upstream to meet the steamer *Bailey* carrying Commissioner Ross and delegates Wilson and Sugrue. The *Susie,* a palatial, twin-stacked, lower river steamer, left Dawson in mid-afternoon and met the *Bailey* near Indian River, about twenty-five miles upstream.

"Running alongside, Messrs. Barrett and Thompson went aboard first to see if the prevailing smallpox was there and presently reported all clear. The committee of eight went aboard to escort the governor from the *Bailey* to the *Susie* which was done amid great cheering and with the band playing national airs. The governor was met on the gangplank by Judge Dugas and then commenced the handshaking which would assuredly have distressed any but a vigorous Western man as the governor. The magnificent saloon of the *Susie* was next visited and found to be set for a banquet. Everyone was invited to line up, and did so. It had previously been agreed that there should be no speaking, but after the generous wine had followed the foods provided the governor was first called on and then others. . . . Then the feast broke up, and the capacious decks were promenaded until Dawson was reached. . . .

"The *Susie* was gay with a hundred flags and streamers galore stretching on the guy wires from stem to stern. The boat felt herself the center of too many eyes to make any common landing. She rose to the occasion and went by Dawson with a play of whistles, then turning the bend below town slowly steamed back to her landing. 'The Maple Leaf Forever' and 'God Save the King' were played by the band aboard, and the vast crowds ashore were answered in their cheering by the shouts of the party aboard. . . . The first to come ashore after the tying at the N. C. docks was the mayor and the city council. The mayor took up his position at the gate of the N. C. warehouse entrance from the river and read an address of welcome to the governor as that gentleman, with many hearty handshakings, made his way through the crowd at that point.

"In reply, the governor said in part: 'Mr. Mayor, and ladies and gentlemen: It is, indeed, a great honor to be so welcomed back to this great metropolis of the northland. The largeness and generousness of the welcome, I take it is indicative of the large heartedness and generous natures of this northern people, and is only what was to be expected of Dawson. It has been said that Dawson and the Yukon were peopled by 'kickers'. That they were a people who would refuse to be pleased whatever was done for them. Never was a greater mistake. I for one can refute the accusation, and if I did not, then this open-hearted welcome would. . . . It is kind of you to say that I have been able to serve you while I have been away, and I want to say that as far as I am concerned it was wholly a labor of love. I like to labor for the people of the west, their generous appreciation is so spontaneous. I only hope to be able to stay and labor a few years longer. But not all the credit for what has been accomplished is due myself. I will give great credit to those whom you chose to assist me and to bear to the capitol your desires and wishes. And those who we went to see, too, must be given great credit, for I will say that they gave what we wanted with very little resistance. The greatest difficulty was to make the people of the East understand what we wanted. How can you make the people of Prince Edward's island understand our needs? . . . They look at our requisition $150 per month for a charwoman, Why they say, that is more than our premier gets [much laughter] and it can't be right. . . . And now, gentlemen, I am happy to be back to this greatest little corner of the empire. The richest, the most progressive, the sturdiest, the most rapidly developing and the most promising land under the flag. I thank you for your immensely kind reception of me.'

"The procession then moved to First avenue where a carriage was waiting to take the governor to his residence. . . . Just before the team was ready to start the traces were unhitched and the crowd took charge and drew the carriage through the crowded street towards the barracks."[30]

Nothing further was heard from delegates Wilson and Sugrue until a meeting of the committee, now twenty-one in number, was called on the afternoon of June 23rd, 1902.

"The meeting was called by the mayor, who is also chairman of the committee, in response to a curt letter from Secretary Black demanding an explanation of the fact that the report of Mr. Sugrue had been in for some time, yet the mayor was so out of sympathy with the movement he persistently refused to call a meeting of the committee or call or preside over a mass meeting to hear the report of the delegates. The mayor read the letter and said that was his reason for calling this meeting. The members of the committee could now do as they pleased.

"Secretary Black rose to explain. He said the letter was excused by the position taken by Mayor Macaulay, who had refused to call or preside at a mass meeting as it would displease Mr. Ross, and regretted having taken part in sending the delegates since with Mr. Ross at Ottawa nothing else was necessary.

"The mayor said he would give the lie direct to such a statement. He had been very busy and had simply neglected taking action on the report. At any rate the meeting was now called and could take what action it wished. . . . The mayor then read the report. . . .

" 'Gentlemen: As there seems in some quarter to be a desire for a report as to the results of our mission with regard to the Treadgold Concession, I wish to lay before the committee a synopsis of our doings at Ottawa.

" 'According to instructions, we met and conferred with Hon. James H. Ross on our arrival, and found him disposed to assist us in every way possible. An interview was arranged with the Premier and the Honorable Minister of the Interior, at which were present Hon. James H. Ross, Ralph Smith, Arthur Wilson and myself. The matter was laid before the premier and Mr. Sifton in its entirety, and the total abolition of the concession was demanded. We found out that the concession had been already granted and that the only method by which we could secure redress was by working with the government, which showed every disposition to rectify the mistakes which had been made.

" 'It did not seem to us that our mission was for the purpose of raising a question between the two parties at Ottawa, but to secure what we could for the benefit of the Yukon territory. This, I venture to think, has been accomplished by us to some extent.

" 'The concession as it stands today differs from the grant which was in existence when we left here, inasmuch that Treadgold is deprived of:

" '1. The right to the exclusive sale of water.

" '2. That he no longer holds the abandoned ground which had reverted to him since January 1, and

" '3. He is deprived of the right to impound water on the various creeks.

" 'These were the main points objected to by the people

of the territory. . . . The only exclusive right reserved to Treadgold [is] for the purpose of generating power with which to pump water to work the auriferous deposits, etc. People believe, or say they believe, that this gives Treadgold the exclusive right to the water of the Klondike, but if read carefully they will see that his powers are very limited. He can only generate power for a certain purpose and even the supply of water that he can use is limited to 5,000 miner's inches. The sale of power, if he so wishes to do, is regulated as to the price by the government, so that he is even restricted here in every way possible.

"'I may say in conclusion that we were received in every way courteously and as far as we can gather, the government, whatever it may have done in the past, and as to that we all hold our opinions, shows a desire to do all that is necessary for the welfare of the territory in the future.

"'With regard to certain remarks as to our snubbing, etc., the opposition, I may say that they are absolutely without foundation. The opposition were more than courteous to us, and were received in like manner. Without laying our grievances before them we informed them of our intention and the methods we intended to pursue, that is, first, to do business with the party in power, and, if unsuccessful, to solicit their aid. As fair-minded men, they realized our position and approved of our intention.

"'We hope that our errand has been satisfactorily accomplished, and thanking the committee for its support in this matter, we remain, equally ready to let the matter drop or to explain more fully to the public in meeting assembled, as the committee sees fit. Yours, John F. Sugrue'"[31]

After some discussion, the committee agreed that it should report back to another mass meeting to be called sometime after the forthcoming holiday celebrations. The mayor refused to preside at such a meeting and could see no reason for further action. Finally, a compromise was reached by which the mayor would call the meeting and someone else would be found to preside. Next, Delegate Sugrue rose to speak in explanation of his report claiming that statements circulating in certain quarters that the delegates had been instructed to ask only for total abrogation of the Treadgold Concession and that it had been a money-making trip were both absolutely false. He had spent $1,500 of his own funds for the trip and had received only $1,150 and his fare from the committee. He didn't make money on it.

During the summer of 1902, protests against the Treadgold and other concessions consisted principally of frequent editorials in the *Dawson Daily News*. In late July, Commissioner Ross had suffered a seizure while aboard the *Columbian* en route to Whitehorse. Left partially paralysed, he remained in the Whitehorse hospital for almost a month and had then been taken to Victoria where he was making a slow recovery. There was no immediate prospect of his return to the government of the Yukon.

James Smart, Clifford Sifton's Deputy Minister in the Department of the Interior, had visited the Yukon during the summer of 1902. In Whitehorse, en route north, he had given a press interview which suggested that he was willing to consider that at least some of the concessions had been obtained through misrepresentation, but later he would claim to have been misquoted.[32] On reaching Dawson, he had spent much of his time closeted in the Administration Building. At one point, he had refused an invitation to visit a group of miners on Hunker Creek and finally, after one of the group spent several days waiting in the Administration Building in hopes of seeing him, had sent the miners a curt note suggesting that they write to him instead.[33] True, he had paid brief visits to Hunker and Bonanza creeks but as the *News* grumbled in an editorial:

"Leaving Dawson in regal state behind four spanking bays, the journey commenced and visits were made where? To the miner at the windlass? To the man delving beneath the surface? To the prospector on the hillside? To the miner in his cabin? No, nothing of the kind. The deputy minister passed from one rich claim owner to another. He examined the property of the man with a steam shovel and neglected that of the man with a pick."[34]

Smart left unexpectedly one morning in early September after the steamer *Dawson* had been held an hour and a half for him. Next day, the *News* fired a final editorial salvo:

"There is rejoicing at the executive mansion for Deputy Minister of the Interior Smart has silently folded his tent and followed the example of the Arab. . . . Take it altogether nobody appears to know why he came, what he did, and his going is a great relief to many who danced attendance upon him while here. There are some things he did that have not been mentioned. He made a temperance tabernacle of the executive mansion, a condition which was reversed before the steamer upon which he was passed the first bend in the river!"[35]

Unknown to Yukoners, the main purpose of Smart's trip was to test the political climate in the Yukon and make sure that the Liberal candidate would win the Federal by-election planned for later in the year. Forced to wait in Whitehorse for a confidential letter from Sifton, Smart completed a long report to Sifton dealing with local politics, the civil service, concessions and other matters. He closed on a personal note:

"I need perhaps not again express my regret that I have been held up here as I was sure that I was clear of the Territory, and I need scarcely say that I would not feel disposed to remain at White Horse for my health alone although a rest will not do me any harm after perhaps the worst experience I have ever had in my official capacity and I will have some sincere sympathy for any gentleman that may be appointed Commissioner of the Territory, whoever he may be."[36]

Treadgold himself visited the Klondike for about six weeks in the autumn of 1902. But, if anything, he was even more uncommunicative than Smart. A *News* reporter gave his version of a meeting in the Administration Building:

" 'You really don't want to know anything about my enterprises,' declared the blushing and modest Treadgold, in reply to the first question.

" 'Yes, but we do, and the public is greatly concerned in your enterprises and the operations on your concession.' rejoined the news gatherer.

" 'No, no,' interrupted Mr. Treadgold, 'you really prefer fiction. You would rather have something of your own fabrication to tell the people. You do not care for my side of the question.'

" 'Not so, Mr. Treadgold, The *News* stands at all times ready to give an impartial interview to anyone, and now has come to you and offers you the same courtesy as it offers others of making your statement of your side of the case, and desires to quote you as you may see fit to speak?'

" 'Oh, for that,' replied the tactful Mr. Treadgold, now warming to the situation with a little of the skill which might have done credit to 'Foxy Grandpa.' 'You certainly are thoughtful, but, I say, you do not need a statement from me, and I have none to make. The matter is of a private nature and regards my own affairs.'

" 'Yes, but the concession you hold and your interests

Clifford Sifton, Minister of Interior in the Canadian government from 1896 to 1905, seen here in September 1900.

have a certain bearing on the public interests and the people are anxious to know about the matter.'

" 'Well,' said the restless Mr. Treadgold, as smiles and blushes and tense lines chased each other in alternation over his face, and he looked earnestly and essayed to hurry on, 'well, so you say, but it is not my custom to speak to the public nor the custom of anyone who has enterprises of moment to handle. Let the public ascertain from what it may see. Let it judge by works rather than words. Works are the best basis of judgment, and, really, I have nothing to say.'

"By this time Mr. Treadgold was scraping and bowing backward into the comptroller's office, and as it seemed somewhat as though he was not enjoying the privilege of speaking for the public, the theme was not pursued further."[37]

Most press interviews with Mr. Treadgold over the next fifty years would fall into the same pattern.

Political changes were taking place in the Yukon, and, at the urging of Commissioner Ross and others, the Yukon was to be given one member in the House of Commons at Ottawa. Only British subjects, perhaps a third of the adult population, would be allowed to vote, but nothing prohibited the non-voters, predominantly American citizens, from taking part in the campaign. The gold rush had been international from the beginning, the mining regulations granting equal rights to everyone over eighteen years of age, regardless of citizenship. The campaign began in the summer, even though the writ authorizing the election was not issued until early September. In late August, the opposition party had chosen Joseph Clarke as their candidate and the Liberals, Commissioner Ross. Ross, still recuperating in Victoria, telegraphed his acceptance of the nomination in late September and resigned as Commissioner. He did not come north to contest the election and played no direct part in the campaign. His opponent, Clarke, a tempestuous politician, always surrounded by controversy, often made bitter, misleading, if not slanderous statements in his impassioned speeches. About a month before his nomination, he had been acquitted of charges of criminal libel and contempt in one of his many appearances in court. Clarke, the supporters of both candidates and the three newspapers (the *News* for Clarke and the *Nugget* and the *Sun* both for Ross) were soon involved in another free-for-all. But, despite the welter of charges and counter-charges on many other subjects, both platforms contained strong planks opposing the concessions:

"Opposition Platform (Clarke):
"4. That all placer ground whether covered by concession or not, be opened to location to the placer miner. That a complete investigation be made of the means and representations by which the hydraulic concessions in the Yukon territory were secured, and where same were obtained by fraud and misrepresentation or issued in error and improvidence or where they contained placer ground that the same be cancelled forthwith and thrown open for location to the placer miner. . . .[38]

"Liberal Platform (Ross):
"Whereas, The supply of water and power to the mines on the creeks is one of the most serious questions of the day in the Yukon territory; and
"Whereas, In the opinion of the convention, the matter of such supply on fair and reasonable terms should best be dealt with by the government itself, and should not be left to private individuals; therefore be it
"Resolved, That the government be requested immediately to make careful examination and obtain reports upon the subject with a view of cancelling forthwith the Treadgold concession and undertaking such a supply as a national enterprise.
"Resolved, That in the opinion of this convention many of the concessions now held were obtained by fraud and imposition; that it is in the interest of this territory that such concessions should be annulled, and to that end that inquiry should be set on foot to ascertain the circumstances of such fraud and imposition, and action taken by the attorney general of Canada in the premises."[39]

Ross won the election of 2 December 1902 but the promises of his platform, at least in regard to the Treadgold and other concessions, were to remain unfulfilled.

The Federal by-election was followed by an election for

five members of the Yukon Legislative Council on 13 January 1903. Originally in 1898, the Council had consisted of senior civil servants but two elected members had been added to it in 1900 and now there were to be three more. The new, ten-man Council would consist of the five elected members and five senior civil servants, the latter the Registrar, Superintendent of Police, Judge, Gold Commissioner and Legal Adviser. Two of the elected members would represent Dawson, two the creeks, and one the southern part of the territory, centered on Whitehorse. Of the fifteen candidates contesting the election almost all were strongly opposed to the concessions and some advocated a government-owned water system to replace the Treadgold Concession. When finally the political campaigns were over, the Yukon had a new federal member and a new Council, and it was known that F. T. Congdon, a former Legal Adviser, would be the new Commissioner, although the appointment was not made until March 1903.

1902 had been a discouraging season for the miners. Production had fallen to $13 million, down from the $20 million produced in 1901 and little more than half the $24 million of 1900. As Treadgold had predicted to Sifton in the summer of 1900, much of the drop resulted from the working out of the richer claims on Bonanza and Eldorado creeks. There had been trouble with the water supply; much of the season had been dry, but occasional heavy showers had flooded workings and played havoc with the miners' dams and ditches. In May 1902, the Mining Regulations had been changed to permit the working of up to ten claims as a partnership, and even more could be grouped provided the Mining Engineer and the Commissioner of the Yukon certified the ground was suitable for hydraulic work.[40] Consolidation was underway, and both the holders of large claim blocks and some concessionaires were requesting large water rights on nearby creeks. Clearly, little remained in the Klondike for the individual miner unless he was content to work as a laborer for one of the new companies or could find a lay on a claim on one of the outlying creeks. For many, it would soon be time to move on but the question was where to?

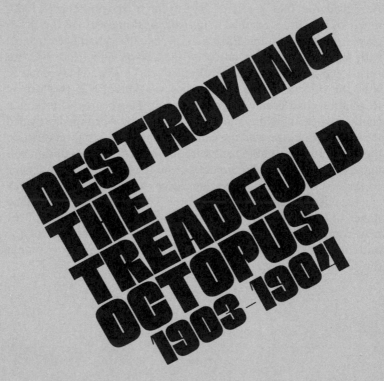

Unexpectedly, on 17 January 1903, the *Sun* carried news of a new gold field in the Tanana district of Alaska, about 300 miles to the west! The report came from Jujiro Wada, a Japanese trader, well-known and vouched for in Dawson, who had left the new find, near the present city of Fairbanks, on 28 December 1902. His information was detailed, and the values he gave for test pannings in the shafts along the new creeks were exciting! Wada, as a Japanese citizen, had been unable to stake a claim himself. Some miners stampeded to the new find while others, sick of mining, resolved to leave the North at the first opportunity. For those who chose to remain, elimination of the concessions, particularly the Treadgold, could help to keep the Klondike alive. Without them, individual claim owners could band together to complete the mining now that the end of the initial high-grading was in sight. In the next phase, creek claims could be dredged and the high-level gravels hydraulicked using water from either a number of small schemes or a district-wide government scheme. Otherwise, the Klondike would die of strangulation as the concession holders added the partially-mined and now abandoned claims to their huge blocks of ground. True, the concessions would be mined when the time was ripe, but few of the present claim owners could expect to benefit from it.

Dawson was too important to be emptied overnight by the rush to the Tanana, but with each day new stampeders slipped out of town. The newspapers carried brief items on the departure of some of the better-known miners together with articles and editorials intimating that the reports from the Tanana were certain to be exaggerated. The newspapers and the merchants had a vested interest in Dawson's prosperity, and they were determined to preserve it. True, their businesses had grown from nothing in the five years since 1898, but by now they were too well established to collect an outfit and head for the Tanana. Something had to be done quickly if they wanted to save the Klondike and their businesses, and the most obvious move was to fight for the cancellation of the Treadgold Concession and the establishment of a government water system. If that could be achieved mining activity was certian to increase!

Working with a newly-formed Miners' Association, the Board of Trade took the offensive. First there was a telegram to the Prime Minister and others in the government including the Yukon member, J. H. Ross:

DAWSON, MARCH 6, 1903

OPPOSE ANY ATTEMPT TO PASS ORDER IN
COUNCIL OR ACT IN PARLIAMENT THAT WILL
IN ANY WAY CONFIRM TREADGOLD
CONCESSION. ARE HAVING MONSTER
PETITION SIGNED AND RELIABLE DATA
PREPARED TO FORWARD TO OTTAWA ASKING
GOVERNMENT AID IN FURNISHING WATER
FOR MINING PURPOSES. PEOPLE ARE A UNIT
IN MAKING DEMAND AND WILL INSIST
UPON GOVERNMENT PROTECTION FROM
MONOPOLY OF TREADGOLD OCTOPUS
      THE DAWSON BOARD OF TRADE,[1]
      H. C. MACAULAY, PRES.

Conditions had obviously changed since last June when ex-mayor Macaulay had found "his time was too much taken up" to chair a mass meeting on the concession. Plans were made to draft the petition immediately and the group expected to obtain 10,000 signatures.

On the day the telegram was sent a committee of four of the newly-elected Council members met with the Acting Commissioner, Major Z. T. Wood of the North-West Mounted Police, to demand an immediate meeting of the Legislative Council in order to petition Parliament on the Treadgold Concession and other matters.

Wood demurred, relying on the opinion of his Acting Legal Adviser, Gold Commissioner Senkler, and suggested the matter could wait until the arrival of newly-appointed Commissioner Congdon who was due shortly. Finally it was agreed that Wood would wire the Minister of the Interior of the demand and that if approval was not granted within a week the committee would wire the Governor General.

Acting Commissioner Wood moved swiftly. The meeting with the Council members had been on Friday and on the Monday following he gave a press interview to announce that W. Thibaudeau, the Territorial Engineer, would be leaving next day to conduct surveys for a government water system. Wood stated that three years of preliminary work had already been done and the results were on file in the Commissioner's office. Water would be taken from the Klondike River at the mouth of Nello River, about 130 miles upstream from Dawson, and brought by ditch and pipe to Hunker Summit, a distance of some 76 miles. Cost of the system would be about $4 million.

"The reason for taking the step I am now doing is the fact that not one but many persons have been pressing upon me continuously the necessity of getting in an adequate water supply in order that the country may be made to produce the gold that it is capable of producing. I have sent duplicates of these maps and data to the government and also to Mr. Ross and I regard it as a certainty that the work will be taken up at once and pushed to a speedy completion."[2]

The *Nugget* was elated:

"The words of Major Wood are of more than usual significance for various reasons. In the first place his statements are always very conservative and he never talks for mere effect. His has been a military training and discipline all of his life and it is characteristic of such that when they do make statements they may be taken as absolutely true and without any element of guesswork about them. A politician will be oily in his demeanor and suave in his manner, making promises that he had not the remotest idea of fulfilling, but with a military man it is different and no surer indication may be that the Klondike will soon have a magnificent water system than the mere fact that Acting Commissioner Wood has said so. If he did not know so he would not have said so.''[3]

The Board of Trade petition, calling for cancellation of the Treadgold Concession and the establishment of a government water supply, was published two days later together with an accompanying statement:

"The Treadgold concession . . . is in the opinion of this board, one of the most iniquitous measures that was ever inflicted upon a people and . . . will work a great hardship upon the people of this territory since it will mean the virtual bankruptcy of all the property holders of Dawson and surrounding territory, and instead of the Klondike becoming the prosperous country we expect it will virtually become the property of Mr. Treadgold and those who are associated with him in his scheme.''[4]

Later, the Board of Trade would receive a reply to their telegram to Prime Minster Laurier but, as the chairman remarked: "The reply was certainly couched in the most diplomatic language, leaving the recipients in very grave doubt as to what exactly was meant.''[5]

Meanwhile, the four elected members of Council representing Dawson and the Klondike had also telegraphed Laurier asking complete cancellation of the Treadgold Concession and received in reply:

MARCH 20, 1903

TELEGRAM OF THE 16TH RECEIVED. WILL
CONFER WITH ROSS AND EVERYTHING I
THINK WILL BE SATISFACTORY
WILFRED LAURIER [6]

In fact, Ross, still recuperating, would not arrive in Ottawa until a few days later, just in time for a brief meeting with Clifford Sifton before the latter left on an extended trip to England.[7]

Later, in early April, an opposition member read the

64

text of the Board of Trade petition in the House of Commons. Prime Minister Laurier replied that he and other government members had received the Board of Trade telegram and that the matter had also been brought to the attention of the government by Ross.[8] All consideration of it would be suspended until the actual petition had been received and there would be no attempt to pass an Order in Council or Act of Parliament in the meantime.

In the Klondike, Rev. Pringle, one of the elected members of Yukon Council, had few illusions over what would happen next when he reported to a meeting on Bonanza:

"The assay office is the most pressing demand. I say it now and I said it then. The Treadgold concession is in fact the paramount question, after all. Because, if Treadgold owns the country, there will be no gold to assay and no need for banks. But the miners want the assay office first, and they want the Treadgold concession cancelled next.

"I am a Liberal and have always been a Liberal. But it seems to me the Liberal government in its administration in the Yukon has driven a coach and four through everything I ever knew that was Liberal.

"We can live in this country if you stop graft. I stand against graft.

"The appointed members of Yukon council refused to sign our telegram to Ottawa against the Treadgold concession because they said it would be a slap in the face of the government. They will vote against us for the same reason when the council meets."[9]

On March 28th, the editor of the *Sun* expected great things from Ross:

"Is he a lightning striker? We should remark that he is. Saturday afternoon he arrived at Ottawa. Sunday he received the members of the House and Senate and made friends for Yukon. Monday he was introduced in the House, upon which occasion he was cheered to the echo. The premier of Canada introduced him. Immediately after the introduction he secured the passage of a Bill granting extended powers to the Yukon council. Tuesday he spent the forenoon in the Department of the Interior looking after matters pertaining to the Yukon. Wednesday he had the price of a free miners certificate reduced to $7.50. . . . What he did yesterday is not known at the time this is written, but the telegraphic advices . . . will tell. If Jim Ross keeps up his present gait it will only take him a week to perform all the seeming impossibilities of the platform prepared here for him, bound him to."[10]

Newly appointed Commissioner Congdon arrived in Dawson by stage late on the evening of 8 April 1903 and was given an official reception the following day. In interviews the Commissioner intimated that he, personally, opposed the Treadgold Concession, but that this was a matter for Ross in Ottawa to act on.[11] He had already made his views on Council meetings clear in an interview at Skagway on his trip in:

"Unless there is special need for it there will be no session of council until the estimates have been made at Ottawa. Deliberation of council must be on these estimates. I do not approve of convening sessions . . . except when necessary. . . . Frequent sessions afford too great a danger for the passage of crank measures that would not be enacted if time was taken to fully deliberate upon them. The best legislation the world over emanates from long sessions convening at stated and and not too frequent periods."[12]

Council member Clarke, aroused over Congdon's attitude and never one to avoid controversy, wrote an open letter to the Commissioner calling for an immediate session to deal with a lien law and a memorial on the Treadgold Concession.[13] After delays, Congdon acquiesced and set 7 May as the opening date.

By now, Territorial Engineer Thibaudeau and his two assistants had returned from a month's study of the Klondike water supply appearing "bronzed from the sun as though they had been with a caravan crossing the burning sands of the great Sahara." They had taken a "thousand and one" barometric elevations over the proposed route but "until he has laid his report before the Commissioner he may not talk of the results of his trip as far as they extend to the purpose for which he was sent out."[14] The party had explored much of the watershed of the main and south Klondike Rivers and had even gone through Davidson Pass, separating the Yukon and Mackenzie river watersheds and the route used by the Peel River Indians on their long winter treks from Fort McPherson to Dawson. Some of the benches and hills of the upper Klondike looked like those near Grand Forks, and Thibaudeau speculated that another paystreak might be present. About a dozen miners were already working on Arizona Creek, near the headwaters of the South Klondike, and,

66

judging by the grub that had already been freighted in, many more would be prospecting next summer. Little more than a week later, Thibaudeau was dispatched to Whitehorse to oversee improvements in the river channel between Whitehorse and Dawson.[15] He was not expected back until after the river opened and his report, if one was even prepared, was forgotten.

The Yukon Council began its session on 7 May 1903 but, involved in organization and other matters, it was May 11th before Dr. Thompson, an elected member, was able to bring the question of the Treadgold Concession before it. After some debate, a committee of seven, three each of the appointed and elected members plus the Commissioner, was appointed to draft a memorial, or message of petition, to the government on the Treadgold Concession and three other matters. Next day, the committee reported back to the council session that, since the Treadgold Concession had already been dealt with by Order in Council, "it is not within the rights of the Commissioner-in-Council, nor is it wise to to offer public criticism of acts already done. In the opinion of your committee interests of the territory will be best served by the Commissioner-in-Council attending to the duties devolved upon him by the constitution, and leaving the performance of the remaining public duties relating to the Yukon territory to those responsible for their care and control. This position is strengthened in comparison with former times by the fact that the Yukon territory is now represented in the Dominion parliament." Acceptance of the committee report was moved, but there were two amendments. The amendment supported by the elected members called for the completion of the memorial; an amendment supported by the appointed members said the opposite, "because it is not within our function to make such a memorial. . . ."[16] Debate over the issue lasted all afternoon, culminating in two tied votes each broken by Commissioner Congdon voting with the appointed members to block preparation of a memorial. The elected members of Council had been frustrated by a Commissioner who, as a private citizen just over a year before, had been an outspoken opponent of the Treadgold Concession. But the fight would not be given up. As Dr. Thompson had expressed it:

"And I promise you that if this Treadgold iniquity is not amended that it will be my duty, and always my duty, to make every effort—to use the public means of this territory, if we cannot raise the private means—to fight this concession. It is a wholesale steal. Until these exclusive privileges are wrested from Treadgold and his associates, I shall not desist from fighting the Treadgold Concession."[17]

During council debate it had been brought out that Treadgold already held key claims covering about two miles of Bonanza Creek and that under the terms of the concession he could continue to hold them for the next thirty years without expense or representation work.

On May 12th 1903, the House of Commons in Ottawa also spent the entire day debating the Treadgold Concession. On a procedural motion, T. C. Casgrain, a Conservative member from Quebec, moved an amendment:

"This House regrets that by an Order in Council of date the 21st day of April, 1902, the government for the ostensible purpose of establishing hydraulic works to supply water for the efficient workings of auriferous deposits have granted to one A.N.C. Treadgold, of London, England, and his associates, vast powers, franchises, and concessions in and upon the beds, banks, valleys, slopes and hills of the Klondike River, Bonanza, Bear and Hunker Creeks, and in and upon the waters of Rock Creek in the Yukon Territory, with the right to establish for the benefit and advantage of the concessionaires in and through the region and district through which these rivers and creeks run, hydraulic, electrical and other systems, and to enter and to take up and operate mining and other lands:

"This House is of the opinion that the said powers, franchises and concessions constitute in favour of the said Treadgold and his associates a gigantic monopoly, which, while depriving the treasury of enormous revenues, is most detrimental to the mining industry of the Yukon:

"And that in so making the said grants and concession by Order in Council, the government have exceeded their authority and have committed a gross breach of the duty entrusted to them under the constitution."[18]

Postmaster General Mulock, the first speaker for the government, regretted that neither Minister of the Interior Sifton nor Ross were present for the debate. Ignoring Ross's election platform, he maintained that if the people of the Yukon were so opposed to the Treadgold Concession they should have elected the opposition candidate. He noted that the Order in Council would not come into force until Treadgold and his associates demonstrated they had adequate financial backing. They had already spent $50,000 on preliminary studies.

The debate continued through the afternoon and evening sessions with five speakers for the Conservative opposition and three cabinet ministers and the Prime Minister for the Liberal government. None of the speakers were miners and there was confusion over what the concession actually entailed and apparent ambiguities in the sections of the order itself. The Liberal speakers maintained that the government was unwilling to undertake a water scheme that might cost one, two or perhaps even five million dollars, and therefore had chosen to encourage a suitable private scheme by granting the concession. True, there had been some unfairness to the miners in the earlier Orders in Council but in the present one these had been righted to the satisfaction of Commissioner Ross and the two delegates, Wilson and Sugrue, all of whom had taken part in its preparation. Treadgold and his backers had the required financial support and once the scheme was completed the miners could be assured of the water they needed to work their claims.

The Conservatives, in turn, stressed the iniquities of a concession that would tie up development in the Klondike for the next six years without any work commitments. Even if Treadgold did complete the scheme he could sell water or not as he chose at whatever price he cared to set. Possible fraud was alleged but there were no specific charges despite taunts from the Minister of Justice. The Conservative argument was backed by virtually all of the blizzard of newspaper articles, petitions and memorials that had already come out of the Yukon. Why even the Liberal Association had protested the concession! Speaking towards the end of the debate, Prime Minister Laurier acknowledged that the Order in Council was not yet in force and that the government planned to investigate the entire matter. At the end of the evening the amendment was defeated 52 to 95. Ross's name appeared as one of 54 paired votes, cancelling that of an absent Conservative member. The House adjourned at 1:15 a.m.

Unknown to the opponents of the Treadgold Concession there was a delayed reaction to the House of Commons debate. In London, about two weeks later, Treadgold hurried to see Sifton who was in the city on the Alaskan Boundary question.

"I have been trying to see you today but they have told me from the Hotel Cecil that you are not in town today; so I shall come in the morning, probably about eleven o'clock, to try to see you.

"The report of the debate in the House of Commons came today and the attitude of Sir Wilfred is so weak that it has thrown my friends into a state of consternation. I don't suppose you have seen it yet. Its* absolutely vital to us."[19]

A few days later, perhaps on the advice of Sifton, the group cabled Prime Minister Laurier:

GRANTEES AND ASSOCIATES INTERESTED
SINCE 1898 IN KLONDIKE WATER CONCESSION
HAVING READ HANSARD DEBATE TWELFTH
MAY PROTEST AGAINST MINISTERS
STATEMENTS THAT ORDER IN COUNCIL IS
REVOCABLE WITHOUT GRANTEES CONSENT
AND THAT COMPENSATION IN REGULATION C
HAS ANY CONNECTION WITH RATES TO BE
CHARGED FOR WATER AND THAT FREE
MINERS HAVE RIGHT TO TAKE WATER
WITHOUT GRANTEES CONSENT.
UNLESS INJURIOUS EFFECT OF THESE
STATEMENTS COMPLETELY REMEDIED
ENTERPRISE INEVITABLY WRECKED.
RESPECTFULLY REQUEST REPLY CABLED
TREADGOLD LONDON
            FOR GRANTEES AND ASSOCIATES
            ORR EWING, TREADGOLD, COLLINSON[20]

They received a laconic reply:

YOU HAD BETTER WRITE AND SPECIFY THE
PART OF THE MINISTER SPEECHES TO WHICH
YOU OBJECT AND STATEMENT OF YOUR
OBJECTIONS
                    LAURIER[21]

_____

*Treadgold's letters were dashed off, often without commas, periods, capitals or even sentence breaks.

70

Disheartened, Treadgold wrote to Laurier, and the group submitted a detailed brief to Sifton with sections by Treadgold, Collinson (a principal backer) and Tancred (the engineer). If a Liberal government could treat them this way what would happen if the Conservatives ever came to power?[22]

The appointment of the commission promised by Laurier was confirmed a few days after the House of Commons debate but agitation continued over the terms of reference of the commission and the choice of commissioners. The commission was instructed to inquire whether the Treadgold Concession "is likely to be beneficial, or injurious to the mining interests of the said Yukon Territory" and there was no mention of possible fraud or misrepresentation. Laurier maintained that the inferences made over the concession were too vague for consideration. He denied emphatically that he had been approached in London during the summer of 1902 or later in Montreal over wrongdoing and challenged the opposition to name the supposed informant.[23] In contrast, in the case of the hydraulic concessions, the commission was to inquire into allegations that they were "procured by fraud and misrepresentation and that the material conditions of the leases have not been observed." As for the two commissioners, one, Mr. Justice Britton, had been a Liberal Member of Parliament before his elevation to the bench in 1899 and the Conservatives predicted a whitewash.[24]

Ross, the Yukon member, had failed to live up to the *Yukon Sun's* billing as a lightning striker after the flurry of activity in his first week in Ottawa. Absent most of the time, for illness or other reasons, he had taken no part in any of the debates on the Treadgold Concession. Eventually in late 1904, he would be elevated to the Senate without either speaking in the House of Commons or returning to the Yukon. In the opinion of the editor of the *Dawson News* he had "proved as impotent as a katydid in a simoon."[25]

Mr. Justice Britton, together with his fellow commissioner B.T.A. Bell, and a staff of three arrived in Dawson on 13 August 1903. At last, the people of the Klondike were to be given an opportunity to express their opinion on the Treadgold and the other hydraulic concessions. The first meeting of the commission assembled on 17 August, exactly seven years from the Carmack party's discovery on Rabbit Creek. The Dawson Board of Trade had retained two lawyers, W. A. Walsh and C. M.

TREADGOLD ACTS THE PART OF
THE DOG IN THE MANGER.

Cartoon against the Treadgold Concession in *Klondike Nugget*,
20 June 1903.

THIS CLAIM TO
BE GIVEN AWAY
NO WATER.

Woodworth, to represent them and most of the other Dawson lawyers were involved, either in the attack or representing the interests of the concessionaires. Over the weekend the commissioners had become personally aware of the bitter opposition to the Treadgold and other concessions and one of their first moves was to limit the time during which complaints could be submitted to less than one week. Later, in his report, Britton would describe the atmosphere at the hearings:

"The counsel who did appear were able men. They represented on the one side, an agitated and excited people who had formed opinions hostile to the concessions long before the Commission issued; and on the other side the concessionaires, who were very thoroughly disliked by their opponents.

"Then, the season was very dry, and there was comparatively little work at mining by individual miners, and so a great many hostile miners thronged the court room and corridors during the sittings. It required considerable moral courage for any miner voluntarily to give evidence against the expressed opinion of the hostile majority in the court room.

"The result of this state of things was, that when Mr. Bell or myself suggested or ruled that a statement was improper or irrelevant or immaterial, or when a question was asked by either that appeared to be like cross-examination, it was treated by some of those present as an unfair interference on the part of the Commissioners."[26]

Taking of evidence began the second day with Walsh reading a preliminary statement against the Treadgold and other concessions on behalf of the Board of Trade. Over the next few days engineers and miners described the difficulties of mining the high-level, White Channel Gravels. All told the same story. An assured water supply was urgently needed on the hills and benches but not under the terms of the Treadgold Concession. The main objections to the concession were that Treadgold had been given his rights for six years, free of any work commitments, and, if and when the water did reach the workings, he could sell it at any price he chose. The price would certainly have to be less than the maximum price of twenty-five cents per miner's inch per hour given in one of the earlier versions of the Treadgold Concession as, at that price, only exceedingly rich gravels could be mined profitably.

Treadgold returned to the Klondike a few days before

the Commission began its hearings. He attended all of the hearings, often sitting behind the jury box. Much of the time his reaction to the evidence would be masked behind a sardonic grin but occasionally he would laugh to himself at something in the testimony. His turn on the witness stand began on 22 August; the *Sun* reporter described his impressions of the first day:

"A.N.C. Treadgold took the stand and spoke publicly for the first time since he became identified with the Klondike. Naturally reticent, he has often been referred to as a sphinx and the appellation was well deserved. No newspaper man has yet succeeded in getting anything from him beyond monosyllables and very few of them. After taking the oath there was a craning of necks, for the sphinx was about to speak, and after he had been on the stand for several hours conclusions that had been arrived at were unanimous regarding several things. First, he speaks of millions as ordinary persons do hundreds; he has figures and data at his finger tips constantly on tap; he disclosed no horns nor hoofs as he has been ordinarily painted; he is highly educated, uses excellent language and made monkeys of his questioners."[27]

Treadgold had no detailed plans or drawings of his scheme with him, these prepared under the direction of Sir Thomas Tancred, remained in London. However, he did give a general description of the scheme he had in mind. It involved taking 5,000 miner's inches from Rock Creek and bringing it by about forty-five miles of ditch and flume to a point where it would be brought across the Klondike River valley in an inverted siphon. From the outlet of the siphon, on the ridge between Bonanza Creek and the Klondike River, two separate flumes, each capable of carrying 4,000 inches of water, were planned; one leading to the hills above Grand Forks and the second to Bear Creek and on to the hills above Gold Bottom Creek. In addition to Rock Creek water an additional 3,000 miner's inches would be pumped from the Klondike River. Power for the pumping station would be obtained by taking 8,000 miner's inches from the Klondike River near the mouth of Bear Creek and carrying it four miles by flume to a hydroelectric plant capable of generating some 3,000 hp. Reluctantly, he revealed the estimated cost of the scheme, a total of about $4.5 million. He refused to commit himself to firm prices for the water delivered on the hills but estimated a maximum price of twenty-five cents per miner's inch per hour, possibly dropping to as low as five cents per inch on Lovett Gulch, close to the outlet of the planned siphon. Treadgold stated that he had the backers, whom he refused to name, and stated that if certain unspecified obstacles were removed the work could begin in March 1904. Questioned what kind of capital he had ready to put into the scheme, Treadgold dived in his pocket and produced a small roll of bills. As he began counting he asked: "Is that the kind of answer you want? That is the only kind of answer a sensible man could give."[28] But Treadgold held back many details and "at one point he appealed to the bench, saying he had never been in court before in his life and thus did not know how far a witness could be made to go in his revelations."[29] Other attempts to question him closely were met with replies of: "Off the point," "I will not answer that," and "No answer," and in most instances he was backed by the commissioners.[30]

A few days later the inquiry turned to the hydraulic concessions that had been protested. The entire character of the hearings changed. No longer trying to look into the future the Commissioners were now concerned with past events involved in the granting of the concessions.

Rules for obtaining the hydraulic concessions had been given in the Hydraulic Regulations of 3 December 1898 and later modifications. The regulations required the applicant to state that he, or his agent, had prospected the ground prior to 3 December 1898 and had found it unsuitable for normal placer mining. Upon a report from the Commissioner of the Yukon that he was satisfied that the applicant, or a person acting for him, had indeed prospected the ground in question and a further report from the Gold Commissioner that the ground requested was unsuited to normal placer mining, the applicant was eligible for a concession. This could include from one to five miles of creek or river frontage with a depth of one mile, although the latter could be extended to the full width of the valley at the order of the Minister of the Interior. Rental was $150 per year for each mile of frontage and the concessionaire was obliged to spend a minimum of $5,000 a year in work on the ground. Default on the requirements of the lease could result in cancellation three months after notice of such had been posted on the location.

A total of forty hydraulic leases or concessions had been granted and at the time of the commission hearings only twenty-seven were in good standing. Of the latter, some eight had been protested before the commission. The concessionaires were a mixed bag; a few, like Anderson and Boyle, had been in the Klondike in 1897 but others had never been within a thousand miles of the concession that bore their name. Some were known to be friends or business associates of Clifford Sifton, Minister of the Interior.

Somehow, for some individuals, the definition of "ground not being worked and . . . not suitable to be worked under the placer Regulations" had been applied to portions of the richest creeks in the Klondike. Reluctantly and often with considerable embarrassment, the concession holders or their representatives took the witness stand to describe their prospecting activities.

Typical among them was J. B. Tyrrell, a geologist and mining engineer, describing his work on the Bronson and Ray Concession on Bonanza Creek. In a statement sworn before Commissioner Ogilvie on 5 May 1899 he had declared:

"That in the month of July, 1898, I prospected a piece of ground, the northerly boundary and the edge of which begins 2½ miles up Bonanza Creek from its mouth, extends up both sides of said creek 2½ miles in a direct line.

"That I did this prospecting for the purpose of determining its value as a hydraulic claim.

"That I made many examinations of the gravel pretty well over the surface of the said piece of ground and found nowhere enough sufficient to warrant me in assuming that it would be a profitable placer mining area.

"That from the indications I observed through such prospects I am of opinion that the ground is suitable only for working on an extensive scale, such as a hydraulic principle or other similar principles.

"That only some process of that kind will render it available for profitable use."[31]

On the same day Tyrrell made his declaration, Gold Commissioner Senkler had written to Commissioner Ogilvie to report about thirty-eight creek or gulch claims, fifty hillside claims and one hundred bench claims lay within the area. About forty of these were in operation and production for the year was estimated at about $120,000 although: "An examination of the dumps exposed on the different claims proves the ground to be low grade with three or four exceptions, so low grade that a large percentage of the claims are worked at very little profit, if any."[32]

On the witness stand Tyrrell was forced to admit that he had arrived in Dawson on 16 July 1898 and that on 7 August 1898 he had been back at the mouth of the Nordenskiold River, some 300 miles upstream on the Yukon River and that during the entire period he had been an employee of the Geological Survey of Canada, a government agency.

Flustered, he had asked: "Is it not possible to work for two men at once?"

"The Bible says not," the Board of Trade lawyer shot back.

Other than that he carried a gold pan and had talked to miners working along the right limit of the ground, Tyrrell could remember little of his prospecting activites.[33] He was whip-sawn over differences between his sworn statement and the Geological Survey report written by R. G. McConnell and himself.[34] Questioned why bench workings on Lower Bonanza were not mentioned in the government report, Tyrrell replied that he had left Dawson at 10:00 p.m. and the workings opposite 60 Below were the first he could examine in daylight. Almost everyone in the room, probably even Tyrrell, realized instantly that there would be almost continuous daylight at the time in question, but the lawyer was more interested in the description of the bench workings and did not bother to follow it up. The bench workings, in the upper end of the Bronson and Ray Concession, were reported to contain gravels running five to twenty cents a pan and nuggets up to $1.35. Yet this was ground that Tyrrell had sworn was "not suitable." Finally Tyrrell was allowed to leave the stand but there was more to bear next day when all three papers commented on his "prospecting feats."

The Board of Trade lawyers met with increasing resistance in their efforts to examine documents relating to the concessions under attack. Initially, Mr. Justice Britton would allow a document to be produced if it was specifically requested, but later H. H. Rowatt, in charge of the files for the Department of the Interior, interposed and refused to show some files to anyone, including the commissioners.[35] One witness, Joe Boyle, was perfectly willing to have the file on the Boyle Concession examined but admitted that he himself had not been permitted to examine it in Ottawa.

Frustrated by the attitude of the commission, another

mass meeting had been called in late August, filling the auditorium.[36] Everyone wanted to speak. The meeting passed a flurry of resolutions condemning the concessions, opposing the present inquiry and calling for the resignation of Ross as the Yukon's Member of Parliament. A committee was chosen to carry the minutes of the meeting to the Britton Commission. In contrast to the Klondikers and the commission members, one individual who was able to work off his frustrations was George Coffey, an old-time miner. In giving evidence, Robert Anderson, a concession holder, had referred to Coffey as "really nobody." The two met on the street the following day and the encounter ended with the police pulling Coffey away from Anderson, who had been knocked into a mud-filled gutter and "whose face looked as if someone had tried to print the map of Lynn Canal on it."[37] Coffey later pleaded guilty to creating a disturbance by fighting on a public street and cheerfully paid a five-dollar fine and costs.

The Britton Commission held two meetings on the creeks, the first at Grand Forks on 3 September and the second on Gold Bottom on Hunker Creek on 5 September. The Grand Forks session, held in the Presbyterian church, was the more informal. At one point, Commissioner Bell left his station in the pulpit, told the secretary not to take notes and allowed a free-wheeling session between Treadgold and the local miners. Treadgold was in great form, and even his old enemy, the *Dawson News,* paid him an oblique compliment: "Treadgold showed that while he is short in supplying water he is long in supplying words. . . . Treadgold answered his own questions and backed up his answers with long arguments. With practice he would make a fair stump speaker."[38]

On Monday, 7 September, the hearings resumed in Dawson amid mounting frustration on both sides. Tuesday morning was particularly difficult. It began when Commissioner Britton grew livid with anger as George Black, one of the attorneys, pressed him for the documents on a concession. Then Joe Clarke, the senior Yukon councillor, took the stand and there was a heated personal exchange between Britton and Clarke over the witness's background. Suddenly it was over. Written arguments could be forwarded to Ottawa during the next two weeks and the attorneys were given ten days to exchange arguments.[39] The sittings adjourned at 12:40 p.m.; at 4:00 that afternoon Commissioner Britton and the stenographer left

Cartoon depicting the Britton Commission's abrupt departure from Dawson in *Dawson News*, 21 September 1903.

Dawson on the *Whitehorse*. Treadgold was one of the small group at the dock to see them off. The rest of the commission staff were forced to cool their heels in Dawson until they were able to get space on a boat later in the week.[40]

In Ottawa a few days later, the conduct of the commission was discussed in the House of Commons. Once again, the government speakers reaffirmed their confidence in Judge Britton as a commissioner and professed themselves unconcerned when "an hon. gentleman like the leader of the opposition reads from some paper published in the Yukon, the 'High Mountain Screecher' or some such name. . . ."[41]

James Sutherland, now Minister of Public Works, thought that a water scheme was necessary but was unwilling to recommend government participation, and furthermore:

"The company which Mr. Treadgold represents is one of the most responsible and respectable companies ever organized to do business in Canada. On inquiry by the government we received assurance from Lord Strathcona that there was no question at all as to the character of the men who formed this company or their financial ability to carry out anything they undertake. The Bank of England could not have had a higher character from Lord Strathcona than he gave to the parties interested in this undertaking. Is it to be supposed that these men, men of the highest character and of the greatest financial ability are going to be mixed up with anything improper? I believe they are going into this hoping that it will result in financial benefit to themselves in working out to successful conclusion the large interests that they have there and that cannot be worked out unless some such undertaking as this is carried out."[42]

In the Klondike, the Britton Commission hearings over, Treadgold and Joe Boyle, with one or two others, set out on a pack-horse trip to examine the possibilities of a water supply from either the North Fork of the Klondike River or the Twelve Mile River.

"The trip was made by taking the old Rock Creek trail, which crosses the divide from the hill back of Dawson, thence going to Rock Creek, then to Coal Creek and on to the northeast. Twelve Mile River was also visited. . . . The party was out fourteen days and had the benefit of the big rains. For a short time at least Treadgold had an actual water question with which to deal. The rains poured down his back and kept his bed afloat at night, put out the camp fires, filled the cooking utensils and made things miserably romantic in general."[43]

Three days later, after a farewell consultation at the dock with his lawyer and some friends, Treadgold slipped aboard the *Whitehorse* by the outer gangplank and retired to the privacy of his stateroom. He was hoping to avoid Waterfront Brown, a Dawson fixture who, since 1899, had made a hazardous living collecting debts or serving writs on debtors attempting to skip town. His rates for this service varied from a usual 20 percent to as high as 90 percent in "difficult cases."[44]

"There was a little excitement yesterday on the *Whitehorse* when the man who is supposed to be the richest person in the Klondike was served with a paper notifying him that the N.C. Co. is suing him for $864.84.

"It was no other than Waterfront Brown who served the king concessionaire with the summons. Brown knocked at the door of Treadgold's stateroom and the latter opened it far enough to see who it was that wanted to get in. When he saw it was Brown he tried to close the door but Brown was there with his foot and the door was kept open for some time. At last Treadgold opened the door and asked, as Brown handed him the paper: 'What is this?'

"He was told that it was a legal summons secured by the N.C. Co. and that Brown had performed all to be required of him. The summons requires an answer from Treadgold within eight days.

"Brown then bowed himself out and let Treadgold tell the man that was with him: 'what a terrible country it is and what beastly people live here. . . .'[45]

"When the boat had gone a few feet the czar came out of the stateroom and descended to the lower deck. He passed forward to the flagpole at the bows. Grasping the pole with one hand at the level of the shoulder, he leaned against it with his feet crossed. With a reflective smile he watched the crowds on the wharves like some paternal despot gazing on his possessions. In this graceful position, he passed from the view of the proletariat."[46]

By now, summer activities were coming to an end. The river would soon be closed and Dawson isolated from the Outside until the winter stages could be put in operation. It was a time when there was little real news and, in place of it, a *Dawson*

Record reporter managed to fill one column of the Sunday edition with comments by an anonymous local merchant:

"This is the beginning of the winter of my discontent. You see, it is this way. Dawson has been flooded with Eaton's and Simpson's catalogues, both being mail order houses of Toronto that supply everything from safety pins up to straw-saving, self-stacking threshing machines, and as is the custom every year many Dawson ladies have sent out to these houses for orders and from now on till the close of navigation they will be coming in by every mail . . . Fully three-fourths of the orders received contain from one to half a dozen articles that fit like a sheet on a broomstick or, in the opposite direction, like a number 2 shoe on a number 5 foot. Then these same people, because they buy a lawn dress in June and a paper of pins at Christmas in my store, think I should fall over myself to exchange all their misfit articles for them. . . . For example a woman with a 44 inch bust will want to exchange a 36 inch waist for one she can button with the aid of a peevie and cant-hook. Another will want to exchange an electric seal coat for one that will fit her and at the same time want the real seal instead of the imitation. And the worst of it is, they snap their jaws like steel traps and look as though they wanted to say 'you mean thing' when I refuse to take their cheap importations in exchange for my goods."[47]

The Britton Commission was gone, their report not expected for some time, but Dr. Thompson, an elected council member, had personally carried the attack on the Treadgold Concession to London in the winter of 1903-1904:

"In London, I met Orr Ewing, the financial backer of Treadgold. He was glad to meet me, and after I had talked with him for considerable time, he declared he never before understood why the people of the Yukon were so persistent in opposition to the Treadgold concession. I told him that with the concession he had the agitation would never cease. He asked if he had my sympathy for investing in the concession and I told him he did while the concession read as it was because the people would never let the matter rest in that state. I pointed out to Mr. Orr Ewing the reasons of dissatisfaction, chief among them being the great quantity of land and water he held, the monopoly of the Klondike river supply, and his mining in opposition with the individual, which in time would be to simply freeze out the individual. He then thanked me for information."[48]

On 29 June 1904, cancellation of the Treadgold Concession was disclosed in a brief exchange in the House of Commons between an opposition member and Prime Minister Laurier:

"Is the rumour circulated in the press as to the cancellation of the Treadgold Concession well founded?"

"It is."

"That is one result of our efforts last season."

"If it pleases my hon. friend, he may think so."

"Would the right hon. gentleman have a copy of the Order in Council put on the table?"

"I cannot see any objection and will state the request to my hon. friend the Minister of the Interior."[49]

The Order in Council cancelling the Concession was accompanied by a letter to the Minister of the Interior from Orr Ewing and Treadgold, dated 2 June 1904:

"Dear Sir: The reason for granting the charter which we received in June 1901 was the belief that we could supply the wants of the Klondike district by the installation of a water system which would develop in extent and usefulness as the necessity for an artifical water supply became more pressing. The modifications which were made at the instance of the delegates who came from Dawson in the spring of 1902 impaired the usefulness of the scheme in our judgment, but if we had been permitted to proceed without further hindrance we should certainly [have] engaged the necessary capital and made the enterprise very beneficial to the claim holders of the district covered by the charter.

"When our enterprise was attacked in parliament in May 1903, we had completed the necessary financial arrangements for the large sum of money required for our work and no doubt existed as to the successful carrying out of our obligations. The attack however, combined with the attitude assumed by the government which also threw doubt on the validity of our charter and imposed on us a complete suspension of operations until the report of the so-called Treadgold commission appointed by the government, should be received has completely paralysed our efforts, undermined the confidence of our financial backers and made it impossible for us to proceed.

"We therefore feel compelled to notify you that we must withdraw from the enterprise as chartered by the Dominion government. In so doing we desire to reiterate to you our conviction that the installation of an artificial water supply is essential for the successful treatment on a permanent basis of the vast alluvials of the Klondike district and we consider it regrettable that the Dominion government should have been influenced by agitation worked up against our charter by a certain section of the Klondike public and should thus have made it impossible for us to proceed with our enterprise on a basis commensurate with the needs of this important district.

"Regretting that after having secured sound financial support for this enterprise and having spent large amounts of trouble and money upon it we have been prevented by the attitude of the government from carrying it to a successful termination in the shape in which it was chartered we are, etc."[50]

The Britton Commission still had not reported, and with the Treadgold Concession cancelled the report was certain to be anti-climatic. Indeed, there was some question whether there would be a report at all despite frequent requests for it in the House of Commons. One of the commissioners, B.T.A. Bell, had died early in March 1904 from injuries received in a fall, and no written report could be found among his papers although it was understood one had been prepared. Mr. Justice Britton, the remaining commissioner, showed little interest in completing a report but ultimately did so, after a decision by the Secretary of State that no report would be required was overruled by the Prime Minister. Delay followed on delay, and the report was not tabled in the House of Commons until the first of August 1904, ten days before the end of the session.[51] The members, weary of the session and exhausted by the summer heat, did not debate the findings. Little remained to debate; the Treadgold Concession was cancelled and Britton had adroitly side-stepped charges of possible fraud and misrepresentation in the granting of the hydraulic concessions. All that remained was the question of whether the holders of the latter had complied with the requirements of their lease.

It had been a limited victory. The hated Treadgold Concession was gone and it seemed certain that in the future the holders of the remaining hydraulic concessions would be forced to meet the minimal requirements of their lease. Unexpectedly, there was fresh hope with new men as Commissioner, the Yukon Member of Parliament, and, most of all, Minister of the Interior. Commissioner Congdon had resigned to contest the federal election of December 1904 and had been defeated by Dr. Thompson, a bitter foe of the concessions. A new commissioner, W.W.B. McInnes, had been appointed in May 1905 despite lobbying for Congdon's reinstatement. Clifford Sifton had resigned as Minster of the Interior in early March 1905 after a dispute with Laurier and had been replaced by Frank Oliver. Beginning in the autumn of 1905, there was a serious attempt to cancel some of the remaining hydraulic concessions but it ended in failure in 1908 when two of the concession holders won an action in the Supreme Court. Later attempts were equally unsuccessful but eventually most of the concessions were abandoned and thrown open, although two, the Anderson (Lease Number 1) and the Boyle (Lease Number 18) would still be in good standing when the dredging ceased in 1966.

TREADGOLD, THE GUGGENHEIMS AND YUKON GOLD COMPANY 1904-1925

Treadgold arrived back in the Klondike in late August 1904 after spending the winter in England. He had lost his battle to hold the Treadgold Concession, but he still held about one-quarter of the claims on Bonanza and Hunker creeks, either openly or through other names. Many were the key claims that would be needed for dumping ground when the White Channel Gravels on the hillsides were hydraulicked—and Treadgold was still dreaming of consolidation. But, in the interim, either mining or representation work to the value of $200 would have to be done on each claim. On arrival, Treadgold gave an interview to a reporter from the *Yukon World,* Commissioner Congdon's newspaper:

"A.N.C. Treadgold, the man whose name has been a byword with the opposition for the past several years and whose efforts to put water upon the hills of the Klondike have met with nothing but the most determined rebuffs at the hands of a select coterie led by a band of misguided agitators, is again in the city, having arrived on the *Selkirk* last night. . . .

" 'I am surprised,' said he . . . 'to see the pessimistic view taken by so many of the people here relative to the exodus to the Tanana country. . . . Don't you know that the more the attention of capitalists is drawn to this northern country the better it will be for it? It would be infinitely better if there were half a dozen centres as well known as Dawson instead of there being but one as is now the case. The discovery of gold in the Tanana and the building up of a city the size of Dawson or even larger can not help but be of great benefit to this camp. The reasons are obvious and perfectly plain to any man of discernment. The camp is certainly neither better nor worse than it was a year ago with every promise of it being better in the future.

" 'Neither do I take the view that the time is approaching when the country will necessarily fall into the hands of the few. This is the time for the individual to hang on. It costs comparatively little to retain possession of a claim and if one wishes to take a chance in the lower country it is no reason why he should sacrifice his holdings here in order to do so. One good thing that has resulted [from] the exodus to the Tanana has been the stiffening of the labor market. Labor should never be cheap here; there is no object in a man migrating to this northern country where conditions are sometimes hard unless he can better his condition financially and that is why I say labor should never be cheap. . . .

" 'Another thing which it might be well to impress upon the minds of the people is that the government has not lost interest in the country. Far from it. What the ministers and many of the members of parliament are saying to themselves is, "What do the people of the Klondike really want?" They are aware that water is desired above all things, yet such a racket was raised over the only proposition that was ever submitted to them that they are in a quandary what to do. Ultimately it will come out all right, and you mark my word for it.'

"Mr. Treadgold did not care to discuss his projects for the future though admitting they were more or less closely associated with the welfare of the Klondike." [1]

He quickly left the Klondike without tipping his hand.

Treadgold was in Ottawa in late March 1905 and believed to be interested in the property of Joseph A. and Ellen Acklen. [2] The property, lying within the Dawson city limits, was centred on a bench directly across the Klondike River from the mouth of Bonanza Creek. It was on a sunny south-facing slope and about 250 feet above the river. Initially, in 1898, the Acklens had developed the property into a successful farm but, with the discovery of gold, farming was forgotten.[3] They began hydraulicking in the summer of 1903 using three sluiceheads of water, and now the Acklens were looking for additional water at the required head of about 300 feet above their workings. An earlier grant on Rock Creek had been cancelled, but by the spring of 1905 they held grants for 10,000 miner's inches from the Twelve Mile River and 1,000 miner's inches from Moosehide Creek, all conditional on the necessary flumes being installed by October 1907.[4] A grant for another 5,000 miner's inches from the Twelve Mile River was pending. The Acklens had announced that their company would spend $3 million on the project.[5] Rufus Buck, the Dawson civil engineer who had surveyed the route of a ditch from the Twelve Mile in 1904, would be busy again in 1905. Water from the Twelve Mile would be brought along the east side of the Moosehide Hills, some seven miles to the northeast of Dawson; that from Moosehide Creek would be carried by a flume, high up on the Moosehide slide, a huge tan-colored smear on the face of Midnight Dome, the backdrop for Dawson City.

Treadgold was back in the Klondike in early June 1905. He was busy "rushing around all summer" and there were many rumors about his new plans. But others, concerned with smaller consolidations or simply finding a job, paid little attention to him now that his concession had failed. Treadgold had an immediate problem with the right of way of the Klondike Mines Railway which would have to cross his Bonanza claims and might interfere with future mining on the ground. The railway, chartered years before, and, launched with a prospectus that anticipated a 25 percent annual dividend, was finally underway after an aborted start in 1902.[6] Immediate plans were to link Bonanza Creek and Dawson but, in more grandiose moments, there were dreams of connecting to a transcontinental line at Edmonton. Work had started on a bridge across the Klondike River and on the right of way up Bonanza Creek. Treadgold was ready:

"A.N.C. Treadgold and the Klondike Mines railway collided this morning. Treadgold did not like the fact that the railway crossed one of his claims in the Nineties Below on Bonanza, so he proceeded to the claim this morning and removed a rail from the track.

Freight train of the Klondike Mines Railway hauling logs. The railway ran from Dawson (background) to Sulphur Springs. Not completed to the Dome until 1906, the railway was left with little to do but haul wood to the newly consolidated Guggenheim operations on Bonanza Creek. It ceased operation in 1914.

"When the tracklaying crew came along this morning on a car drawn by a locomotive it found the track torn up. Treadgold disputed the right of the locomotive to cross his property, and stood on the track, and demanded the authority of the party.

"Jerome Chute, railway contractor, politely picked up Mr. Treadgold and lifted him off the track and deposited him some feet from the track. Treadgold in the meantime made an effort to free himself, but not until the more skookum Mr. Chute deposited him beside the track as aforesaid.

"The railway crew relaid the track, while Contractor Chute held Mr. Treadgold. Treadgold afterwards returned to the middle of the track and refused to get off to let the engine pass onto his claims.

"Dave Curry, foreman, took Mr. Treadgold in charge, and knelt upon the chest of Mr. Treadgold until the engine passed.

"The story of the incident soon spread over the town, and was the subject of considerable talk. Treadgold objects to the railway crossing his claims and the railway people insist their franchise gives them a right and that they intend to have their rights. The two sides of the question of franchise and damages are to be argued in the territorial court Monday on a motion for injunction and damages."[7]

The question was still festering when Frank Oliver, the new Minister of the Interior, visited Dawson in late August 1905. The minister, walking along the railway route, was joined by Treadgold and the railway people who walked along with him "making representations as they went. The two sides told their story, and finally became so eager to talk that the minister had to call them to order and tell them not to quarrel before him, but if they had anything to say to him to say it. They said many things. The minister expressed many emphatic statements on the situation, and gave the impression that he would see that in so far as he is to have anything to do with it that there will be a full understanding and a clearly defined course of rights."[8]

The issue was finally resolved in the spring of 1906, but by then gold production was falling rapidly and much of the population had deserted Bonanza Creek and Grand Forks. The railway, eventually extended to the Dome, was left with little to do except haul wood for the Guggenheims and proved a financial disaster for the English backers.

Treadgold left Dawson at the first of November 1905. The *Dawson News* commented:

"A.N.C. Treadgold, the man of diminutive stature and the big ideas, who plays the title role in the concerto and does all the visible hustling at the Dawson end, was here all summer putting in every moment this season in most energetic action. He visited water sources, toured the creeks, bought numerous new properties along Bonanza and did other things on a giant scale and it is said he has a plan to contrive to get the privilege to bring water from the upper Klondike or the Twelve Mile and the Klondike combined, or some such source to the placer fields of the camp in great quantities. It is generally surmised and locally believed that Treadgold and the Acklen water concern are one. Last year the Acklen people built miles of ditch and said they had millions back of them. This year they did nothing visible to the public.

"Now Treadgold has hied himself to Ottawa or London, his usual winter haunts and is supposed to be on the same feverish hotfoot drill there that he maintains in the Klondike. Treadgold has pursued his dream in the Klondike for about eight years and seems undaunted."[9]

Rumors flew all that winter but the first definite news of Treadgold's latest plans came with the arrival of C. A. Thomas and a party of six other engineers in mid-March 1906.[10] A ditch fifty to sixty miles long was to be built to carry 5,000 miner's inches of water from the Twelve Mile River to the mouth of Bonanza Creek. The Yukon Sawmill Company had contracted to set up a portable sawmill about twenty-five miles from the mouth of the Twelve Mile before the spring breakup. Two or three steam shovels would be used in the construction of the ditch and some of the Twelve Mile water might be used to generate power for dredges understood to be on order. Thomas had little to say about dredges except that the company would be lucky to get them with factories Outside overrun with orders for steam shovels and other machinery for the Panama Canal. Thomas declined to name the backers of the scheme, but there were persistent rumors from Outside concerning the Guggenheim interests.

Even the *Dawson News* felt differently about Treadgold now:

"Treadgold is instructive. He is a lesson all in himself. Through him we come to a better understanding of ourselves and by him can be proven the falsity of the repeated assertion that the opposition of the people of this country to all forms of concession came from the envy of wealth. When Treadgold acquired the well-remembered Treadgold concession, war was declared, and knew no surcease until after years of distressing agitation the concession became a thing of the past. Today, Treadgold, or those whom he represents, owns miles upon miles of even richer Klondike placer ground than that in the original concession—and not a word unfavorable or critical is heard. Why? All that he now has, he has acquired in the regular manner—in a way open to us all if we have the backing or cash, while all that he had, was secured by special concession, by favoritism, by a special exercise of the powers of government. What he has is felt to be rightfully his; what he had no man felt he had a right to possess. The one was graft: the other is felt to be individual property. What he has, he has acquired in what men regard as honest fashion; what he had was secured by certain wire pulling manipulation four thousand miles away.

"The immense Treadgold interests lately secured have provoked not the slightest opposition in any quarter. Vast water rights have been given, but they were first properly advertised as being regularly applied for under provisions of the law open to all alike. Immense ditch rights have been given, but they also were secured in similar fashion. Miles of claims have been absorbed—under the placer mining regulations available to us all. And the difference in results is remarkable. While Treadgold is once more the ostensible holder of more valuable rights and properties in the Klondike than any other man, there is neither the alleged envy seen on a former occasion, nor enmity to the great wealth he represents. On the contrary, there is a keen desire to see his ditches built and filled with water and to see his trains of pack mules bringing in the gold for shipment.

"Clearly, then, the former opposition was never personal to Treadgold. When the name was being bandied from pillar to post, it was evidently the concession and not the man that was aimed at. When the size and wealth of the former Treadgold grant was being held up to public disapprobation it was not the wealth nor the prospective fortunes provoked the contumely. And it will be noted that each step of progress now taken by the Treadgold people is chronicled with approval commensurate with the former indignation sounded at everything done, in short, Treadgold proves the temper of the people here to be 'Special privileges to none: equal opportunities to all.' ''[11]

Property acquisitions continued, and at the end of March 1906, two of the larger operations on Bonanza Creek, the Fuller Norwood and the Anglo-Klondike mining companies, were reported sold to Treadgold for transfer to the new company.[12] The price for each was believed to be about half a million dollars.

Supplies began streaming in with the first boats, and late in June a shipment of pre-cut timbers for three dredges arrived on a barge pushed by the *Columbian.*[13] Pits for the dredges were prepared, two at claim 104 Below and one at 90 Below on Bonanza.[14] Preliminary work was underway on the power plant on the Twelve Mile River, some twenty-five miles northeast of Dawson, and the sawmill located in the timber on the Twelve Mile had been in operation since late April.[15] Water for the power plant would be tapped from the Little Twelve Mile River, amid the jagged peaks of the Ogilvie Range, and carried 5½ miles by ditch and flume to a point above the power plant in the main valley. Water would be delivered to the power plant at an effective head of 650 feet and the initial installation would be about 1,650 horsepower. Later, a ditchline, about seventy miles long, would carry Twelve Mile water to the mines on the hillsides above Grand Forks.[16] Other projects underway included completion of the Acklen Ditch from Moosehide Creek to a reservoir above the Acklen Farm and a dam across Upper Bonanza Creek at 57 Above.[17] The latter, keyed into a four-foot

Yukon Gold Dredges Numbers 1 and 2 under construction at 104 Below on Bonanza Creek in 1906. Hydraulic workings in the background are on the Acklen Farm property, across the Klondike River.

Shovel Number 2 at work on Yukon Gold's Twelve Mile Ditch in August 1906. Wood was cut along the route for use as fuel.

deep slot into the soft bedrock would be 225 feet thick at the base narrowing to 20 feet at the top. When full it would hold over 3½ million gallons of water and up to 2,000 miner's inches could be delivered to the White Channel Gravels above Grand Forks by flume and ditchline built on the hillside above the creek.

By now, it had been acknowledged that the Guggenheims were behind the new scheme, and two of the Guggenheim sons visited the Klondike in early August 1906. Before their arrival, the Dawson newspapers were full of background information on the family. The founder of the dynasty, Meyer Guggenheim, born in Switzerland in 1828, had emigrated to America as a youth and later made a fortune in the embroidery business. Involved as a partner in an unsuccessful mining venture in Colorado, he had personally salvaged the mine and then expanded his interests into smelting. Later, in 1888, he built a smelter for his seven sons at Pueblo, Colorado, at a cost of $1¼ million. The sons, operating as M. Guggenheim's Sons, continued to expand the enterprise and would ultimately become principals of American Smelting and Refining Company. In

97

addition, other mining ventures were carried on by their Guggenheim Exploration Company. Two of the sons, Daniel, executive head of the latter company, and Solomon, together with their wives visited the Klondike.[18]

Treadgold chartered a special train on the newly-completed Klondike Mines Railway to take them on a tour of their extensive workings on Bonanza and Eldorado creeks. In addition, the party visited the Bear Creek dredge, installed the summer before by the Canadian Klondyke Mining Company on the Boyle Concession in the Klondike River valley.

Commissioner and Mrs. McInnes held an afternoon reception for the party at the Commissioner's Residence:

"The reception was a splendid revelation to the strangers of the possibilities of life in the Klondike. The mansion was a bower of beauty. At every turn were the richest of flowers. Brilliant native blossoms of a score of varieties mingled and vied with as many charming flowers indigenous to other lands. . . . Amid the fragrance and the beauty of the scene was the constant strain of sweet music. The orchestra was half hid by palms and a bank of growing plants.

"The guests . . . were introduced to the host and the hostess and the guests of honor in the west salon. . . . The visitors moved into the central drawing room . . . where they chatted for a few moments or enjoyed the pleasure of the cushioned divans or great easy chairs. Across the spacious hallway was the tempting dining hall, ablaze with shining glasses, brilliantly tinted punch bowls and the sparkling beverages all set off with the snowbanks of unflecked linens. . . . Seductive ices, delicious cakes and palate-tickling sandwiches conspired to dispel the ennui or aid the crimson brew exhilarate. Fragrant draughts of coffee were served . . . while Mrs. A. E. Wells supervised the modest installments issued at the punch bowl. Some of those of the more severe side of humanity did the heavy work with the ladle. . . .

"The honored ones were most happily entertained, and no pains were spared, to make the occasion all that might have been expected by the most fastidious Klondiker, and to make it far more than visitors from afar in the world of old and established and known ways might ever imagine possible to behold within the shadow of the Arctic circle."[19]

Dawson and the Klondike were still overwhelmed by the extent of the Guggenheim activity when the party, accompanied by S. H. Graves, President of the White Pass & Yukon Route, left next evening on the *Whitehorse,* specially chartered for their visit. Surely with all their activity the Klondike would boom again ending the steady drop in gold production from more than $22 million in 1900 to the current $5 million. Construction was going ahead rapidly; the three dredges were to be completed that fall and the powerplant was scheduled to go into operation in the spring of 1907. By late summer, crews were at work stringing the transmission lines from the Twelve Mile plant to the dredges. Treadgold himself was busy acquiring more property, and during the summer many of the smaller properties had been transferred to the Guggenheims, now operating under the names of Yukon Consolidated Goldfields Company and Northwest Hydraulic Mining Company.

The Guggenheims had not announced any financing scheme, and the work was being carried on under a number of company names but what did it matter? Obviously, the Guggenheims had the resources to develop the scheme privately if they wished to do so, and if they chose to finance it publicly there should be no difficulty in floating the stock. In mid-October 1906, a huge grouping of claims was recorded for Bonanza, Eldorado and Hunker creeks and it was realized that the Guggs now controlled most of the ground Treadgold had sought for his concession. How Treadgold fitted into the scheme had not been revealed but it seemed certain that, as the promoter, he must have been suitably rewarded. The consolidation was complete. The next step would be dredging of the creek ground followed by hydraulic mining of the unworked portions of White Channel Gravels on the hill claims. But, even at this time, Treadgold had additional holdings that had not been included in the consolidation. Perhaps these would be included later or possibly he was already dreaming of a new consolidation that would be his alone.

By October 1906, most of the crews had been paid off, and there was a slack period until late November when the muskeg had frozen and the first snowfall provided the cover needed for winter freighting. Huge woodpiles grew beside the thawing plants that would prepare the ground in front of the dredges. At Twelve Mile Landing, some eighteen miles northwest of Dawson, the 3,000 tons of material landed from the steamers and barges could soon be hauled the remaining thirty miles up the

Twelve Mile River.[20] A winter road had been cleared and the tussocks of moss that carpeted much of the valley bottom levelled off. Roadhouses were built at ten- to twelve-mile intervals, and the hauling began.

Heavy sleighs were used, each pulled by six horses and capable of carrying sixteen tons. First priority went to the steel penstocks and other material needed to complete the power plant and, following this, material and supplies were spotted along twenty miles of the ditchline leading to the Klondike. The loads included lumber from the Twelve Mile sawmill to be used in sections where the water would be carried by flume and specially-cut staves of redwood lumber, together with hardware, for the sections of stave pipe. Many of the crews would spend Christmas and New Year's in the company camps and roadhouses.

A Japanese merchant from Dawson, Kawakami, or "The Mighty Atom," was hard at work building a public roadhouse at the foot of the Twelve Mile Hill. This was five miles downstream from the powerhouse, where a steep road climbed out of the valley bottom to reach the ditchline, almost 1,000 feet above the river.[21]

The young American engineers had done their work well. By early 1907 everything was ready to go when the spring thaw released the water needed to operate the powerplant and ditchlines. Moosehide Creek was the first to open, and after a careful inspection by C. A. Thomas, the Guggenheim's resident manager, water was turned into the Acklen Ditch in late April.[22] Less than a week later there was a break in a section of flume crossing the Moosehide slide, and water poured down the hillside and into the Yukon River near the Dawson city garbage pier. The break was quickly repaired and watchmen stationed on the line. The following afternoon lawyers for Yukon Consolidated were in court seeking an injunction against Mrs. Lizzie Schmidt to prevent further interference with the ditch.

In the case that followed, Mrs. Schmidt, owner of the An Las quartz claim on which the break had occurred, acted as her own lawyer. She claimed that the ditchline interfered with the development of asbestos showings on her claim and no company, not even the Guggenheims, was entitled to stand in her way. The judge, unimpressed by Mrs. Schmidt's legal talents, ruled that she had a right to mine her claim but that it should be done in such a manner that it did not interfere with the ditch and flume crossing

Hauling logs to the Twelve Mile sawmill, March 1907.

Top—Freighting equipment and pipe for the Twelve Mile power plant, February 1907.

Bottom—Twelve Mile sawmill from across the log pond, 1907.

it. Neither blowing up the flume, nor cutting batter posts, nor digging under them could be considered bona fide mining, and her demand for $75,000 from the company "looks like what we call in this country, a hold-up."[23] The injunction stood, and Mrs. Schmidt was fined $100 and $919.75 costs. Later, she would rebuff peace feelers from the company and continue her battle even after her An Las claim was sold at a sheriff's sale for $80 in March 1908.[24]

There were other problems. At the new dam on Upper Bonanza, the discharge pipe had buckled, and the crew of 400, some of whom had been at work for almost two months, was cut back to about thirty men.[25] The Twelve Mile power plant was still not ready, but the new dredges could be tested briefly using power from the Dawson steam plant. The Twelve Mile plant was completed on the evening of 28 May 1907 and tested the following day. It ran smoothly and was left in service.[26] All three dredges were started up, and if an official opening was planned it was quietly forgotten. It had been a remarkable achievement. Tens of thousands of tons of equipment and material had been assembled and shipped into the Klondike by ship to Skagway, rail to Whitehorse and river steamer to Dawson and Twelve Mile Landing. During the middle of winter everything had been freighted to the sites and assembled. Once the river closed for the winter the only connection to Whitehorse and the Outside was by stage, and only small, light items could be transported on the sleighs. Miraculously, all the pieces had been fitted together and the entire plant was in operation before the Yukon River opened and the first boat of the 1907 season reached Dawson.

Much of the ground ahead of the dredges was permanently frozen and would have to be thawed. Hardest to contend with were the sections of creek bottom riddled with abandoned underground workings, many now filled with solid ice. Already, the manager of the original Discovery dredge had found that an encounter with a pillar of ice would rack the dredge more than a month of ordinary work: "It is like putting the dredge against so much granite."[27] Initially, steam thawing (modified from the method used in underground mining) was used, although it was hoped that this could soon be replaced by a system of stripping using water under high pressure to remove the muck followed by natural thawing of the exposed gravels.[28] In steam-thawing, locomotive-type boilers, commonly of 150

PUBLIC ARCHIVES OF CANADA

Top—Panorama of the Twelve Mile River valley, looking south from the intake of the siphon carrying Tombstone River water across the valley of the Little Twelve Mile River. Yukon Gold's power plant is in the centre foreground and, on the hillside, the Twelve Mile Ditch continues south beyond the penstock, where smoke is visible in the distance.

Bottom—Twelve Mile power plant, seen from the stable in March 1907.

Top—Steam thawing plant, with steam points in place, preparing ground ahead of Yukon Gold Number 5 in September 1911. The Bonanza Creek siphon, carrying water from the Twelve Mile Ditch, has been opened to permit the dredge to work through.

Bottom—Nailing battens on the Twelve Mile power plant flume, May 1907.

horsepower, were fed from huge woodpiles surrounding each one. A system of main and branch pipes, all boxed and insulated, led out from each boiler with rubber hoses leading to the steam points that were connected at eight-foot intervals along the branch lines. There were two common patterns for setting out the points, eight-foot rectangles and nine-and-a-half-foot triangles. To start a steam point, a steel bar would be driven into the ground until frost was encountered and then the steam point, with a 5/16-inch orifice for the steam at the tip and a head that could be driven with a sledge hammer, started in the hole. A point could generally be advanced about two feet per hour; two-man crews, one to hammer and the other to keep turning the point with a wrench, were kept busy working the group of points assigned to them. Steam pressure in the boilers was generally 100 to 150 pounds per square inch and the crews tried to keep the pressure at 25 pounds at the points themselves. The operation went on in a maze of metal and rubber pipes and, underfoot, the ground was a morass of water, thawed muck and vegetation. Under such conditions, accidents and scalds, either from broken lines or blowouts of boiling muck from around the points themselves, were all too common. The method was expensive, averaging about 14.5 cents per cubic yard for the years 1909 to 1914. Attempts were made in 1906, 1907 and 1909 to develop a method of stripping followed by natural thawing but the company found they were unable to prepare ground fast enough for the dredges and, for the moment at least, the expensive steam thawing continued.

The dredges were large, floating sluicing plants, weighing about 800 tons, that carried their ponds with them as they mined.[29] Their scow-like hulls and superstructures were heavily braced against the stresses developed by the heavy machinery. Digging was done with a continuous bucket line, each bucket having a capacity of five cubic feet. The buckets discharged into a hopper within the dredge and from there the gravel was fed into a huge, revolving, inclined screen about six feet in diameter and twenty-eight feet long. The gravel was washed and broken under a water spray as it worked along the screen. Any fragments less than one inch in diameter passed through the screen and over a series of tables, or sluices, where the gold was recovered. Coarser material worked to the lower end of the screen from where it was carried out well behind the dredge by an inclined belt or tailings stacker. Finer tailings that had passed over the tables were discharged from short sluices behind the dredge. The forward end of the steel girder, or ladder, that carried the bucket line was suspended by cables and pulleys from the heavy posts of the front gantry; it could be raised or lowered by a winch. Another winch (both were operated by the winch-man from the winch-room atop the dredge) drew the dredge along a cable anchored to deadmen on shore, so that the dredge dug in an arc, pivoting on a huge steel pin, or spud, at the rear of the dredge. After the gravel and approximately four feet of bedrock had been dug from one position of the spud, the spud would be lifted, the dredge winched into position for the next cut, the spud dropped and the new cut started. As the dredge advanced, crescentic piles of tailings, capped by slabs of bedrock torn from the bottom of the cut grew behind it. Each dredge was under the supervision of a dredgemaster and the normal crew on each shift consisted of a winch-man, an oiler in charge of the machinery and one or two men on shore in charge of the deadmen and cables. Both the yardage handled and the recovery reflected on the skill of the dredgemaster in handling his operation. With the short season controlled by the availability of power from the Twelve Mile plant, every effort was made to keep the dredges operating on a twenty-four hour basis with a minimum of down time for maintenance.

Activity speeded up during the summer of 1907. Dredging and hydraulic mining were underway, the latter at some of the smaller operations purchased the year before. The dam on Upper Bonanza was completed and the water was being delivered to Gold Hill, near Grand Forks, by two ditch lines and an inverted siphon across the valley of Bonanza Creek. The inverted siphon consisted of a U-shaped line of steel pressure pipe, with a minimum diameter of twenty inches, leading from the intake down to the creek bottom and up the opposite slope to the workings where it was directly connected to two hydraulic monitors, operating on a head of 150 feet of water.[30] Four more dredges, all with seven-cubic-foot buckets, were under construction, two on Hunker Creek and two on Bonanza. In addition, a large crew continued work on the Twelve Mile, or Main, Ditch.

To supplement the dredges, the Yukon Gold engineers had designed mechanical elevators to mine areas with coarse gravel and broken bedrock considered too blocky for a dredge to

Yukon Gold's Elevator Number 3 at claim 3 Above on Bonanza Creek, summer 1908. Hydraulic monitors were used to drive the gravel into the elevator pit, from where it was hoisted and sluiced. Exposed bedrock was cleaned by hand, one man cleaning 15 to 20 square feet per day. Later it was found that dredges could handle the ground more efficiently, and the elevators were abandoned.

handle.[31] Essentially, they were continuous bucket lines, like those of the dredges, operating from a sump, and their capacity was about 3,500 cubic yards per day, roughly comparable to one of the first dredges with their five-cubic-foot buckets. Eventually, three elevators were built and installed on Lower Bonanza Creek. They operated from 1908 until the end of the 1910 season, when it was realized that a dredge could mine the same ground at a much lower cost.

Now, with the operation in production, there was a consolidation and, in mid-June 1907, claims held by the various Guggenheim companies were all transferred to a new one, Yukon Gold Company.[32] From this time on, all the Guggenheim operations in the Klondike were carried on under the name of Yukon Gold, locally referred to as the Guggs, and earlier companies, including Yukon Consolidated Goldfields Company and Northwest Hydraulic Mining Company, were dissolved a few months later. Yukon Gold Company, incorporated in the State of Maine on 28 February 1907, was originally capitalized at $25 million, divided into 250,000 shares with a par value of $100. At the end of 1907, 116,572 shares of $100 each were reported issued and outstanding. Solomon Guggenheim was president of the new company and directors were four of the Guggenheim brothers, together with A.N.C. Treadgold, J. Hays Hammond, A. Chester Beatty, O.B. Perry and C.K. Lipman. Financing was still private; no plans for public financing had been announced. Hemmed in by Yukon Gold operations, little remained for individual claim holders or the smaller operations on Bonanza and Hunker creeks. Many were selling out, often as soon as the richest portions of their ground were mined. Most of the sales were for cash at prices less than $50,000.[33]

Work went ahead steadily in the Klondike but there was an unexpected blow from Outside with the financial panic of 1907. There had been uncertainties and warnings throughout the year but in mid-August the stock market was hit by heavy selling. More problems followed and until late in the spring of 1908, the Dawson newspapers would carry many articles about conditions Outside including bank and trust company failures, currency shortages, marches by the unemployed, riots and the use of troops to control them, together with statements by President Theodore Roosevelt of the United States and other government officials attempting to calm the situation and restore confidence.

In early November 1907, Daniel Guggenheim gave his views in an interview in New York. The financial troubles had been started by "shrewd, long-headed bear operators" overselling hundreds of thousands of shares that they did not own. Things had now reached the "hysterical stage" with people disposing of their holdings regardless of their actual value. As an example he cited Guggenheim Exploration with its valuable Klondike holdings, ready to produce next season, and yet the stock was selling at 120, far below the 200 of a year before.[34]

In the Klondike, Yukon Gold's Resident Manager, C.A. Thomas, assured the community that the money had already been appropriated and that work would go ahead despite conditions Outside.[35] Some 2,000 men would be employed, mainly on the Twelve Mile Ditch, and a crew of 100 was already at work in the winter freighting.

Battered by the financial panic and falling metal prices, the Guggenheims chose to float an issue of 700,000 shares of treasury stock of Yukon Gold Company. In preparation the share structure was expanded to 5 million shares, par value $5, with Guggenheim Exploration Company, who had already spent over $8 million on the project, holding the 2,800,000 shares already issued. The float was understandable; more money would be needed before the property could be brought into full production and gold was one metal that still had a firm price. In contrast, the choice of Thomas W. Lawson, a stormy petrel of the financial world, to handle the issue was incredible. Possibly the Guggenheims reasoned that his backing would recommend them to the public at a time when their fortunes were at a low ebb and their name under increasing attack.

Lawson was a Boston financier who had been involved in a running battle with Wall Street, the mining and oil barons, and the government for years. Typical of his attacks was one made before the Minneapolis Commercial Club in July 1905:

"I have several millions of dollars myself, and I wronged the American people getting it. But I did not know it at the time. When the time comes I will give all this money back to them.

"John D. Rockefeller is worth $500,000,000, and I can sit down and show you in a week's time how he got every penny of it. There is no secret about it. Every dollar that John D. Rockefeller has he got dishonestly.

"If I live I am going to make the American people sell every dollar's worth of stock they have. By that time they will know better than to buy back."[36]

In 1908, he expressed a different opinion in a letter to *Everybody's Magazine:*

"You talk of what I owe the people. What do I owe to the gelatine-spined shrimps. What have the saffron-blooded apes done that I should halt any decisions to match their lightning change, chameleon-hued loyalty? The people . . . particularly the American people are a joke—a system joke. When in all history have the people done aught but rail, or stand shivering by, while their enemies crucified those who battled for their benefit?

"I cut off my friends and the friends of those dearest to me. I directed upon myself and those dearest to me the cursed machinations of the most vicious human wolves. I spent an enormous fortune, so that today the remnant makes the cavity appear an abyss. I replaced a big, broad love for, and faith in, the people with a contempt so great as to make me wonder how both could be bred in the same human soul. And even this awful price I would have willingly paid if I could have gained the end I started for. Yes, even now I would continue paying the same price on and on to the end if—and there's the rub—if it had done good. But it has done no good."[37]

Lawson's promotion, conducted in late March 1908, consisted of four advertisements entitled "Fair Finance" run consecutively in the leading newspapers of the United States, Canada, England, France and Germany. The name of Yukon Gold Company or the Guggenheim connection was not revealed until the final advertisement, twenty-four hours before the stock was offered on the New York Curb Market.

The first advertisement, titled "Fair Finance 1," addressed to President Roosevelt, the people, capitalists and the press, asked all to watch for news that would cause the capitalists, at least, "to sit up—straight up—and take notice."[38] Fair Finance 2, addressed "To Every Man and Woman With Savings," told how Lawson had advised the "Captains of Finance" to use publicity in the sale of stocks and that:

"My condition that I be allowed to 'paw over'
the goods of 'the Street' was conceded, and I quickly
found enough rare good ones for a test. . . .

111

"Men and corporations of great wealth and business responsibility have been induced to contribute 20 per cent of one of their most important investments to the public at 50 per cent of its actual sure worth, or 25 per cent, of its perhaps worth, for the purpose of proving to the public, in an unmistakable way, that from now on the people are to get a square deal in American finance. . . .

"In 38 active years in finance . . . I have never known of any investment where large dividends were combined with sufficient safety to justify an honest man who really knew finance in advising say a woman of ordinary means to exchange her Government bonds or savings bank deposits for it. . . .

"This remarkable investment which is to be offered to the people is really free from any hazard. It could have been sold at any time during the past two years and can be sold now to Wall Street itself at much more than the price at which it is to be offered to the public. It is as safe as any investment can be. It represents one of the greatest successes of its present owners, who are in the very front rank of the world's greatest Captains of Industry. . . .

"In other words, in my chapter to-morrow I will demonstrate, absolutely, that this remarkable offer is really what it appears upon its face to be—an opportunity for the people to accumulate millions, and that this opportunity is given to them solely for the purpose of most successfully inaugurating a new system of finance."[39]

Next day, Fair Finance 3 revealed even more. The offer was to be 700,000 shares of a gold stock with a par value of $5 with the remaining eighty per cent of the stock held by a holding company, controlled by the most successful group of mining capitalists in the world. The complete story would be told tomorrow and it:

"will be unique inasmuch as it will be the first time in history of stocks where a story relating to a security of great worth will read like the yarns usually spun in glaring advertisements by irresponsible, wildcat, stock-promoting swindlers."

Lawson advised:

"First, that every small investor . . . place in the hands of any of the members of the leading stock exchanges or of their local bank or banker, all or a substantial portion of his savings, at the same time an order to buy, at say, not over $7.50 per share, whatever number of shares the money will pay for, but in every case to attach to these buying orders positive instructions not to execute the order until after further directions. Next, carefully read to-morrow's statement and investigate the correctness of all the assertions and proofs submitted and, if the verdict is as it will be, that this is an investment such as heretofore have only been given to 'insiders'—captains of finance—then affirm the order. But I bear down on this: If the slightest doubt remains about this investment being a nugget, cancel the order, and no loss will accrue and no harm will have been done. . . .

"My advertising has interested vast numbers of people everywhere in what is to be described to-morrow when all will be able to judge for themselves of the desirability of investing, but not until Saturday, that is, not until everyone has had twenty-four hours' opportunity to satisfy themselves of this stock's worth, can anyone secure a share at any price, for every share is owned by the corporation I refer to. I do not own a share."[40]

Yukon Gold Company was named in the Fair Finance ad the following day. Lawson considered Yukon Gold the surest and choicest investment in the Guggenheim group:

"First—The product of gold mining is always worth at least one hundred cents on the dollar in the money of any nation, with the market always unlimited.

"Second—Because 'Yukon Gold' is a 'dredging and hydraulic' instead of a 'deep mining' proposition, which means that it cannot be affected unfavorably by flood, famine, earthquakes or 'bad times'.

"Third—Because the quantities of gold contained in the Yukon property are definitely known.

"Fourth—Because the cost of mining on this property could always be accurately estimated.

"Fifth—Because this group had been liberal and far-sighted in their expenditures for 'the plant' to an extent heretofore unequalled in any gold mining proposition in the world—that is, this group will have invested, when their present plans have been completed (they are nearly complete now), $12,000,000, and three years of labor, not only fearlessly invested, but so wisely that if 'the Guggenheims' had accomplished nothing else in 'business' this one effort would have marked them as great public benefactors.

"Sixth—Because it was positively known that the enterprise was an immensely profitable investment.

"For the above reasons leading bankers have eagerly sought to secure the whole or a large portion of the Yukon stock to offer to the public. For the same reasons the group have always refused to part with any of it.

"The only reason that makes it possible to secure any of this stock now is, first because it is now a complete success and, second, because the group have been convinced that just at this time, when the people are filled with distrust of all things corporationwise, it will be of inestimable value to the whole investment and corporation structure to spread through the land into the hands of thousands of small and large investors a fraction of the stock of their enterprise at less than one-half of its actual worth. . . .

"While I do not yet own a share of Yukon stock, I have, nevertheless, a tremendous interest in the success of this project of disposing of this stock. If it's the success it should be, I increase my power to procure bargains from the great captains of finance for the people, and when the 700,000 shares I have been instrumental in securing for the people at one-half or one-third their worth are in great public demand at two to four times what the people have paid for them, I will have added largely to my public following.''[41]

Other material in the ad included a summary of a letter by O.B. Perry, General Manager of Yukon Gold, estimating that the gravels should yield $50,000,000 in gold of which $36,000,000 should be net profit. Another by Treadgold gave an estimate of $58,540,000 and a net profit of $43,950,000 for the higher grade gravels along the creek bottoms and hillsides of Bonanza and Hunker creeks.

There was no prospectus or financial statement on the operations of Yukon Gold to date. In the text of his ad Lawson admitted that ''duplicate parts'' of the statements by Perry and Treadgold had been cut out because of advertising costs. Unabridged copies would be sent to anyone who wished them, but exactly how they would obtain these before the stock went on sale the next morning was not specified. Despite his worry over advertising costs, Lawson did find it possible to include a listing of the important Guggenheim companies and their capitalisation together with a pooled list of directors, company officers, representatives and agents.

A second ad on the same page of the *New York Times* carried the title ''Fair Finance—Warning,'' and in it Lawson warned that, despite rumors to the contrary, not a share of Yukon Gold stock could be obtained until the following day, and further:

''Everyone may rest assured of the following course:

''The stock will be put on sale Saturday at 5½, 5¾, 6, 6¼, 6½, 6¾, 7, 7¼ and 7½, and under no circumstances will be allowed to go beyond 8 until every share of the 700,000 has been disposed of—fairly and openly disposed of.

''I pledge myself to this, and it will be possible for me to keep my pledge, for, until the last share has been sold, the business is completely and absolutely in my hands. . . .

''I give this warning that the public everywhere may know that under no circumstances will there be a runaway market in this stock until after the

115

700,000 shares are in the hands of the public. Then the public themselves through their brokers in the open market, will make their own price.

"Bear in mind that all that is necessary for a would-be buyer is to give his order to any Stock Exchange or Curb house or local banker with instructions to buy Yukon Gold at not over 7½."

Ads by other brokers offered their services in securing shares, one noting:

"The fact that our senior partner . . . has until recently, and for 13 years past, been private secretary to Thomas W. Lawson, and that our firm makes a specialty of the securities of the only company to which Mr. Lawson has loaned his name, and of which our senior partner is Vice-President, the 'Lawson Mexican Company', should mean that we are not handicapped in such a rush as is slated for to-morrow."[42]

The Sunday edition of the *New York Times* described the sale: "The interest stirred up by the Lawson advertising brought a big crowd to Broad Street before the market opened yesterday morning. When the trading started . . . there was a mob on the sidewalks and up and down Broad Street on both sides of the stretch of asphalt at the corner of Exchange Place given over to the curb brokers, which was pretty nearly as big as the crowd which hooted down the Suffragettes a month ago. Like that day, an additional audience leaned out of the windows of near-by skyscrapers and every vantage point within shouting or signalling distance of the crowd of fighting and yelling brokers. . . .

"The curb men were nervous over the possibilities when the hands of the curb clock got around toward ten yesterday morning. Scarcely a curb house in the Street lacked orders, either to buy or sell the Lawson stock, and no one was sure that orders were not big enough to run away with the market. The Police Department showed its anxiety by sending down to the curb two mounted men and seven patrolmen, bossed by three Sergeants.

"There are no stringent rules on the curb . . . and when some one in the packed mass of brokers yelled out an offer at eight minutes before ten the market broke loose. Lawson's agents had distributed selling orders among about twenty curb brokers, who were scheduled to put out the stock at prices ranging up from 5½ to 7½. Their first shouted offers brought buyers down on them in masses. For the first few minutes every man with stock to put out was the centre of a fighting swirl of brokers, who rushed the sellers back and forth across the asphalt from one side of the street to the other. . . . The police let the buyers and sellers fight it out without interference. . . . In the scrimmages around the sellers the small men of the curb had little chance to get their orders filled, and . . . several of the traders went down in the crowd. Clothes were torn in the scramble, and a broker was lucky who saved his hat."[43]

The excitement simmered down after the first half-hour. No one knew the total number of transactions but the accepted estimate was 350,000 shares and the closing price was 6¼ to 6½.

"Fair Finance—Yukon $10" appeared in Monday's papers and Lawson reported that all 700,000 shares had been sold in two hours. However, rather than leaving Yukon to the street he had decided to stay with it a week longer:

"to show [the growlers] that to keep a stock in great demand, at, say 10 for the present, even though it has all been turned over to the public at an average of 7 . . . is as easy as it is to sell 700,000 shares in two hours, when the combined efforts of 'the street' cannot market half that amount of stock in two weeks. . . .

"Therefore, I say again to the public everywhere; Buy Yukon at any price under 15 as an investment, and I say to all who have already bought, don't part with any of your stock under 10. I ask both classes to watch the movements of Yukon in all the different markets where it will be most actively traded from now on, and to judge by its price whether some of us know as much about market operations as we do about talking to the people through the press megaphone."[44]

Despite Lawson's claims, all had not gone well, and next day, when the stock had dropped to 5½, Solomon Guggenheim issued a statement:

"In view of the misleading reports regarding our attitude with respect to the marketing of shares of the Yukon Gold Company, I consider it but just to ourselves and to all concerned that we make our position plain.

"Arrangements for the sale of 700,000 shares of treasury stock were made by our Mr. Daniel Guggenheim just before his departure for Europe. We have no criticism or complaint as to the manner of working the stock, and have never attempted to repudiate any statements published by Lawson concerning the property.

"We have absolute faith in it. Every statement contained in our publications is fully justified by the reports of our experts. Our judgment is based not only on their reports but on a personal examination of the situation made by my brother Daniel and myself in the summer of 1906. It was after that visit I accepted the presidency of the company, which I now hold, and we have never sold any of our shares."[45]

On April Fools' Day, Lawson had another ad in the *New York Times:*

"As I have said so many times, Wall Street is a queer place—very, very queer; but when one knows Wall Street—I know every hair on its beautifully combed head—its queerness is mighty fascinating.

"One always likens Wall street to a rosy-cheeked kid. It pouts when it gets no jam, it pouts when it gets lots of jam, and it pouts while it waits for jam. Some of us have dallied with Wall Street in all of its moods, and some of us wouldn't give up dallying for a front seat in Azure Land.

"Wall Street hoped I would bump my forehead on Yukon. Instead I just drove the jam cart right up to its curb and told all hands to sail in—and they did. Then they got mad—piping mad—and swore they wouldn't play and that they would be blessed if they would let me play. Then they proceeded to sell at a loss some of the Yukon I let them have at a bargain. Queer, queer Wall Street.

"I knew what Wall Street would do on Yukon, because I have known Wall Street so long I always know what it will do. Wall Street thought it would fool me into buying back its Yukon at a profit to Wall Street, but I remembered that when Wall Street makes up its mind to get mad, it doesn't care whether it makes a loss or not. So I reasoned this way:

"Every share of Yukon is worth ever so much more than what I sold it at. I have sold it to many thousands of investors. They bought it because I showed them it was the best sort of an investment. They, these investors don't care a picayune whether Yukon sells at 5 for a day or two, or not. In fact, they will rather like to have it sell down there because then they can buy some more. Therefore, why not let that part of Wall Street which is real mad over my Yukon success drop the remainder of its stock which it bought Saturday, at say 5 to 5½ for a quick turn? Then have it stand by and watch what it sells at 5 to 5½ go marching along up to say 8. Truly Wall Street is a queer lot—of course I mean only a section of Wall Street. To-day or to-morrow when I go down and call Wall Street's attention to how demurely Yukon is trotting along up, a man from Mars would never dream that Wall Street was mad with me—never."[46]

Yukon Gold stock traded at a high of 5 or fractionally above for the next ten days and then fell to 4½ or below. Volume was less than 10,000 shares a day after the first three days and the *Wall Street Journal* quipped, "At one moment on Tuesday the celebrated Yukon crowd consisted of a boy with a sandwich board and two brokers busily quoting stock to one another."[47]

Ten days after the float, Lawson was back with an ad that promised to explain the reason the stock had not risen in a following ad, but the promised ad, printed the next day, concluded that to do so "would be unwise and perhaps to some, unfair."

The statement would now be published later "at the beginning of an aggressive market campaign" when "all will clearly understand how easily the best laid stock market plans can be temporarily interfered with by not-possible-to-be-foreseen accidents."[48]

The promised campaign began in early August with an ad that prophesied:

"In this market fortunes will be picked from
every bush if would-be pickers will only follow the
advice of those who have never yet missed a big
pickin'."[49]

This time the stock was National, a holding company
that would use its vast funds to control the price of other stocks
including Yukon Gold. Once again, Yukon was to be boomed to
10, but, despite frantic advertising through much of August,
Lawson was only able to push it to a high of 6 for one day. Again,
the Guggenheims were attacked for their association with Lawson
in the float. They had received perhaps half of the money they
expected—and desperately needed—from the float, but both they
and Yukon Gold would suffer from bad publicity for many years.

The price of Yukon Gold stock never rose to the
promised 10; below 4½ for most of the last four months of 1908,
it rose to a high of 6 in the summer of 1909 but soon dropped
below 5 again and later drifted down gradually to just over 2 in
1913.

In the Klondike, Yukon Gold started up the Twelve
Mile powerplant early in May 1908. The first two dredges were
working before the end of the month, the other five following
over the next few weeks. Some 800 men were already at work and
it was expected that the crew might reach 2,000 later in the season.
There was also trouble, this time over the bringing in of contract
labor from Outside.

The steamer *Dolphin* (of Alaska Steamships, a
Guggenheim-controlled company) had slipped into Vancouver
harbor in early June 1908 to pick up 100 contract laborers for the
Klondike.[50] Under the terms of their contract, the men agreed to
work ten hours per day, seven days per week at a wage of $2.25
per day plus board. Transportation would be provided to and
from Vancouver, provided the worker completed the four-month
season to Yukon Gold's satisfaction, and free board would be
provided in the case of temporary layoffs. Overtime would be
paid at the same rate as the usual shift. The worker was expected
to supply his own blankets and pay a charge of $2.25 a month for
medical coverage. Late in June 1908, a mass meeting was called in
Dawson to protest the use of contract labor at $2.25 per day when
the going minimum wage in the Klondike was $4 per day. Ex-
Commissioner Congdon, now in private legal practice in Dawson,

was appointed to negotiate with Yukon Gold, and he negotiated an agreement which provided that there would be more local hiring and that contract workers could work for the going rate of $4 per day provided they repaid Yukon Gold the cost of their transportation from Vancouver. However, many of the 350 men who had started for the Klondike had deserted on the way in or on reaching Dawson, and the company insisted that those who remained pay part of the additional expenses resulting from delays on the trip in. The tangled expenses of the men who remained with the company were not settled until late August.

Most of Yukon Gold's operations went well in 1908. All seven dredges were in production, and there were three mechanical elevators and smaller hydraulic operations using water from the Bonanza Creek drainage. Only the attempt to replace steam thawing with natural thawing had failed; the natural thawing experiments which had gone on since 1906 were abandoned at the end of the season. Steam thawing would be modified and made more efficient over the next few years, but still it required huge woodpiles, and with the denudation of the nearby forests fuel was becoming increasingly expensive. There would be no breakthrough until cold water thawing, developed in the Nome area of Alaska, was introduced in the Klondike in 1919.[51]

The Twelve Mile or Main Ditch was not expected to be in operation until the 1909 season. It would not be needed sooner because Yukon Gold's plans called for large sections of the Bonanza Creek bottom to be dredged before the ground was buried by the immense fans of tailings that would spread from the hydraulic mining of the White Channel Gravels on the hillsides. From intakes on the Tombstone and Little Twelve Mile rivers in the Tombstone Range, the ditch followed the valley wall of the Twelve Mile River for about nine miles below the powerhouse, then crossed the Tintina Trench, marked by a ten-mile-wide low area between the Ogilvie Mountains and the Moosehide Hills. On reaching the Moosehide Hills, the ditch snaked its way along the contour of the northeast flank to a point overlooking the Klondike River valley opposite the mouth of Bear Creek. An inverted siphon more than three miles long carried the water across the Klondike valley. From the outlet another ditch followed the ridge above Bonanza Creek and then, by means of another inverted siphon, conducted the water across Bonanza Creek to the White Channel Gravels on the west side.

Assembling redwood-stave pipe on the Lepine Ridge section of the
Twelve Mile Ditch in 1907.

One visitor described the difficulties of a summer inspection trip along the route of the Ditch:

"As viewed from afar the panorama of wooded valleys, and the distant range that serves as a watershed, afford no suggestion of the natural obstacles to be overcome, but a closer acquaintance soon demonstrates that the forest is but a scant growth of small trees, just fit for telephone poles, not big enough for lumber, struggling to assert a stunted life amid the vast morass covering the face of the land. A soggy blanket of moss mantles the ground, which is held in the grasp of a perpetual frost. Under the moss is ice; the moss forms an insulating blanket so that even the short warm summer does not thaw the frozen ground lying beneath this dark green coverlet. In places the ice melts slightly and pools of water form. Everywhere the surface is wet and sloppy. Our horses splashed through it. We stumbled over the spongy mass. It is a dismal swamp, which becomes almost impassable when torn by traffic. Wherever a trail was worn by use, it became a quagmire and it was best to turn our horses to the untrodden moss alongside; in this their feet would sink to a depth of six or eight inches, for below that was the frozen ground; while in places, where the moss was cut and worn away, the thaw had

Ditch construction on the hillside above Bonanza Creek in 1909.

reached deep enough to make progress impossible. And these conditions obtained not only on the flats, but on the slopes. The water is held by the moss as by a sponge, so that even over an undulating topography there were no running streams."[52]

In building the Twelve Mile Ditch, correct gradients had to be maintained in order that the water would flow at a uniform rate. Ditch was the cheapest construction but where the topography precluded its use other alternatives used to carry the water were open flume, redwood-stave pipe, where the head did not exceed 125 feet, and steel pipe in the inverted siphons crossing the larger valleys. The water would be delivered to Gold Hill, overlooking Bonanza Creek valley at Grand Forks, at an effective head of 375 feet above the creek. Some 70.2 miles of construction were involved, comprised of 38 miles of ditch, 19.6 miles of flume, and 12.6 miles of wooden-stave and steel pipe. Many miles of the ditch would be over frozen ground carpeted with a thick cover of moss and scattered, twisted and stunted black spruce. Once the moss cover was disturbed, natural thawing would quickly change the ground into a foul-smelling quagmire of black organic muck. If a ditch was to be built, the permafrost itself would have to be utilized to maintain the walls.

Ingenious schemes were developed. In areas underlain by a mantle of muck over bedrock, the ditch was shaped carefully and then lined with a wall of inclined poles covered by a layer of moss up to a foot thick that was in turn covered by fine dirt or other tamping material. In areas underlain by silt, the silt could be used as the bottom of the ditch if moss could be made to form a blanket that would protect the upslope side. Crossing areas underlain by soft schist bedrock, typical of much of the Klondike hills, the ditch had to be lined with moss covered by puddling dirt to prevent leakage. On rock slopes with no lower bank, the lower wall was built as a continuous rock-filled crib, and the ditch was sealed with moss and puddling dirt as before.

Six steam shovels were used on the Twelve Mile Ditch and they, like the other supplies, had been positioned along the ditchline during the winter when the ground was frozen. The shovels could dig between two and three hundred feet of ditch a day. Local wood was gathered for fuel, and the ditch and shovel crews would combine to move the shovel ahead, either on rails or by the use of lifting jacks and blocks.

The standard flume, 6 feet wide and 4 feet deep, was

built of lumber cut from spruce timber growing in the valley of the Twelve Mile. Sills of the bents supporting the flume were set in firm ground, either bedrock or else gravel or other material that would not settle on thawing. In some cases, shafts had to be sunk with the use of steam points to reach an acceptable footing. The deepest, one of eleven sunk for the bents supporting a section of pipe on the Lepine Creek crossing, was a slot, 64 feet deep and 29 feet long at the base, but only 9 feet wide at the top to allow for the 2-in-12 slope on the spruce bents.

The wood-stave pipe, of 42 or 48 inches diameter, consisted of 30 staves around the perimeter, each pre-cut from 3-by-6-inch California redwood stock. The assembled pipe was bound with half-inch bands of round iron spaced from just over 1 inch to 10 inches apart, depending on the calculated pressure at the point in the line.

The inverted siphon crossing the Klondike River valley was the largest single job on the project. Crews of over 300 men were employed for two summers, and the last rivet would not be driven until early October 1908. Over three miles of wood and steel pipe was used and a mile-long section of this across the Klondike flats would be under pressure exerted by a head of 1,000 to 1,500 feet of water. Steel pipe up to 11/16 of an inch in thickness was used, much of it lap-welded with the bends and angles carefully calculated during fabrication. Most of the pipe was ordered from Pittsburgh, but 1,400 feet was purchased in Germany. Some 36-foot sections of the German pipe weighed more than four tons. Across the Klondike flats, which overflowed each spring, the steel pipe was carried on pile bents. The river was crossed by a three-span steel bridge 285 feet long. Piers for the bridge were of piling surrounded by mortised timber and shod with steel as protection against the trees and logs that would be torn from the bank or drift piles by the swollen river during the brief spring run-off.

The Twelve Mile Ditch was nearly completed by late September 1908. As work on each section was completed and the camps closed, the 1,200 odd men engaged poured into town.

Treadgold, in the Klondike briefly, commented:

"I deem the work done by the men here one of the greatest accomplishments of the kind in the history of the world. . . . I should say that it is a triumph of young manhood. . . . Older men would not have had the courage and

Top—Pipe for the Klondike siphon on wagons, Front Street, Dawson, 1908.

Bottom—Intake of the Klondike siphon viewed from the bridge across the Klondike River at Bear Creek, 1908.

127

perhaps have looked too much for a precedent. The work is a splendid demonstration of what pluck, hustle and energy can accomplish. In two or three years more the entire equipment will be operating at its best, and the splendid results then will be patent.''[53]

Early in October, Angus McDonell, field marshal of the project was given a surprise party at the mess house in Dawson and presented with a gold watch charm depicting a Klondike cabin and mining scene, set with a single sparkling diamond to represent the sun.[54]

After 1906, Treadgold does not appear to have been involved in Yukon Gold operations to any great extent. He was back in the Klondike in mid-July 1907, in time to testify at an Exchequer Court hearing over the cancellation of the Anderson Concession.[55] He told the court that he had held an interest in the concession since 1898 and that, in this matter, he was not a representative of either Yukon Gold or the Guggenheims. He remained in the Klondike for about two months and made the usual round of inspection trips with Yukon Gold officials, including a five-day horseback ride through the dismal swamp along the route of the Twelve Mile Ditch.[56] In mid-September 1907 he left for London, taking five malemutes with him, accompanied by the Bredenberg family.[57] Edward Bredenberg had looked after Treadgold's Klondike interests for many years but now he had sold his own holdings and, for the moment at least, there was nothing to keep him in the Klondike. In September 1908, Treadgold returned for a brief visit that coincided with the completion of work on the Twelve Mile Ditch. He would be back again in the summer of 1909 but his activities would be unrelated to those of Yukon Gold, although he remained a Director of that company for many years.

Early in 1909, Yukon Gold completed preparations to use water from the Twelve Mile Ditch in their hydraulic operations.[58] Initially, the water would be used on Lovett Hill, lying between Bonanza Creek and the Klondike River, until a siphon crossing at the Bonanza Creek valley had been completed near 25 Below. Much construction was planned, mainly on the Bonanza section of the ditch; C. A. Thomas predicted that there would be work for anyone who wanted it.

The spring start-up was marred by the failure of the siphon across the Klondike River valley as it was being filled.[59] A

Failure of a section of steel pipe in the Klondike siphon during a test filling, May 1909.

section of the heavy steel pipe about 100 feet above the valley floor burst along a defective weld and water, under a pressure in excess of 400 pounds to the square inch, sliced off trees to six in inches in diameter for 200 feet on either side of the break. The Klondike River was in flood, so the replacement section, seven feet long and weighing over a ton, had to be taken to Ogilvie Bridge, from where a team of horses worried it along what remained of the disused AC Trail (Alaska Commercial Trail) on the north side of the river. Repairs were completed in less than a week. Finally, on 4 June 1909, water from the Twelvemile was used to operate two hydraulic monitors tearing down the White Channel Gravels on Lovett Hill.

The 1909 season was a successful one for both dredging and hydraulic operations. In September, an initial dividend of 10 cents per share was declared; and Yukon Gold proposed to pay 40 cents per year, for an 8-percent return on the par value of $5 per share.[60] In December, the second quarterly dividend was declared, and shareholders were offered rights to purchase 297,000 shares (presumably the remainder of the Lawson float) on the basis of one additonal share at $5 for each ten shares held. The amount raised, close to $1½ million, would be used to reduce Yukon Gold's indebtedness to Guggenheim Exploration Company.[61]

Yukon Gold had completed their main construction during 1909. In 1910, the crew was down to about 600 men, less than a third that of earlier years. The young engineering staff remained, and continual improvements were made to increase the efficiency of the operation. Late in the 1911 season, two new steel-hulled dredges, both with seven-cubic-foot buckets, were put into operation. Number 8 went to 6 Above Bonanza and Number 9 to 7 Eldorado. In the same year, the company expanded to Gold Run Creek, south of the Dome, with the purchase of the Chute and Wills Company ground and the Crueger Concession for a reported half a million dollars.[62] Dredge Number 6 was moved from Lower Bonanza Creek to the Gold Run ground in late 1913.

In late February 1913, Dredge Number 1, on Lower Bonanza, was dynamited and sank in its pond.[63] Violence of this kind was unknown in the Klondike, where doors were seldom locked, and hurried arrangements were made to post armed guards on the other dredges in case the dynamiter should try to strike again. The company posted a reward of $5,000 for evidence leading to the conviction of those involved. The dynamiter had broken the lock and stolen a case of powder from Yukon Gold's powderhouse, located near the road between Dawson and Guggieville, and later broken into a nearby cabin to thaw the frozen explosive. Numerous ski tracks near the stricken dredge cast suspicion on a small group of Swedes who, between them, appeared to own the few pairs of skis in the area. The principal suspect, nicknamed the Educated Swede, had often been seen skiing near the dredges, but until now the crews doing winter repairs had paid little attention to him. Suspicions were one thing

Hydraulic mining on Cheechako Hill near Grand Forks. Streams of water from hydraulic monitors, viewed here from across Bonanza Creek, are tearing down the White Channel Gravel deposits, formerly mined by underground methods; dumps from the earlier work dot the hillside. The water for the monitors is supplied by the Twelve Mile Ditch.

---

but there were no definite leads in the case until R. E. Franklin, Yukon Gold's Electrical Superintendent, returned to Dawson in mid-March and planted a primitive listening device, or bug, in the cabin where the Swedish group often gathered. Crouched outside in the cold, he listened and took notes while the group made fun of the police and the Guggs, and he later heard the suspect say that he had chosen Number 1 since it was closer to town and his ski tracks would be easier to explain. The Educated Swede, actually a Norwegian, was arrested soon after that. Although Franklin's evidence was never given in court, a jury convicted the suspect on the basis of a long chain of circumstantial evidence, including his movements at the time of the dynamiting and his ownership of a typewriter and paper used in writing threatening notes to Yukon Gold and Canadian Klondyke.[64]

A dynamited dredge was a problem that Yukon Gold could deal with, and Number 1 was back in service in May 1913, but there were other nagging problems—with their neighbour Joe Boyle and his Canadian Klondyke Mining Company. From the time Boyle regained control of Canadian Klondyke in the summer of 1909 there had been continual conflict between the two companies. It was a battle without compromise, perhaps because of Boyle's personality, and each side was prepared to obstruct the

Top—Yukon Gold Number 1 after she was dynamited in late February 1913. Rebuilt with a false bottom to cover the hole in her hull, she was back in operation with the fleet in mid-May 1913.

Bottom—Ice dam formed across the bows of Yukon Gold Number 4, in February 1913, to permit repairs to the hull. Ice was allowed to form to about eight inches thick, and then half the thickness was chipped away across the width of the trench. When the ice thickened again, the chipping was repeated. The process was continued until the required depth was reached.

operations of the other regardless of cost. Yukon Gold's frustration at being hemmed in by Boyle, later combined with the difficulties of operating during World War 1, presaged the eventual withdrawal of Yukon Gold from the Klondike.

Over three decades, Yukon Gold gradually shifted equipment and personnel to other operations in Alaska and Idaho and later to the placer tin fields of Malaya. The withdrawal began in March 1912 when Dredge Number 7, having completed working its ground on Upper Hunker Creek, was dismantled and moved into Dawson, ready to be shipped to the Iditarod district of Alaska as soon as the river opened.[65]

Late in the 1915 season, Dredge Number 9, one of the new steel dredges, was halted on 26 Eldorado Creek when Yukon Gold was unable to come to an agreement with claim holders upstream; in December 1916, the dredge was dismantled for shipment to Murray, Idaho.[66]

In the 1917 season two more dredges—Number 5, located at 7 Eldorado, and Number 8, the other steel dredge located at 43 Bonanza—completed mining their ground. Both were later dismantled, and in 1919 they were shipped from Dawson (via the Lower Yukon River and St. Michael) to Seattle and then to their final destination in Malaya.[67]

Two more dredges were dropped in 1918. Number 2 at 31 Bonanza completed its ground and was dismantled; the equipment was stored at Guggieville.[68] Number 3 on Bear Creek completed the 1918 season and was not put back in service in 1919.[69] In 1922, it was stripped so that a watchman would no longer be required for insurance purposes.[70]

Yukon Gold suspended dividend payments in late 1918. The president, now William Loeb, Jr., wrote in explanation:

"This action is absolutely necessary in order to conserve our cash resources. The estimated income for this year is a disappointment, as it has been to all gold companies, due to the abnormally high and constantly rising cost of labor, material, supplies and freight. Owing to the high wages paid to the miners of base metals, efficient miners are attracted away from the gold mines and the labor left in the gold mines is only 60 per cent efficient, and not obtainable in sufficient numbers.

"Notwithstanding these increasing burdens on the industry the value of our product is stationary. If these were not war times and we were free to exercise our business judgment and

George Coffey (centre), Hydraulic Superintendent and, after 1920, Resident Manager for Yukon Gold, at his home at 14 Below Bonanza in the summer of 1906.

leave patriotism out of account, the proper course to pursue would be to leave the gold in the ground, to be mined when times were more normal. As long as we can show a profit or break even, we consider it our patriotic duty to keep up the production of gold, one of the most essential of war metals, trusting that the government will see the necessity of coming to the relief of this industry."[71]

But even with World War 1 over and labor available once again, Yukon Gold's Klondike operation continued to shrink. Towards the close of the 1919 season Dredge Number 1 was laid up at Guggieville and the bucket line removed; there were no definite plans to put the dredge back in service.[72] In September 1920, Number 4 completed working its ground at 62 Below on Hunker Creek and was sold to North West Corporation for use in that company's Dominion Creek operation.[73]

In the 1921 season only the hydraulic plant and the one remaining dredge, Number 6 on Gold Run Creek, were in operation.

The company was also active in the Keno Hill area,

about 130 miles east of Dawson, where high-grade silver-lead deposits had been discovered in 1918. Operating through a subsidiary, Keno Hill, Limited, the company had acquired ground in 1919 and considerable direct shipping ore was mined over the next few years but then the company became inactive, their properties operated by lessees.

At the end of the 1923 season, Dredge Number 6 ceased operations and was abandoned. Hydraulic operations continued until the end of the 1925 season; George Coffey, Resident Manager, left Dawson a few days before Christmas.[74] Coffey, manager of the Anglo-Klondike Mining Company when it was taken over by the Guggenheims in 1906, had been manager of Yukon Gold's hydraulic operations for most of the period. On his departure, Grant Henderson, son of Robert Henderson, was left in charge; in March and April 1926, he busied himself salvaging copper wire from the powerline between Twelve Mile and Gold Run.[75] About a year later, Henderson announced that all the Klondike holdings of Yukon Gold had been taken over by a new Treadgold consolidation.[76]

From their beginnings in the Klondike, Yukon gold operations had grown to include gold dredging in Alaska, California and Idaho, lode mining in Nevada and Yukon and finally placer tin dredging in Malaya. In late 1939, the company was reorganized as Pacific Tin Consolidated Corporation after operating briefly under an intermediate name. Yukon Gold's Klondike operation yielded about $25 million from the dredging of about 49 million yards of gravel and just over $6 million from the hydraulicking of about 34 million cubic yards; a grand total of over $31 million. Total dividends paid from the initial dividend in 1909 until dividends were suspended in 1918 amounted to $2.82½ per share or a total of $9,858,110.[77] Dividends did not resume until 1936, long after the Klondike assets had been sold. The enterprise appears to have been successful but it fell far short of the promises of the Lawson campaign of 1908 when Treadgold estimated that the high-grade Klondike gravels alone would yield a gross value of $58,540,000 in gold of which $43,950,000 would be profit.

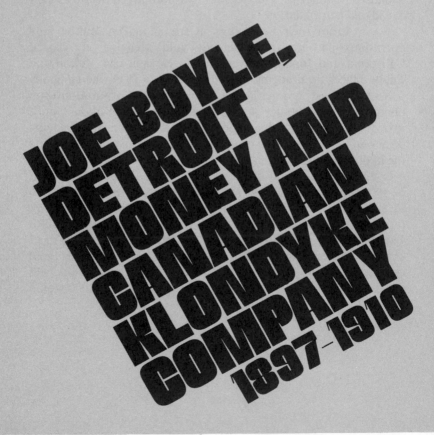

JOE BOYLE, DETROIT MONEY AND CANADIAN KLONDYKE COMPANY 1897-1910

6

The Boyle Concession, Lease Number 18, covering about forty square miles of the Klondike River valley between the mouths of Hunker and Bonanza creeks, was protested at the Britton Commission hearings in August 1903. Joseph Whiteside Boyle had been associated with the concession since the initial application in 1897, and he still held an undisclosed interest in it. In his testimony to the commission he was forced to acknowledge that no serious attempt had been made to develop or mine the ground. The cancellation of the Treadgold Concession in June 1904 and the continued agitation against the remaining hydraulic concessions put whatever interest he still held in the concession in jeopardy. Early in 1905 it was announced in Ottawa that the Detroit Yukon Mining Company, already mining on nearby ground, would take over and mine the concession. Canadian Klondyke Mining Company was formed for the purpose, and the first dredge was installed in the summer of 1905. A few years later, Joe Boyle would gain control of both the new company and the concession through an involved series of lawsuits and would run the enterprise as the King of the Klondike until the collapse of his empire less than ten years later.

At the Britton Commission hearings in the summer of 1903, Joe Boyle and Frank Slavin testified on the sequence of events leading up to the granting of the Boyle Concession in November 1900.[1]

Slavin was an Australian heavyweight boxer who had made an unsuccessful bid for the world heavyweight boxing championship in London in 1891. In June 1897, after a defeat in San Francisco, Slavin and Boyle (together about a year, with Boyle acting as manager and sparring partner) had drifted north making a scant living from exhibition bouts.

There had been rumors of a gold strike in the Yukon since the winter before, and either in Victoria or—more likely—Juneau the pair learned more of the Klondike. With little to lose, they collected an outfit and crossed the White Pass, reaching Dawson about August 1897. Once there, there seemed little they could do; all the valuable ground appeared to be staked, and they had no interest in working for wages. Boyle had nineteen dollars and Slavin three, and their mining equipment consisted of a Yukon stove, picks and shovels.

They were soon associated with Swiftwater Bill Gates, who had already made a fortune on Claim 13 Eldorado and would make and lose many more in the years ahead. Slavin and Boyle did not stake any claims. In late September 1897, Boyle went Outside with Swiftwater Bill in advance of the famine expected that winter. Slavin told the Britton Commission that he remained behind, spending much of his time searching for unstaked fractions.

On the first of December 1897, without any definite arrangement with Boyle, he applied on behalf of Boyle, a man named Genest, and himself for a concession in the Klondike River valley between the mouths of Hunker and Bonanza creeks. At the hearing, the Board of Trade lawyer wondered aloud whether Slavin "asked for only eight miles because of thinking that was all they could work with their capital."[2] Slavin's answer was lost in the laughter. In applying for a concession, Slavin was probably following the example of Robert Anderson who had made a similar application for the lower part of Hunker Creek in September 1897. Slavin's prospecting had consisted of sinking one shaft on a placer claim about 100 yards outside what was later to become the boundary of the concession and inspecting two other shafts. Leaving the Klondike soon after, Slavin travelled to Ottawa, arriving there sometime early in 1898.

In Ottawa, Boyle, the businessman of the pair, took charge. A new application was submitted for the Klondike Concession in early February 1898. This time Boyle and Slavin were joined by Genest's employer, J. J. Guerin of the Canadian Yukon Company of Montreal, on Boyle's understanding that the company would provide the money required for the first year of the lease. Early in March 1898, James Sutherland, a Liberal MP whose riding included Boyle's home town of Woodstock, Ontario, wrote to Sifton on behalf of the applicants: "Will you kindly get the papers in the Boyle matter and fix it up in some way so that they can get away tomorrow."[3] It was not that easy, and, despite more letters from Sutherland, there were still delays. Finally, in mid-April, after an unsatisfactory phone call to Guerin, Boyle sent a letter asking Guerin if he intended to carry out the verbal agreement made with his representative.[4] A few days later, Guerin (he was also a Montreal physican and minister without portfolio in the Liberal government of Quebec) wrote back denying the agreement as understood by Boyle.[5] On receiving Guerin's letter, Boyle wrote directly to Sifton asking that the concession be granted to himself and Slavin.[6] Slavin later told the Britton Commission that this application, in Boyle's handwriting and on House of Commons letterhead, was prepared for them by H. B. McGiverin, an Ottawa lawyer.[7]

Slavin also testified that he and Boyle had met Treadgold in Ottawa early in 1898 before Treadgold had been to the Klondike. Slavin understood that there had been negotiations between Boyle and Treadgold for a quarter interest in the proposed concession. Before leaving Ottawa in May 1898 Slavin had received some money from Boyle—he was uncertain whether the amount was $180 or $280—on the understanding that it was his share of an initial payment by Treadgold. Slavin had nothing on paper to show for the transaction, but papers were never required between the pair; Boyle was his partner and he trusted him implicitly.[8] The partnership had continued until May 1899 when Boyle bought out Slavin's interests for a reported $20,000.[9]

Joe Boyle followed Slavin back to the Klondike, arriving in Dawson on 7 July 1898. At last he would be able to examine the ground of the proposed concession which he had

Joe Boyle at Dawson in the summer of 1916.

probably only glimpsed at a distance from the Eldorado trail the year before.[10]

But first, there was a more immediate problem to be dealt with. A Mr. Stewart, claiming to have authority from the Acting Crown Timber Agent, had a crew of fifty men at work cutting timber on the ground of the proposed concession. Treadgold, who had arrived in the Klondike a few weeks earlier and was acting as Boyle and Slavin's representative, had been unable to get the cutting stopped.

Boyle and Treadgold protested to the Commissioner of the Yukon, Major Walsh, and to his Gold Commissioner, Thomas Fawcett, but were unable to get satisfaction. Walsh acknowledged to them that·there had been a letter from Sifton dealing with the proposed concession but stated that he had passed it on to Fawcett's office. Somehow the letter had disappeared and no one was prepared to act without it.

The gravels of the proposed concession might or might not be of value but the timber certainly was and Boyle, anxious to have both, left the Klondike after six days, hurrying to Ottawa in hopes of persuading Sifton to issue the timber berths to him. Sifton was out of town when Boyle reached Ottawa almost a month later but after a meeting between Boyle, McGiverin and Sutherland, the latter acting for Sifton, all three sent letters to Sifton requesting that the timber berths be issued to Boyle.[11]

Boyle's direct approach paid off and Timber Berths 25 and 26 covering the timbered flats of the proposed concession were issued soon after. Returning to the Klondike in September 1898, Boyle had spent the winter on the ground of the proposed concession, sinking and watching others sink shafts.

There were many delays, and Lease Number 18, covering the Boyle Concession, was not issued until November 1900. On 11 June 1898, before Boyle had set foot on the ground, the Klondike valley between Hunker and Bonanza creeks had been withdrawn from staking by a request from Commissioner Walsh to Gold Commissioner Fawcett. This request, misplaced by the time Boyle reached the Klondike in early July 1898, had been repeated on 12 July 1899 by the Commissioner's office. Later, on 28 August 1899, Sifton's office had written to Boyle and Slavin stating that it had been decided to issue a lease to them and requesting a definition of the ground they were interested in as soon as possible. On 5 October 1899, another letter informed them that each would get a frontage of four miles along the Klondike River and that they had sixty days to supply a description of the ground and the required reports. The descriptions were furnished on 21 October 1899. On the 26th, Boyle submitted an affidavit that the ground had been prospected prior to 3 December 1898 and had been found unsuited for placer mining. The prospecting consisted of one shaft sunk to a depth of twenty-four feet that showed from five to twelve cents to the pan and shafts sunk since the original application to depths of eighteen to twenty-six feet. Boyle's affidavit did not mention Bear Creek or its tributary Lindow Creek, both lying within the area requested and being mined by others at the time. A few days after receiving Boyle's affidavit, Commissioner Ogilvie wrote to the Minister of the Interior that it had been proven to his satisfaction that the applicants or a person acting for them had been on and prospected the ground prior to 3 December 1898, a condition that must be met before a lease could be issued under the regulations in force at the time.

Boyle then engaged T. D. Green, a local surveyor, to complete the required survey of the lease. The plan Green prepared omitted both Bear and Lindow creeks. When Boyle submitted Green's plan on 18 December 1899 he requested that the boundaries of the lease be extended to the limits of the valley, a discretion allowed the Minister of the Interior under the regulations of 3 December 1898. Commissioner Ogilvie appears to have approved this extension originally and then, a month or so later, moved to restrict the boundary to the one mile in depth usually granted.

Ogilvie marked the one mile limit with a blue dotted line on one copy of Green's plan and noted on the plan his approval "subject to dotted line." But the marked plan remained in the Gold Commissioner's office in Dawson and Sifton's office in Ottawa was apparently unaware of Ogilvie's attempt to limit the size of the concession.

Later, in October 1900, when a question arose over the description to be inserted in the lease, the Assistant Gold Commissioner wired to the Secretary of the Department of the Interior:

PLEASE WIRE EXACT BOUNDARIES, LENGTH
AND BREADTH OF 'BOYLE CONCESSION,

KLONDIKE RIVER.' DOES IT EXTEND FROM
SUMMIT TO SUMMIT

The reply from Acting Minister Sutherland was:

YES, SUMMIT TO SUMMIT

The lease, incorporating these boundaries, was issued on 5 November 1900. Slavin had already sold his interest to Boyle in 1899, and on 17 November 1900 an assignment of Boyle's rights to the lease to H. B. McGiverin of Ottawa was accepted and registered in the Department of the Interior. Boyle still retained an undisclosed interest in the lease; Judge Britton ruled out questions as to what interest, if any, Treadgold held in the concession.[12]

In his testimony to the Britton Commission, Boyle was questioned closely about the work done on the concession since the original application. Like most of the other concession holders, Boyle had little of substance to report. He was forced to acknowledge that only three test holes had been put down on the property in the winter of 1898-1899 and that two of these were sunk by a prospector contemplating staking. In addition, he thought some prospecting had been done on the hill between Bear Creek and Quigley Gulch by his partner and others but he had not visited the site and was unable to remember the names of the other men involved. A building described in his affidavit was actually a roadhouse built by someone else, the owner paying twenty-five dollars a month for the right to cut timber on the concession. True, Sir Thomas Tancred had been retained at a cost of 2,000 to make a survey for the installation of an hydraulic plant on the ground, but McGiverin, now the holder of the concession, had already been notified that this expenditure could not be accepted as part of the $5,000 for mining operations required annually under the terms of the lease.[13]

In November of both 1901 and 1902, the mining inspectors had reported that nothing had been done on the ground in preparation for a mining operation. Later, in the spring of 1903, there had been a single shaft sunk in Jackson Gulch. Started in a wash of tailings coming down from mining on a claim farther up the gulch, the claim owner had already testified that he considered it simply an attempt to harass his operation by forcing him to restrain the tailings.

143

The witness had amused both the commissioners and spectators with his description of Boyle's operation as involving two men working with a boiler scarcely larger than either of the two dogs used to haul wood for it.[14] Obviously, even if the Britton Commission report turned out to be a whitewash, as so many in the Klondike were predicting, there was going to be increasing pressure for cancellation of the Boyle Concession.

Boyle personally lacked the resources needed to develop either the Boyle Concession (Lease Number 18) or the Quartz Creek Concession (Lease Number 9), in which he also held an interest. Since his return to the Klondike in the autumn of 1898, Joe Boyle had been involved in a number of business ventures, including a sawmill on his Klondike timber berths, a steam laundry and the arranging of prize fights at the DAAA (Dawson Amateur Athletic Association).[15]

In November 1898, Boyle and Slavin's advertisement for cordwood began to appear in the *Nugget,* and later, in February 1899, that for their Arctic Sawmill at the Upper Klondike Ferry offered: "All kinds of dimension lumber—lowest prices in the Klondike." The mill, moved about six miles east to the mouth of Hunker Creek in late 1899, was destroyed by a forest fire in June 1901.[16] It had not been rebuilt immediately. In the interim, Boyle issued permits to cut wood on his Klondike timber berths, charging $3 to $4 a cord for firewood and $1.50 to $2 for each building log.[17]

None of his schemes had developed the capital needed to start mining on his own, and attempts to bring in other backers had not worked out satisfactorily. Treadgold had tried to buy the Boyle Concession but Boyle refused to sell. In late July 1902, Treadgold wrote to Sifton of his offer, perhaps hoping that the Minister would pressure Boyle into making a deal:

> "McGiverin will tell you of the very generous offer we made to Boyle; the fellow flatly refused it. How he proposes to get out of the hole I cannot think. Probably by fooling with the holders of the Rock Creek Grants; both his hydraulic lease in the Klondike Valley and his timber berths are so hopelessly involved and at your mercy as well that it is difficult to see how he could refuse such a splendid offer as McGiverin made to him."[18]

Sifton had other reasons for concern; after a visit to the Klondike his Deputy Minister had reported to him:

"I think the grants that have been made to Boyle, and the way he deals with them, has caused more unpopularity for the government than has all the other grants that have been made."[19]

Despite pressure and problems, Boyle clung stubbornly to his concessions, unable to do anything himself but ready to contest any activity, either mining or logging, that might infringe on his holdings.

During the winter of 1903-1904 a small amount of lay mining and wood cutting was done on the Boyle Concession.[20] Strictly speaking, neither would be acceptable as part of the $5,000 in mining operations required by the terms of the lease, but the work on the concession might serve to delay cancellation until something better could be arranged. Frank Slavin, living in a cabin beside the road through the concession, was acting as a watchman to stop unauthorized wood cutting. In late March 1904, he had stopped and challenged two men pulling a hand sleigh loaded with wood and had been badly beaten in the ensuing fracas. At the trial that followed, both men testified that the wood in dispute came from an abandoned cabin which they had purchased for wood, and that when Slavin had threatened them they had defended themselves with lengths of chain used to hold down the wood. They considered this justified since Slavin was a professional fighter. The pair, judged defiant and guilty of using excessive force, were sentenced to three or four months respectively on the police woodpile, and countercharges against Slavin were dismissed. Popular opinion was with the pair, probably in resentment over the Boyle Concession; more than 2,000 persons signed a petition requesting that the pair be pardoned.[21]

By the spring of 1904, Boyle was being sued by his wood cutters for wages and by Sir Thomas Tancred for his Klondike timber berths and other property. Tancred's lawyers claimed that the berths and other property had been given as security on a loan of £6975 made to Boyle in September 1900 and on which Boyle had made only one interest payment.[22] The loan had been involved in a scheme to develop the Quartz Creek Concession in

145

which Boyle held an interest, but the project had collapsed and Tancred had been unable to get a satisfactory accounting from Boyle. Sifton, at Tancred's request,[23] had had Boyle's holdings investigated by his officials but had declined to act directly in the matter, suggesting that McGiverin give a Declaration of Trust for the Timber Berths. Boyle lost the case and, in June 1904, was given two months to settle, failing which the timber berths and other property would go to Tancred.[24] Boyle left the Klondike in late July 1904, hoping to make arrangements Outside for the working of the Boyle Concession.

Nothing was going right for him. The *Whitehorse Star* reported another minor incident on the trip out:

"Joe Boyle, who passed through Whitehorse yesterday morning, is in Hogan's alley parlance, 'up to snuff' and is one of the last men on earth whom any fakir would approach to sell a gold brick or divining rod.

"Yet Joseph is not by any means so astute as he gives himself credit for being. Otherwise he would not have carried six ounces of gold dust and nuggets in the interior realm of his pants unaccompanied by a certificate of exportation.

"But between here and Caribou the wily officer whose duty it is to see that no gold is taken out contrary to law got next to Joseph likewise his poke. And there is where Joseph and his poke were separated, the gold being taken by the officer and Joseph going on alone, the mercury of his self-estimation thermometer having dropped down into the bottom of the bulb.

"Joe did not deny having the gold when questioned and said it was the product of his own claim which he was taking out as a sample. P.S.—He didn't take the sample."[25]

Boyle's luck improved when he reached Ottawa. By September 1904, he and H. B. McGiverin were involved in negotiations with a Detroit group over mining the Boyle Concession. The group, headed by Sigmund R. Rothschild, a cigar merchant, operated under the name of Detroit Yukon Mining Company. The company was already mining on the Williams Concession on Hunker Creek and Claims 19 and 20 on Bear Creek, an enclave in the Boyle Concession. On the Bear Creek property, the company planned a light railway to carry the gravels to the Klondike River for washing. Four small locomotives and the cars, reported to have cost about $100,000, had been landed at Dawson in early June 1904. [26]

Mining the Boyle Concession was certain to involve some form of water system and, in late November 1904, Treadgold, busy trying to piece together a new water scheme from the wreckage of his Treadgold Concession, was lobbying to Sifton again:

> "Now we who have the necessary water are willing under certain conditions to give sufficient water to work the lease on a large scale; these conditions are that the Detroit parties who wish to acquire the lease should make such arrangement or agreement with us, before the lease is transferred, as will secure for our water company the direct interest which it requires to have in the lease. . . . I refrain at present from laying stress on the undivided interest to which I am entitled in Lease 18 and on the large amount of money which I have advanced to Mr. Boyle; both of these are ignored in the proposed sale to the Detroit parties by Mr. Boyle; but independent action on my part might involve in each case legal proceedings which ought not to be necessary against Mr. Boyle, the lessee from the Crown of an important property like Lease 18. . . .
>
> "The agreement is also of little substantial benefit to Mr. Boyle himself. It provides for the payment to him of $500,000 in shares and royalty—a promise of the future which likely will bring him little or nothing; I have shown him this; he is partly convinced and he should be given to understand that he must be reasonable in his demands, lest he stand in the way of the development of the country in more senses than one." [27]

Sifton, by now wary of Treadgold and his many proposals, declined to act. Rebuffed by Sifton, Treadgold attempted to insinuate himself in the final stages of Boyle's negotiations to be held in Detroit. [28] He thought he had succeeded but unexpectedly there was a telegram from Boyle, who had gone ahead, that the agreement had been signed and there was no longer any point in Treadgold's coming to Detroit.

Under the agreement, a new company, Canadian Klondyke Mining Company, had been formed with a capitalisation of 30,000 shares at $25 par value.[29] The Detroit group would hold 20,000 shares and Boyle 10,000, and Boyle would receive $250,000 in the form of a 25 percent royalty on the gross gold production.[30]

Shortly after reaching Ottawa in August 1904, Joe Boyle had begun booming the idea of a Dawson hockey team "who could beat anyone" touring Eastern Canada. The idea caught on, and the team, now challengers for the Stanley Cup, arrived in Ottawa on 12 January 1905, the day of their first scheduled game. Somehow the team, still exhausted from the trip, managed to hold the score to 9 to 2 but in the second game a few days later the team, still dead on their feet, were overwhelmed 23 to 2. Boyle, acting as sponsor and manager, accompanied the team on a series of exhibition games in Montreal and the Maritimes. The team, possibly more interested in entertainment than hockey, lost many of their games. At the end of the series, Boyle remained in Ontario, apparently not taking any part in the operations now getting underway on the Boyle Concession.[31]

On his arrival in Dawson in mid-April 1905, Otto Brener, a major shareholder in both Detroit Yukon and the new company, Canadian Klondyke, announced that plans for the summer included installation of a dredge and power plant on Bear Creek plus other improvements, costing a total of $325,000.[32] Construction of the dredge was to be supervised by J. Moore Elmer, the father of dredging in the Klondike, who had installed the first primitive dredge at 42 Below on Bonanza in 1901. The Canadian Klondyke dredge, built by the Marion company, was to be electrically operated and would have seven-cubic-foot buckets. Parts began arriving at the first of July and the completed dredge and power plant went into service on 13 August 1905 when Commissioner McInnes "touched the button which opened the fair."[33] The dredge, weighing about 500 tons and built on a wooden hull 100 feet long by 28 feet wide, had been assembled in thirty-three days. The power plant, consisting of three 150-horsepower marine-type boilers supplying a steam turbine directly connected to a 400-kilowatt generator, in an even shorter time. There were a few minor adjustments required after the initial start-up but, following these, the dredge, capable of digging 5,000 cubic yards per day, operated into October.

View of Dreqge
At Bear Creek

**Front view of dredge, Rothschild Number 1, later renamed Canadian
Number 1, in operation at Bear Creek, about 1905. The first
electrically-operated dredge in the Klondike, she was financed by the
Rothschild group of Detroit who, at the time, controlled Canadian
Klondyke Mining Company and the Boyle Concession.**

Actually, there was still no work on the Boyle Concession itself as the dredge had been installed on Detroit Yukon's Claim Number 20 Bear. The ground was rich, and for years rumors persisted that the new dredge had paid for itself in the first sixty days of operation.[34]

The Detroit Yukon group returned to the Klondike early in April 1906.[35] This year Otto Brener would be mining his own ground on French Hill above Eldorado Creek; Fred Rothschild, son of Sigmund Rothschild the principal backer, was to be general manager of the operation.

The dredge was started up on the 9th of May and it ran until the 23rd of October, handling an average of just under 3,000 cubic yards per day. The ground ahead of the dredge had been prepared by using water from the spring runoff to remove the moss cover. Only a little frozen ground remained and the dredge was able to cut through that, although some gold was lost when the chunks of frozen gravel passed over the screen of the dredge without disintegrating.

The summer was a busy one; about 80 men were employed.[36] Four Keystone drills operated ahead of the dredge, two more dredges were reported on order, and the company was investigating power schemes to replace the wood-fired thermal plant. The Klondike took to the Rothschild family, especially when it was realized that Fred was an accomplished pianist.[37] The father, Sigmund, arrived early in July and spent the remainder of the summer at the growing camp at Bear Creek. Under the management of the Detroit group, the Boyle Concession was finally being mined and when Fred Rothschild and Otto Brener left the Klondike in late October 1906, Canadian Klondyke seemed certain of a successful future under their leadership. Early in 1907 there was speculation that the Detroit group might sell to the Guggenheims, and in March Joe Boyle began an action to restrain the Detroit group from acting as directors and calling for the appointment of a receiver. Boyle claimed that the Detroit group had entered into an agreement to sell 10,000 shares, a one-third interest in Canadian Klondyke, to the Guggenheims and that on completion of the deal they no longer held control of the company.[38] Despite Boyle's action, Fred Rothschild returned to the Klondike in June 1907 to supervise the dredge operation. In mid-July, there was word that his father, Sigmund, the "old gentleman" who had charmed his crews and the Klondike the summer before, had died in New York.[39] The dredge, working in thawed ground across the Klondike River from the mouth of Bear Creek, operated until early October with a production slightly below that of the season before.[40]

Boyle's legal action against the Detroit group was heard before Judge Riddell in the fall assizes, October 1907, at Sandwich, Ontario.[41] Boyle contended that the Detroit group had failed to put $500,000 in cash into Canadian Klondyke Mining Company as called for in the original agreement, and that therefore their shares were not fully paid up. Instead of cash, called for in the articles of incorporation filed with the government in Ottawa, the group had simply transferred two claims and some mining machinery of dubious value belonging to the Detroit Yukon Mining Company in exchange for their Canadian Klondyke shares. Sigmund Rothschild, chief negotiatior for the Detroit group, was gone, but others who had been present testified that there had been a verbal agreement with Boyle over the transfer of the claims and machinery. But they were unable to produce either written evidence or supporting witnesses.

Otto Brener, present at one of the meetings where the agreement was supposedly discussed, was called to the stand in a surprise move by the plaintiffs, and he testified that the purchase of the machinery had not been discussed at the meeting in question. Continuing, Brener stated that although he was a large shareholder of Canadian Klondyke he did not learn of the transfer until a year after it had taken place.

Judge Riddell found in favor of Boyle:

"There never was any agreement that this machinery should be taken for $500,000 in cash or in stock. The acting directors of the Canadian company were all directors of the Detroit company and the pretended sale was in fraud . . . of the Canadian company and of the plaintiff, its largest shareholder. It may be that those guilty of this fraud would be shocked to hear the transaction thus bluntly described, but that is the only name that fits."[42]

He ordered the Detroit group to pay in $500,000, less the value of the claims and machinery, which he placed at $15,000 and $50,000, respectively.

In late March 1908, C.S.W. Barwell, a Dawson surveyor who had testified for Boyle, returned to Dawson with more news on the continuing battle between Boyle and the Detroit group:

"Under the terms of the judgment rendered during the winter by Judge Riddell the shares of the five Detroit men were declared wholly unpaid. The Detroit men attempted to pay in $190,000 cash and the remainder by offsetting notes, accounts and other matters of the kind between the Detroit-Yukon company and the Canadian Klondyke company, the old and new companies, respectively, handling the Boyle Concession property.

"Boyle contended the payments had to be made fully in cash and that the cash could be used in squaring the accounts and that a meeting of the company could direct the payment of the notes and the like.

"A general meeting was held in January which proved a lively one. Boyle attended and claimed that he and some of his friends, under terms of the judgment, were the only holders of fully paid up shares.

"Then the Detroit men began to hold a meeting of their own right there in the building. Joe and his cohorts, not to be outdone, had a meeting in the same building.

"Each side held elections and the like to their liking, and Joe's forces declared the officers, banks, lawyers and all such changed. The two rival concerns afforded enough life for an opera situation. Joe obtained a writ demanding the property and books. The other people then obtained the injunction restraining Joe in his ambitions and the case is now up to Judge Riddell."[43]

Early in March 1908, Judge Riddell ruled that the judgment must be paid in cash and that, following this, Canadian Klondyke could decide how the indebtedness was to be paid off. Turning to the two boards of directors he restrained the Detroit board from paying out any moneys on notes in dispute, or for any purpose without an order of the court, pending a trial, and the Boyle board, in turn, undertook not to act.[44] In May 1908, Judge Riddell authorized the directors of Canadian Klondyke to forward $10,000 for working expenses to the Klondike where Fred Rothschild was already on hand to supervise operations.[45]

The legal action took a new turn; the Detroit group, refused permission to offset notes which they held against the $435,000 judgment, had deposited the $435,000 in a Detroit bank and begun an action in the U. S. courts to recover notes aggregating $285,000. Judge Riddell, in turn, had appointed

Boyle the receiver of the company and steps were taken to compel the deposit of the funds in Canada. Before Boyle could qualify as receiver, Judge Riddell's decisions were set aside at a hearing before three judges of the Divisional Court at Toronto. They considered "that there was nothing in the conduct of the directors of the Canadian Klondyke company or in the method of carrying on the business of the company which justified Justice Riddell's order appointing a receiver. . . ."[46] The court directed that an issue be framed in which Boyle could try the question of whether the judgment had been paid or not.

Undaunted, Boyle took the case to the Court of Appeals but once again the opinion, handed down in April 1909, went against him and this time there were some stinging comments:

"It is urged for the appellant (Boyle) that the payment was a fraudulent one. It is difficult to understand what is meant by such an argument, unless it is advanced to draw off the mind from the real facts of the case. The money was actually received and now stands to the credit of the company, in a financial institution of the highest standing in Michigan. It can make no possible difference that it was paid in the invariable way in large transactions by the way of check instead of good coin. There is no sort of warrant for the claim advanced by the appellant that the money should have been paid into court. . . .

"It is said that the payment was not a real one. It is very difficult to perceive anything real in the appellant's contention. . . .

"There is nothing in any of the actions alleged which would justify such an extraordinary course as the taking of the management of the affairs of the company out of the hands of the shareholders into the court, or into the hands of a receiver. The board of directors are a body of business men elected by the shareholders, entirely competent to carry on the business of the company, and quite able to meet the most extraordinary demands that could be made against them, as is shown by the payment of the judgment."[47]

Perhaps, despite their victory, the Detroit group felt that it was not worth continuing the battle, and in late May 1909, at the Sandwich Assizes, where Boyle had entered two new actions, an agreement was announced which gave Boyle complete control of Canadian Klondyke Mining Company.[48] Under its terms he was to buy out the 20,000 shares of the company held by the Detroit group for a total of $400,000, without interest, and of this amount, $45,000 was already owing to him as a share of gold production under the former arrangement. Payments were to come from the proceeds of the dredging, $100,000 each in the 1910 and 1911 seasons and the final payment in 1912. Boyle controlled it all, and, for the moment at least, he was not at war with anyone. The Detroit group had equipped the property for him and now it was his to develop as he wished. Five years before, all he had to show for his mining was a six-ounce sample of gold dust and even that had been confiscated when he left the Yukon!

Joe Boyle, "looking fine and husky as ever" returned to the Klondike in September 1909 accompanied by his wife and daughter.[49] Despite the court battles, the Detroit group had kept the dredge in operation for a full season each year and Boyle was able to report: "The present dredge never did as well as it has this year. This is saying a good deal. The dredge always has been a good payer."[50] His plans for next season included the installation of two new dredges, if the material could be delivered and assembled in time, and the installation of a 2,000 hp hydroelectric plant on Fish Creek, a tributary of the Klondike River.

Meanwhile, Boyle was able to keep the Bear Creek dredge operating until late November by turning steam into the dredge pond. The steam was developed by a boiler fed with stumps cleared ahead of the dredge.[51] When the dredge was finally shut down on November 20th, it had operated for a total of 195 days, a record season for the Klondike. Boyle claimed that he was able to operate his dredge at a cost of under fifteen cents per cubic yard dredged, less than half Yukon Gold's costs. The dredge, operating twenty-four hours a day, had been shut down for maintenance and repairs less than 8 percent of the time and had mined a total of 681,616 cubic yards, an average of 3,558 cubic yards per day.[52]

Soon after the dredge shut down, Joe Boyle and his wife left for Ottawa, taking with them a $50,000 gold shipment to be used by the Mint in the first coins struck from Canadian-produced gold.[53]

In March 1910, Boyle sent word that he had contracted for the world's largest dredge and that it would be installed during the coming summer.[54] Busy with the design and arrangements for the new dredge, Boyle did not return to the Klondike until mid-July 1910, arriving on the same steamer as A.N.C. Treadgold.

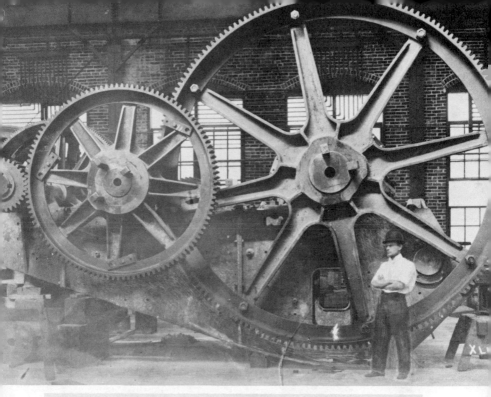

Fabrication of machinery for one of Joe Boyle's big dredges, probably
Canadian Number 2, at the Marion Steam Shovel plant.

Top—Reduction gears used to drive the rollers beneath the
revolving screen.

Bottom—One of the steel spuds, 65 feet long and weighing 27 tons.

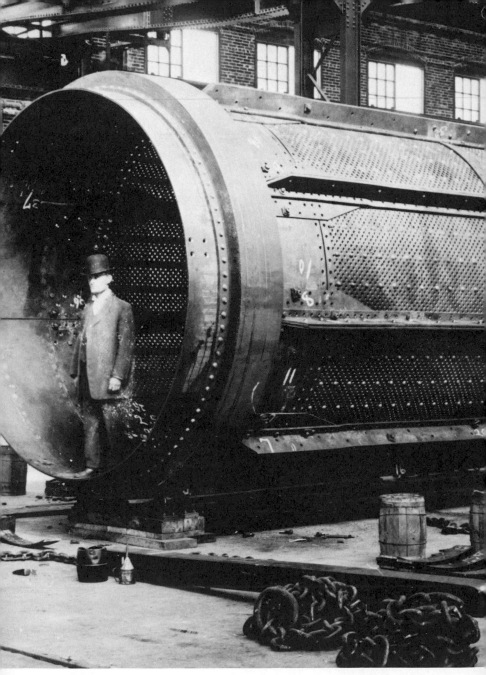

The revolving screen, or trommel, used to wash the gravel in Canadian Number 2 was 9 feet 9 inches in diameter, 49½ feet long, and weighed 63 tons.

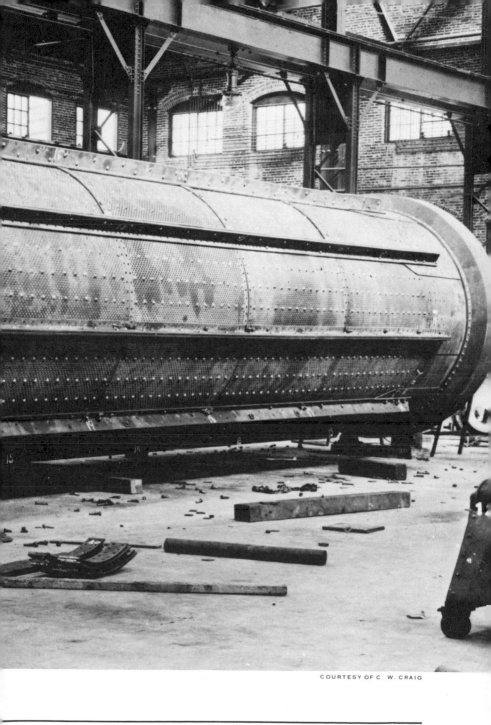

Number 1 dredge had been in operation since late April; parts for Number 2 had already begun to arrive in Dawson and the pit for it was ready.

Boyle's Canadian Number 2, with fifteen-cubic-foot buckets dwarfing the seven-cubic-foot buckets of Number 1, was assembled about a mile west of Bear Creek. First came the wooden hull, 130 feet by 49 feet, followed by the heavy machinery. One of the largest pieces was the steel spud, sixty-five feet long and weighing twenty-seven tons, used to fix the position of the dredge in its pond.[55] Loaded on two extra-heavy wagons, one under each end, a crew using half a dozen horses and blocks and tackle secured to anchors and deadmen worried the long load around the Klondike bluffs. Once past the bluffs, twenty-four horses were used to pull the load on the straight sections of the road. More than a hundred men had been employed under Boyle's personal direction and the cost of the dredge was estimated to be between $300,000 and $400,000.

Finally, on 4 November 1910, the power was turned on and the dredge began to dig its pond for the winter.[56] The seventy-one buckets on its bucket line were capable of digging over 10,000 cubic yards per day and could handle gravel from twenty feet above to forty-five feet below the surface of the water in the pond. For the moment, electric power came from the Coal Creek plant, a lignite-fired thermal plant about fifty miles downriver from Dawson, installed by an English company. In the 1911 season, power would be available from a new hydroelectric plant that Treadgold was installing on the Klondike River, some fifteen miles to the east of Bear Creek.

Always one to plunge ahead, Joe Boyle was gambling that his huge Number 2 dredge would be able to operate profitably in the immense yardage of low-grade Klondike River gravels lying within the boundaries of his concession. Bedrock on the ground was deep, in places up to forty feet, and there were huge boulders, up to three or four feet in diameter, to contend with. Already, there was evidence that smaller dredges, such as his Canadian Number 1 and the Yukon Gold fleet, were unsuited to this type of ground.[57] On Bear Creek, where Number 1 had started up in 1905, the gravels were richer and the dredge had recovered about $123,000 in a part season of about sixty days, complicated by inevitable starting-up difficulties. In contrast, in 1910, as Number 1 moved out into the main valley of the

Canadian Number 2, the world's largest dredge, under construction near Bear Creek in the summer of 1910. Its 15-cubic-foot buckets, more than twice the size of those on Number 1, would prove capable of handling the coarse gravels on the Boyle Concession.

Klondike, production for the whole season, 233 days, was only $128,000, little more than half that of the year before.

Boyle's personal finances had improved. In the 1904

Teams hauling the spud for Canadian Number 2 from the docks to Bear Creek. The spud was steel, 65 feet long, and weighed 27 tons.

NUGGET SALOON.

E. O. Ellingsen.
— Photo —
248.

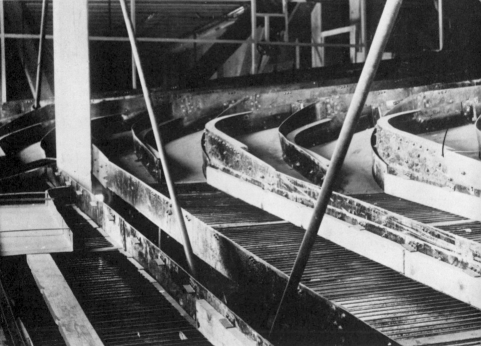

Assembling Canadian Number 2.

Top—Filling the dredge pond around the completed dredge, October 1910.

Bottom—A section of the sluice tables on one of the large dredges, where gold was recovered from gravels washed through the revolving screen.

Top—Detail of the bucket line. Originally Canadian Number 2 was fitted with a line of 71 buckets, each having a capacity of 15 cubic feet, but later a line of 68 buckets of about 16 cubic feet was used, similar to Canadian Numbers 3 and 4. Each of the larger buckets weighed 4,600 pounds; the lower tumbler weighed 28,000 pounds.

Bottom—Moving the assembled digging ladder into place. It was 97 feet in length and weighed 108 tons.

An open-cut mining operation. Once the high-grading had ended, the more efficient dredges reworked much of the same ground.

agreement with the Detroit group, he was to receive 25 percent of the gold returns, up to a total of $250,000; he had been given $32,500 in advances. Later, during the litigation, direct payments to him were suspended, but the Detroit group had paid out more than $70,000 to cover his obligations, including Treadgold, $27,249.37, Tancred, $35,000 and McGiverin $6,124.92. On gaining control, Boyle continued to credit himself with 25 percent of the gold return and began to draw against it. The total of $250,000 was reached during the 1910 season and, at the time, more than $80,000 of it still stood to Boyle's credit on the company's books.[58]

If his Canadian Number 2 dredge proved successful, Joe Boyle's personal empire should be secure. True, there were continuing squabbles with his neighbour, the Yukon Gold Company, but Joe Boyle was never one to be afraid of a lawsuit—in fact he appeared to enjoy them. Perhaps because of this, many who opposed him in the courts could still consider him a personal friend. He enjoyed life in the community, and the community in turn profited from the splash of color and excitement he added to it.

The *Dawson News* told of an interesting addition to the community in late summer 1910:

"The Boyle Brothers have received from Detroit a Flanders motor car seating four people including the driver. It is equipped like a Democrat wagon, having the rear of the bed so arranged that the top can be removed and room afforded for storage of light packages. The machine has twenty horsepower, and is declared just the thing for this country. The only other auto in use here this season is a Zust, an Italian car, owned by O. B. Perry."[59]

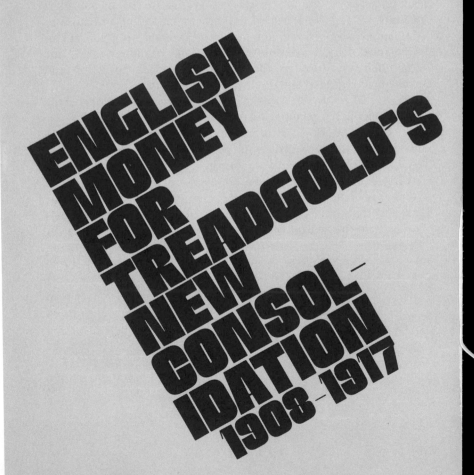

ENGLISH MONEY FOR TREADGOLD'S NEW CONSOLIDATION 1908-1917

7

Treadgold and his English backers had not transferred all their Klondike holdings to the Guggenheims in the 1906 consolidation, and by 1908 they were acquiring new ground in open competition. The split with the Guggenheims may have resulted over a number of things, including Treadgold's withholding ground, his complex and convoluted business methods, or his antipathy towards dredging, and the use of steam thawing ahead of the dredges. For the moment, Treadgold remained a director of Yukon Gold, but there were reports years later that it had cost the Guggenheims a million dollars or more to buy out his interests.[1] Treadgold's other holdings included interests in the Anderson and Boyle Concessions.[2] In early June 1908, Dredging Lease Number 23, covering a portion of the Klondike River valley, was issued directly to Treadgold. The ground lay at the junction of the Yukon Gold holdings and Canadian Klondyke's Boyle Concession ground; it could be mined by either company.[3]

Treadgold spent the summer of 1909 in the Klondike.

A. N. C. Treadgold (with coat over arm) and Edward Bredenberg (in front of poster) at Murray's Hotel, 33 Below Discovery on Dominion Creek, about 1907.

After his departure on the last sailing of the *Lafrance* in mid-October, the Vancouver and Victoria papers carried speculation over a new consolidation and possible backers. As usual, Treadgold himself had nothing to say, but speculation by other Yukoners centered on a hydroelectric plant somewhere along the Klondike River and mining on Upper Dominion, Quartz and Last Chance creeks. Soon after Treadgold's departure, Gus Bredenberg, acting as Treadgold's agent, filed for 2,000 miner's inches of water to be taken from the Klondike River, one-half mile upstream from the mouth of Rock Creek.[4] Presumably, the water would be used in working the Anderson Concession.

The speculation proved correct, and in mid-March 1910 work began on Treadgold's new scheme, a hydroelectric plant on the Klondike River, about fifteen miles east of the mouth of Hunker Creek.[5] Numerous power schemes had already been proposed for the Klondike; Treadgold had taken over one initiated by Grey, Dolan and Strong, three Dawsonites, who had held a water grant since mid-1908, perhaps as a front for Treadgold. W.J. Rendell, a local civil engineer, had completed a survey of a ditch line in 1908. In the fall of 1909 a crew of about twenty men were put to work on the project in order to meet the work requirements of the grant.[6]

Water would be taken from the North Klondike River, about six miles from the mouth, and carried by canal about six miles to a point above the Klondike River where a plant would be installed using the effective head of about 228 feet. The canal, eighteen feet wide at the bottom and twenty-eight feet at the top, was designed to carry up to 15,000 miner's inches of water, triple the capacity of Yukon Gold's Twelve Mile Ditch. Initially, it was planned to develop 10,000 hp but there would be provision to expand the plant at a later date.

One hundred fifty tons of equipment and supplies, including two steam shovels, had been freighted to the site before breakup, and work was soon underway directed by Harry Boardman, formerly chief electrician with Yukon Gold. The shovels, part of the equipment brought in by the Detroit Yukon company in 1903 and later unloaded on Canadian Klondyke, were finally being used on a project they were suited for. Worked in two ten-hour shifts, each shovel proved capable of digging up to 300 feet of ditch per day; one completed a record 800 feet in forty hours. By 1910 about 300 men were at work on the project.[7]

Treadgold did not return to the Klondike until mid-July 1910 but there had been news of him in late April:

"Arthur Newton Christian Treadgold no longer is single. The king of Yukon promoters forsook the single life and fled into the realm of matrimony as unostentatiously as he closes a ten million dollar deal in Klondike placers.

"It has been some time since the foremost of Yukon organizers took the marriage vows but Klondike has just received the news. Mr. Treadgold seldom takes any trouble sending out unessential information to the proletariat so the news of the wedding was fated to come to Dawson by the slow process of conveyance by returning Klondikers. . . . The bride is a wealthy American girl, a woman of rare beauty and accomplishment. . . . It is understood that she is 20 to 25 years of age.

"No Yukoner is better known than Mr. Treadgold. He is conceded the greatest individual rustler [sic] and organizer

Yukon has known and now is winding up details on the second largest mining company ever projected for Yukon. . . ."[8]

Arriving without his bride, Treadgold took command of the project, working day and night with scarcely any office staff. In addition to the plant and ditch, two new power lines were strung. One went from the plant to Hunker Summit and on to Dominion Creek; a second line went to the Bonanza Basin Gold Dredging Company's dredge lying idle just east of Dawson. Treadgold now controlled this dredge.[9] It had been installed in 1905 by a group with St. Louis backing, but the dredge was poorly suited to the ground and had operated with indifferent success between major modifications.

Treadgold was believed to hold many placer claims on Hunker, Dominion, Sulphur and Quartz creeks, acquired either directly or by others acting as his agent, but the extent of his holdings would not be known until he chose to reveal it or the transfers were recorded at the Gold Commissioner's office. Work continued on the ditch and power plant until halted by cold weather in November. Later that month Treadgold slipped out of Dawson on a special White Pass stage.[10]

Freighting began over the winter trail from Dawson to the North Fork power plant in February 1911 with the movement of 700 tons of material, chiefly steel pipe for the penstocks.[11] In addition, White Pass stages had carried fifty tons of cement over the winter road from Whitehorse to Dawson, the largest shipment ever handled on the winter route. A crew of about 100 hurried the final details of the project, and on 8 May 1911 the first unit of the plant was turned on.[12] Everything ran without a hitch and the plant began supplying power for Canadian Klondyke's two dredges almost immediately. In addition, there was a contract to supply power to Yukon Gold's seven dredges, but that company refused to accept the power until meters had been installed.

During the winter, Treadgold had been busy in New York and London arranging financial backing for his new consolidation. In early August 1911, it was announced that the Consolidated Gold Fields group, through an American subsidiary, had acquired a large interest in Treadgold's enterprise, already financed in part by H. C. Hoover and A. C. Beatty.[13] The new company would be known as Granville Mining Company; for the moment, there would be no public stock issue, the funds having been subscribed privately. Hoover, a consulting mining

Top—North Fork power plant. Started by Treadgold in 1910 and completed in 1911, about the time this photograph was taken, the plant supplied power until the dredging ended in 1966.

Bottom—Interior of North Fork power plant, 17 December 1913.
In 1935, the building was extended to house a third unit, and the plant was operated until 1967, when it was replaced by a diesel plant in Dawson. Since then, some of the equipment has been removed and the building is currently used by an outfitter to store hay.

171

engineer (and later a President of the United States), was associated with the Govett group of companies in London; Beatty, also a consulting engineer in England, had once been assistant exploration manager for the Guggenheims. Treadgold, Mrs. Treadgold and M. H. Orr Ewing, one of his original backers, arrived in Dawson early in September 1911.[14] Work had already started on another ditch to bring water from the Klondike River to the foot of Dago Hill on Hunker Creek. A new sixty-five-ton Vulcan shovel, brought in and assembled earlier in the summer, was used on the project.[15] Treadgold was busy overseeing his new empire until a few days before Christmas 1911 when he, Joe Boyle, and Gus Bredenberg left Dawson in a special sleigh, racing to overtake the regular White Pass stage somewhere on the winter road ahead of them.[16] They finally caught it south of Indian River and the party, now including Boyle's wife and daughter who were on the stage, would spend Christmas on the road to Whitehorse.

In London, there were negotiations between Boyle, Treadgold and the principals of Granville Mining. Boyle had a going dredging operation and if Granville could consummate a deal with him it would give the company a source of income until their own mining operations got underway. In late March 1912, Joe Boyle, now back in New York, telegraphed that there had been an amalgamation of interests.[17] Boyle would control operations north of the Dome and Treadgold those to the south. Additional information on the scheme was disclosed in mid-August 1912 in connection with the listing of Granville Mining on the London Stock Exchange:

Promoters of the company were Treadgold, Hoover and Beatty; the share capital of 1,200,000 shares (nominal value £1,200,000, or $6,000,000) was issued to the promoters as the purchase price. An additional £1,000,000 ($5,000,000) in 6 percent debentures would be convertible into shares until the end of 1917. Of these, £460,000 ($2,300,000) had been issued or contracted, and a further £440,000 ($2,200,000) was proposed.

From the money raised, Granville would lend nearly £300,000 ($1,500,000) to Boyle's Canadian Klondyke Mining Company to enable that company to build two more dredges with sixteen-cubic-foot buckets. In return for the $1,500,000 loan and for giving Canadian Klondyke rights to the properties north of the Dome, Granville would receive 29 percent of the capital stock of

Canadian Klondyke and an option to convert the $1,500,000 debenture into an additional 20 percent of the stock.

Canadian Klondyke, in turn, guaranteed Granville a minimum income of £48,000 ($240,000), which was comprised of £18,000 ($90,000) in interest on the Canadian Klondyke debentur £15,600 ($78,000) in dividends on the 29-percent stock interest and £14,400 ($72,000) in interest on £240,000 ($1,200,000) in Granville Power Company bonds. The total minimum income of £48,000 ($240,000) would be almost sufficient to cover the interest of £54,000 ($270,000) on the Granville debentures.

Using the remainder of the money raised, Granville Mining proposed to add to their holdings south of the Dome on Quartz, Sulphur and Dominion creeks and to equip their ground for working. Granville estimated that their ground, exclusive of that turned over to Boyle, contained more than 600 million cubic yards of gravel, half of which was estimated to contain values of about thirty-one cents per yard, recoverable at a cost of about twelve cents per yard.[18]

Treadgold estimated that the net income over fixed charges for Granville Mining should be £17,025 ($85,125) for 1912 £48,600 ($243,000) for 1913 £175,650 ($878,250) for 1914; £292,900 ($1,464,500) for 1915; and £367,900 ($1,839,500) for 1916. Production beyond 1916 was "a matter entirely of equipment, its holdings of workable gravels being so large as to admit of a large number of separate workings, each of which should add materially to the revenue. . . ." He concluded:

"Your company is not pioneering in the Klondike district, as is shown not only by the work of the Canadian Klondyke Company, above referred to, but also the results of the Yukon Gold Company, of which I am a director. The Yukon Gold Company has paid out in dividends from 1909 to the present date nearly £800,000."[19]

One point glossed over in the Granville prospectus was that the transfer of "certain properties which [Granville] owns in the vicinity of the Canadian Klondyke Mining Company" would include the North Fork power plant, owned by the Granville Power Company. Capital stock of Granville Power, all held by Treadgold, would be turned over to Boyle; Boyle would guarantee $1,200,000 in 6-percent, 15-year Granville Power Company bonds to be issued to Granville Mining Company.[20] In addition, the agreement between Granville Mining and Boyle called for the issue of $300,000 of Granville Power bonds to Boyle, "provided he shall by then have performed all of his obligations hereunder." Later, in April 1913, Granville Power was renamed Canadian Klondyke Power Company, Limited.

Finally, in July 1912, a portion of the claim holdings Treadgold had amassed were revealed in the transfer of large blocks of claims to subsidiary companies. Included were 177 claims on Dominion Creek transferred to The Dominion Mining Company, Limited; 29 on Quartz Creek to The Calder Mining Company, Limited; 22 on Upper Eldorado Creek to The Deep Vale Mining Company, Limited; 64 on Dago Hill and 22 on Last Chance Creek to The Dago Hill Mining Company, Limited; and 13 bench claims on Lower Dominion Creek to The Big Creek Mining Company, Limited.[21]

Treadgold was back in the Klondike in mid-August 1912, leaving his wife behind in Skagway to await his return.[22] A new problem awaited him. It had begun at the end of May 1912, when F. T. Congdon, acting for Treadgold, had entered an action against Peter Rost, a claim holder on Dominion Creek, claiming that Rost had not fulfilled an agreement that required him to obtain a block of claims on Dominion Creek for Treadgold. Rost was advanced $33,780 to purchase the claims, but now he was refusing to turn them over to Treadgold.[23]

The case was called early in September 1912, and it dragged on for two weeks. Treadgold, on the stand for four days, proved a difficult witness. As the *Dawson News* reported, "Mr. Treadgold answers most of the questions from memory and touches on a vast number of points in connection with his dealings with Mr. Rost. Efforts to get answers to some of the questions in cross-examination resulted in slow progress with the case."[24] Finally, Judge Macaulay, losing patience, suggested the parties agree on a settlement.[25] The attempt failed, and Macaulay's judgment, delivered a month later, dismissed Treadgold's action. The only agreement between the two parties had been a letter in Treadgold's handwriting:

"Lower Dominion, 25 Aug., 1909
"A.N.C. Treadgold, Esq.
    "Dear Sir: In consideration of your assistance in consolidating my position on Dominion creek I agree

to give you the exclusive right to purchase all my interests on Dominion creek and its hillsides and benches for the price and sum of two hundred thousand dollars, payable as to ten thousand dollars on October first of this year and as to the remainder in stock of a company to be formed by you to acquire and work Dominion creek or such parts of Dominion creek as you may consider advisable. I will give you all the assistance in my power to ascertain the values of all the ground on the creek and to acquire such claims as you may consider desirable, turning over to you all claims which I have acquired or may hereafter acquire with your help at the price paid by me for same. You shall form the company at your discretion as to place and time of incorporation and amount of capital, and my stock shall be issued to me fully paid and you shall decide when it may be desirable to merge the company in a larger company.

"Yours faithfully,
"Peter Rost
"By E.
"Peter Rost

"Witness:
"Elizabeth Rost."[26]

In his judgment, Judge Macaulay commented:

"The plaintiff is a mining promoter who has successfully organized large mining enterprises in this territory and is still engaged in further organizing and promoting large mining companies to work the gold bearing gravels in this district; is a graduate of Oxford University, England and is, and has been, a successful mining promoter.

"The defendant Rost is a man unable to read or write except for the fact that he has learned to write his own name, but, as I gathered from the evidence, has had an experience of between 30 and 40 years mining in Australia and this territory, and apart from the fact that he had no education, appears to me to be a shrewd mining man and possessed of more than the ordinary amount of intelligence and a man who thoroughly understood the business of mining in a practical way.

"The defendant Rost depended entirely upon his wife, who seems to have a fair education, to transact any business for him that required to be in writing, and generally to look after his clerical affairs."[27]

The Rosts contended that the letter prepared by Treadgold did not set out the agreement as they understood it, and that Treadgold, despite numerous promises, had never returned with a new agreement. Finally Treadgold's agent, Tom Patton, had appeared with a new agreement in late November 1910, on the day Treadgold left by stage. The Rosts, wary by now, realized that they, as well as the claim owners bought out, had been included in Treadgold's remark to Rost: "Peter, our course is plain, we shall promise them everything—and give them nothing," a statement that Mrs. Rost could mimic in a near-perfect imitation of Treadgold's Oxford accent. They refused to sign the new agreement and sought legal advice. Treadgold balked at the alterations suggested by the Rosts' lawyer. A year later, in November 1911, Treadgold had offered Rost 38,000 shares, $5 par value, in The Dominion Mining Company. Rost, uncertain of their value, if indeed they had any, refused to accept the shares. Judge Macaulay concurred with Rost on the value of the stock and ruled that Rost was within his rights in refusing it. Further, Judge Macauley nullified the offer in the Rost's letter of 25 August 1909. He declined to turn over the claims in question to either party, indicating that a new action would be needed to establish ownership. Both sides prepared for the appeal, to be heard in Vancouver in the spring of 1913, but, at the last minute, the case was settled out of court with Rost's acceptance of an offer from Treadgold's side.[28]

Treadgold faced other uncertainties. Laurier's Liberal government, in power since 1896, had been defeated in 1911, and George Black, a prominent Conservative and long-time enemy of the concessions, had been appointed Commissioner of the Yukon early in 1912. Certainly, there would be differences in dealing with the new government. Another disturbing change was that Joe Boyle now controlled everything north of the Dome, including the new North Fork power plant. The working styles of the two men were different. While Treadgold preferred working quietly behind the scenes, Boyle was always a centre of controversy. At the end of the summer of 1912, there was trouble and it was predictable. Boyle was deadlocked with Commissioner Black over who should control the sale of any surplus power generated by the North Fork plant,[29] and Treadgold—even though his money had built the plant—was powerless to intervene. Treadgold could only hope that Boyle's actions would not endanger his own plans for the Indian River side of the Dome.

Treadgold went Outside in November 1912. Involved in property negotiations, the lawsuit with Rost, and trouble with Joe Boyle, there had been little opportunity to get his own mining projects underway. A little was accomplished: A small crew had been at work ground-sluicing near 33 Below Lower Discovery on Dominion Creek.[30] There was always next year. Treadgold had no idea that his many worries, now only small clouds on the horizon, would gather in a catastrophic storm that would drive him from the Klondike and leave him bankrupt.

Joe Boyle and his wife followed Treadgold to London, arriving early in January 1913, and new negotiations began between Boyle and his companies on one hand and Treadgold and

Ground sluicing on Dominion Creek, probably on ground controlled by Treadgold's North West Corporation. After the brush was stripped off, water was directed over the frozen black muck and the thawed organic material was carried away by the existing streams. Once the underlying placer gravels were exposed, natural thawing would begin, reducing the amount of steam thawing required.

Granville on the other. Boyle was in a strong position. He had received the agreed sum of $1,350,000 from Granville by 1 November 1912, his two new dredges were almost completed, and he had full control of the North Fork power plant and most of Treadgold's other interests on the Klondike side of the Dome. Granville Mining, in contrast, had only an agreement signed by Boyle (as an individual and on behalf of one of his companies).[31] Nothing was resolved, but later, in mid-March 1913, Boyle, now back in Canada, cabled Herbert Hoover that a new company had been formed and that he expected to complete everything and deliver the bonds by the end of that month. The debentures were never issued, and, in later years, Boyle would link this to Treadgold's failure to clear up the titles and complete the transfer of the last of his holdings in the Klondike watershed. Treadgold and Granville Mining were to be hapless spectators to Boyle's activities over the next few years, even though Boyle was using their money, their properties, and their plant and equipment.

Granville Mining, left with an uncertain income from Boyle, not quite enough to cover their interest charges, and with no production from Treadgold's operations on the Indian River side of the Dome, unexpectedly found itself in a precarious financial situation. At first, nothing was done, but finally, on the suggestion of a director representing Consolidated Gold Fields, the board decided that Granville Mining should become a holding company.[32] Treadgold could form a company and raise money to mine the gravels on the Indian River watershed; Boyle's Canadian Klondyke could continue mining on the Klondike side. As a holding company, Granville would control 75 percent of Treadgold's new company, North West Corporation, and a possible 49 percent of Canadian Klondyke Mining Company.[33] A London comment referred to the move as "an unscrambling of the Granville egg."[34]

Treadgold set to work to organize his North West Corporation while a market was being created for the shares. The selling campaign was kicked off with a lunch in Treadgold's honour given at the Liverpool Street Station Hotel in London by a broker who held a chain of options on North West shares.[35] Treadgold, enthralled by his latest consolidation, took no interest in the champagne and caviar used as bait. A total of £150,000 was raised, much of it by Treadgold from his friends. Treadgold, still certain that dredges were inefficient, did not specify the mining method to be used on North West's ground. In the Klondike, Treadgold's crews spent the 1913 season doing preparatory stripping on Dominion Creek.[36]

A statement released to the newspapers in late 1913 purported to give details of the financial structure of Granville Mining, Canadian Klondyke and North West Corporation.[37] Actually it was little more than wishful thinking. It described the situation that would exist if only Boyle could be persuaded to issue the Canadian Klondyke debentures. The second annual meeting of Granville Mining was held in London early in 1914. At it, there was the proud announcement that Boyle's Canadian Klondyke had dredged total of 6,363,000 cubic yards during the 1913 season and recovered 85,899 ounces of gold with a gross value of $1,331,000. Boyle estimated his costs at $480,000 leaving an operating profit of $851,000. Granville expected to receive more than the $240,000 guaranteed by Boyle, but the amount would not be known until final returns for the season were received. The chairman concluded his remarks on a cheerful note:

"If Mr. Treadgold is as successful in converting anticipations into realities as Mr. Boyle has already proved himself to be—and we have no reason to doubt that Mr. Treadgold will be equally successful—the Granville Mining Company need have no misgiving as to the future and can look forward with confidence to receiving a satisfactory return upon the capital invested in the Klondike district."[38]

Granville Mining held their third general meeting in London on 10 November 1914. In reporting on Canadian Klondyke Mining there was now a note of uncertainty:

"The accounts show that the value of gold won for 1913 was $1,299,333, whilst the operating expenses amounted to $443,966. After deducting bond interest and other outgoings there was a net profit for the season of 1913 of $752,557. Mr. Boyle's report has not yet been received, but it is understood that the profit was utilized for capital expenditure. It is expected that this year's profit will be free for dividend."[39]

There was another note of concern in the accompanying brief, and otherwise routine, auditor's report: "We have not seen the securities for the investments in the Canadian Klondyke Mining Company, Limited and the Canadian Klondyke Power Company, Limited."

Treadgold's North West Corporation had continued

their stripping operation on Dominion Creek during the summer of 1914. There was still no production, let alone income, from the operations. Treadgold had announced that two track-mounted Lubecker excavating machines would be shipped to the Klondike for use on the Dominion Creek ground. One machine would be used simply as an excavator while the second would carry a washing plant as well. The ground would be ready by the time they arrived the following summer.[40]

New problems arose for Treadgold in March 1915, when his Yukon employees started a legal action for their unpaid wages.[41] The needed $63,000 was finally advanced by Consolidated Gold Fields on the condition that the men's time checks would not be transferable. (People such as Joe Boyle sometimes bought up back wage claims in an attempt to get control of a company, and this provision of the agreement headed off that maneuver.)

There was a note of optimism at the North West meeting held in London on 1 July 1915. In his speech, the chairman of the company, A. Chester Beatty, noted that the company had recently raised a further £75,000 in 7 percent debentures, convertible into stock at par. An additional £75,000 could be issued with the unanimous consent of the directors. Stripping (by using surface waters channelled over the ground) had removed 3⅓ million cubic yards of muck, and the ground was ready for mining by the excavating machine; one machine had already been shipped and was due in Montreal shortly.

The company rejected the use of dredges:

"The objection, however, to the dredging method is that it requires large capital expenditure, that it is not possible to see bedrock, and that a certain amount of gold is lost by the incomplete cleaning of the bedrock, where the bulk of the values naturally occur. To overcome these difficulties, Mr. Treadgold, your Managing Director, in co-operation with a number of local men of experience, have adopted a well-known excavating machine, which has been successfully demonstrated as an excavator, and have fitted this machine with a washing plant. . . . Its ability as a digging machine has been actually demonstrated, and it will be of great value for stripping the overburden in connection with the washing, even if it does not prove practicable to continue the actual washing operation with the machine. I may say, however, in connection with the capabilities of this machine to wash as well as recover material, Mr. Treadgold and other men who are familiar with the Klondike conditions and operations, feel absolutely assured in their minds that this machine will be an unqualified success.''

Continuing, the chairman noted that Mr. Treadgold and his friends had now raised the sum of £225,000 and ''have fully equipped the property as regards stripping, thereby laying the way for the final equipment by machinery, of which the machine which we have just shipped is the first unit. We may not be able to follow out literally the suggestion of the Chancellor of the Exchequer to furnish silver bullets, but we certainly hope to be able to furnish some gold ones in the battle that is now being waged for civilisation. [Cheers.] I now move the adoption of the report and balance sheet.''[42]

The first Lubecker excavator arrived in Dawson in late July 1915 together with David Elliott, Treadgold's shovel expert. Rushed from Liverpool, it had made a remarkably quick trip considering wartime conditions and a submarine scare on leaving England. The machine weighed about 170 tons and advanced on sets of rails spaced about twenty feet apart. Digging was done by a bucket line, dragging inwards toward the machine, and the tailings were deposited from a stacker much like that on a dredge. The machine would operate in a long cut, shuttling back and forth to strip the gravels that had been thawed by the sun's heat since the last pass; it was capable of digging seventy feet above to seventy feet below its track level. The Lubecker was expected to handle up to 15,000 cubic yards per day, equal to one of Boyle's big dredges, but at one third to one half the cost.[43]

In the autumn of 1915, the machine was moved to a site on Dominion Creek, that had been prepared for it, assembled, and tested for a few hours. Elliott, interviewed in Skagway in mid-November while en route back to England, reported that the machine had worked well, although minor parts of the machine needed to be strengthened or improved. Unfortunately, there had not been sufficient electrical power available for a good test.[44]

The second machine, equipped with a washing plant, arrived in Vancouver in late September 1916. The White Pass, making a special effort, had managed to get most of it to Dawson on one of the last boats of the season. The new machine, weighing 270 tons, ''includes many heavy pieces, among them two or three huge cylindrical parts twenty to thirty feet long, and five to six

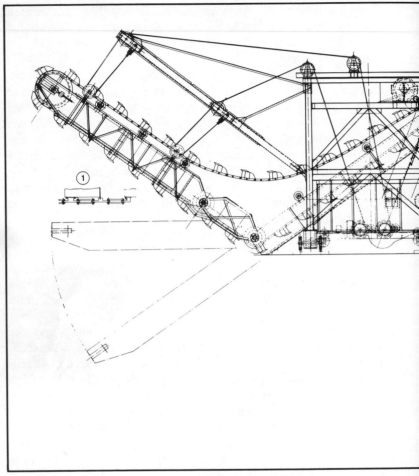

Treadgold's Lubecker chain bucket excavator, which he intended to replace the gold dredges.

feet in diameter; also several long, heavy steel stackers, girders, plates and wheels and other parts. All are painted red.''[45]

The scramble to get the machines into the Klondike was in vain; the first was never put back in service, and the second sat in Dawson, customs duties unpaid, for over ten years. Eventually it would be stripped of small parts, such as electric motors.

Granville Mining Company simply drifted during much of World War 1. Initially, there had been an income of $132,000

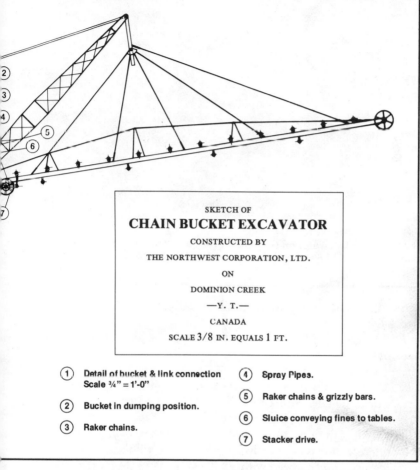

SKETCH OF
CHAIN BUCKET EXCAVATOR
CONSTRUCTED BY

THE NORTHWEST CORPORATION, LTD.

ON

DOMINION CREEK

—Y. T.—

CANADA

SCALE 3/8 IN. EQUALS 1 FT.

(1) Detail of bucket & link connection
Scale ¾" = 1'-0"

(2) Bucket in dumping position.

(3) Raker chains.

(4) Spray Pipes.

(5) Raker chains & grizzly bars.

(6) Sluice conveying fines to tables.

(7) Stacker drive.

every six months from Boyle's companies but this had ended in mid-1915, despite the guarantees, and there was no production from Treadgold's North West Corporation. Herbert Hoover became fed up with Treadgold's machinations and withdrew from Granville, leaving only F. A. Govett to represent the Govett interests. Finally, in April 1917, Granville was placed in receivership and the receiver, Edward Dexter of London, in turn applied for receiverships for Canadian Klondyke and North West Corporation. Treadgold was forced aside and F. P. Burrall, an American engineer who had been in the Klondike for Granville since 1915, took over field management of North West to

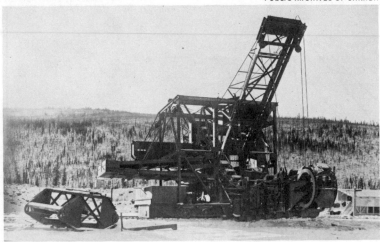

The Lubecker excavator on Dominion Creek in 1915. Tested late in the season, it dug "a few wheelbarrow loads" before being shut down and forgotten.

---

determine what, if anything, could be salvaged from the tangled wreckage.[46]

Treadgold struck back at the move in a letter to his backers:

> "In 1915, the 'three parties' contrived to issue a prior lien debenture as a means of raising further funds—unwisely, but definitely in furtherance of a selfish plan to partition the Klondike in their own interest. It was especially offensive to me who had formed and financed with £150,000 in 1913 the North West Corporation, thereby relieving the Granville Mining Company of financing, and leaving it a holding company only. In further indulgence of their selfish aims the 'three parties' in 1917, as Canadian Klondyke Company still failed to issue its $1,500,000 debenture, promised to Granville Mining Company in 1912, instead of pressing for its issue in the Klondike, applied for a receiver for the Granville Mining Company in the High Court here [London] through the prior lien debentures, which were, it was pretended in jeopardy. The court granted their application. The Granville receiver

appointed on 1st May 1917 at once applied for a receiver against the North West Corporation and was himself appointed receiver and manager. He then applied in the Klondike for a receiver of the Canadian Klondyke Company and his application was in September 1917 granted. So the Klondike stands, one part of it owned and worked and paying dividends to the Yukon Gold Company of New York, and the other very much larger part lying smitten by the receiverships covering all of it with their blight."[47]

Treadgold had lost his new consolidation. First Boyle had made off with the North Fork power plant and all of Treadgold's holdings on the Klondike side of the Dome and now the receivers had taken everything on the Indian River side. His money and that of many of his friends was gone and there was little prospect of regaining control. Still dreaming of consolidation, he fought the receiverships in the courts. The low point came on 26 February 1920 when Treadgold was adjudicated a bankrupt with liabilities totalling £446,134.[48]

The excitement that Joe Boyle brought to the Canadian
Klondyke operation continued into 1911. Boyle had stayed in the
Klondike over the winter of 1910-1911, and he kept his two
dredges operating until mid-December, making a total of 233 days
for Number 1. After repairs, the two dredges were away again on
22 April 1911 using power from the Coal Creek thermal plant
until Treadgold's new North Fork power plant began generating
in early May 1911. Treadgold was in England and not expected
back until late summer; for the moment, Boyle was manager of
the new power plant as well. His new Number 2 dredge with the
sixteen-cubic-foot buckets was working steadily at close to rated
capacity and seemed certain to be profitable. Boyle was able to
keep it going until 19 December 1911. A few days later when
Boyle left the Klondike, racing off in a special sleigh with
Treadgold and Gus Bredenberg, he knew that his company would
show an operating profit of over $130,000 for the 1911 season.[1]

     Early in 1912, after he had negotiated the amalgamation
with Granville Mining Company, Boyle had ordered two new

dredges, sister ships to his giant Number 2. In addition, under the agreement, he had taken over Treadgold's holdings on the Klondike River side of the Dome (including all the shares of the power company, soon to be renamed Canadian Klondyke Power Company), the new ditch Treadgold had started from the Klondike River to Hunker Creek, and the Bonanza Basin dredge.

And all the while, Boyle was forming new companies and shuffling his holdings among them. The first new company was Boyle Concessions, Limited, incorporated on 18 May 1912 with members of a Windsor, Ontario, legal firm as directors. A month or so later, 28 June 1912, Boyle Concessions purchased most of the assets—but not all—of the Canadian Klondyke Mining Company.[2] On 15 March 1913, a *new* Canadian Klondyke—Canadian Klondyke Mining Company, *Limited*—was incorporated, with Boyle and members of the same Windsor firm among the directors.[3] The new company then purchased the assets of Boyle Concessions, Limited on 25 March 1913. Next day, the original Canadian Klondyke Mining Company, the one incorporated by the Detroit group in 1904, had its name changed to Yukon Exploration, Limited.[4] While these changes were taking place, agreements were being made with other companies, such as Granville Mining, with Boyle often acting both as an individual and on behalf of one of the companies. Later, when difficulties arose, it became a shell game for Boyle's adversaries to guess which company the real assets lay under at the time of signing and what obligations, if any, were passed to the successor companies.

In late May 1912, pits for Canadian Klondyke's two new dredges were started on the Discovery Claim on the Bonanza Basin group on the Klondike River, less than a mile from Dawson, but work halted abruptly when Commissioner Black pointed out that he, not Boyle, owned the surface rights to the ground.[5] By July an agreement had been reached, and Canadian Klondyke had 185 men at work on two square pits, each 175 feet on a side and 15 feet deep. A shovel was at work in each, and four narrow-gauge engines and strings of cars were used to haul the gravel from the pits. The Klondike Mines Railway had trains running day and night hauling material between the Dawson wharves and the site. Their loads included huge timbers of British Columbia fir, free of knots and other imperfections, and specially selected to withstand the enormous stresses that would rack the dredges as they dug the coarse gravels of the Klondike flats. Howard

Brenner, who had supervised the erection of Canadian Number 1 in 1905 and Number 2 in 1910, was back on the job again.[6] The framing was done by early August and the company began advertising for carpenters, promising that all available would be put to work. By mid-August, about 300 men were at work on the two dredges.[7]

Joe and Mrs. Boyle arrived back in the Klondike in late July 1912 and Boyle took charge of his expanded empire. Aside from the dredging and construction already underway, one of the first new projects was a ditch about sixteen miles long, called the South Fork Ditch,[8] that would bring water from the main Klondike River to the North Fork plant. Always in a hurry, Boyle had gone ahead without the necessary water grant and, at the end of August, was forced to cancel plans to use an eighty-man crew on the ditch until the question of the grant was settled with Commissioner Black.[9] The Commissioner contended that he, not Boyle, should control the conditions of sale for any surplus power generated and that Boyle still had not supplied the required

<small>YUKON ARCHIVES. MACBRIDE MUSEUM COLLECTION</small>

Canadian Klondyke Mining Company's dredges, Canadian Numbers 3 and 4, under construction in the Bonanza Basin area near the mouth of the Klondike River, 2 August 1912. Yukon Gold's Guggieville shops are in right background, Ogilvie Bridge at left.

information concerning Granville Power's present operations. Later, Black added a warning: "The government will accord fair treatment to all persons dealing with it and, no matter how powerful the corporation nor what pull it may have had nor what special privileges have in the past been allowed it or to the person controlling it, so far as I am concerned the same compliance with the law and regulations will now be required of it as of individuals."[10]

Joe and Mrs. Boyle left Dawson in mid-December 1912 in an attempt to drive through to Whitehorse in their 20 hp Flanders car, part of a publicized attempt to travel from Dawson to London in eighteen days. Poor road conditions and a 1,500-pound load in the car forced them to switch to a White Pass stage for the last portion of the trip to Whitehorse. A few days later their attempt was upstaged by the arrival in Whitehorse of Commissioner Black and C. A. Thomas of Yukon Gold in the latter's 60 hp Locomobile driven by chauffeur George Potter. Running time from Dawson was 35½ hours. "Tires were worn down to the canvas and nearly everything loose that was not riveted" but after repairs they started on the return trip. The car, by now a "locoed-mobile," had to be abandoned just north of the Pelly River, and the travellers arrived in Dawson by stage on New Year's Eve.[11]

Commissioner Black described the downfall of the car as a "simple accident to the machinery, one that might have happened on a city boulevard. An insignificant looking but most important little part of the carburetor called the float . . . sprung a leak. It had leaked when in use in Dawson last summer and had been repaired temporarily with solder instead of being replaced. . . . On the return trip the solder worked loose. . . . We patched it up on the road with candle wax which was not very satisfactory. While we had the car in the barn at Scroggie Creek we undertook to repair it by heating the solder unfortunately greatly increasing the aperture, putting the machine entirely out of business. . . ."[12]

Despite the difficulties with the Flanders on the winter road, Joe Boyle reached London about 11 January 1913. There were new negotiations with Granville but now Boyle's holdings were being shuffled between his companies, and the issue of the $1,500,000 debenture would have to wait until he returned to Canada. Promises were easy to make: Joe Boyle already had

Joe Boyle with his Flanders 20, probably en route from Whitehorse to Dawson, April 1913.

Granville's money and full control of everything north of the Dome, including the power plant, while Granville, in contrast, had only an uncertain agreement with him. Granville had no hold on him. Besides there were other interests to be acquired in London. In mid-February 1913 he cabled his brother Charlie, acting manager of Canadian Klondyke, that he had leased the plant and operations of The Northern Light, Power and Coal Company.[13] The company owned the Dawson utilities—Dawson Electric Light and Power, Dawson City Water and Power and the Yukon Telephone Syndicate—plus a coal mine, thermal plant and railway at Coal Creek, about thirty-five miles northwest of Dawson, and the steamer *Lightning*, used in the coal trade on the Yukon River. Built on an incredible mixture of dreams, promotion and greed, the company had a turbulent history. At the time of Boyle's lease it had already spent over $2 million on various projects, had been in default on bond interest for several years and was involved in an on-again-off-again legal action against the former owners of the property. The company had strung a power line into Dawson from their Coal Creek thermal plant and the latter had been started up in August 1910.[14] Initially, the plant had a 2,000 KVA capacity but it was hoped to expand it

First auto over the winter trail from Dawson to Whitehorse, in December 1912. The party (from left: George Potter, driver; Commissioner George Black; and C. A. Thomas, resident manager of Yukon Gold) made the trip in 35 ½ hours running time in Thomas's 60-hp Locomobile.

to 9,000 KVA once there was a market for the power. The plant, fired by lignite mined from a thin and much-disturbed seam, was a marginal operation at best, but there was hope that it could produce power early in the spring and during the fall freeze-up when the hydroelectric plants were unable to operate. If power could be supplied during these critical periods there was a good possibility that the dredging season could be greatly extended.

One afternoon in late April 1913, Joe Boyle and Joe Jr. drove into Dawson in their Flanders automobile after a week on the road from Whitehorse. Both men were mud-spattered and brown from the spring sunshine. Best time on the trip had been between Whitehorse and Carmacks where one run of nineteen miles had been made in a record time of just under two hours. They had gone off the track numerous times but fortunately the Flanders, now stripped and weighing only 1,680 pounds, could be manhandled back onto the road.[15]

Joe Boyle's troubles began about a week later when the Dawson thermal plant (one of the utilities leased from the Northern Light, Power and Coal Company) burned on Saturday night, 3 May 1913. The engineer in charge reported that he had noticed the steam pressure in the plant dropping, had stepped out to tell the fireman, and returned to find a sheet of fire playing about the switchboard. He was badly burned in an attempt to extinguish the fire and had been lucky to escape alive.[16]

At the time, the main generator in the plant was running in parallel with the North Fork plant, and the two were carrying Boyle's Canadian Number 2 and the Yukon Gold dredges. It was a heavy load, and the fuses had blown the night before but, on that occasion, the engineer had been close to the switchboard and was able to put out the fire with a chemical extinguisher.

The fire on 3 May destroyed the thermal plant and the city pumping plant, and only a bucket brigade had kept the flames from spreading to buildings nearby. Joe Boyle was soon on the scene directing his line crews, and power was restored to Dawson by midnight, some three hours later.

Canadian Number 3, the first of the new dredges, was started up on the evening of 9 May 1913 with Joe Boyle at the controls. All ran smoothly, and after a few stops for minor adjustments the dredge began to work downstream on the Klondike River, mining the gravels that the old Bonanza Basin dredge had been unable to handle efficiently.[17] Canadian

Number 4 was run on 20 May.[18] This time, Mrs. Charlie Boyle had the honour of turning the power on in the presence of a number of her friends, including Mrs. George Black. Canadian Number 2 had been working since late March; Canadian Number 1, dismantled the fall before and rebuilt on Claim 21 Below on Hunker Creek, was expected to be away before the first of June. Other than the fire at the Dawson thermal plant, things were going smoothly; 1913 promised to be a banner year.

From his earliest days in the Klondike, Joe Boyle had always been active in community affairs. Now, with the wealth from his ever-growing placer empire he could do even more. From 1913 until he left the Klondike, there would be an annual children's picinc about the first of July. Using either the Northern Light Company's *Lightning* or a chartered steamer, Boyle would take the children of Dawson on a picnic to Swede Creek, about six miles upstream. Children under five were expected to bring their parents with them and those under twelve were given the option of inviting their parents if they chose to do so. It was always Joe Boyle's day and, romping and playing with the children, he enjoyed the outing as much as they did. Then, in the Christmas holidays, there would be a trip to the North Fork power plant for the high school students. A convoy of cars would carry the students and their teachers to a roadhouse near the plant and the group would travel from there by sleigh over the winter road.

Joe Boyle at one of his annual picnics for the children of Dawson.

There would be a dance at the plant and the group would return to town by the same route a day or so later.

For those who were young in the Klondike during those years, Joe Boyle was, and will always be, a figure of heroic proportions. But with his flamboyant nature, he could not achieve the same popularity in his business dealings. From the small beginnings when he first returned to the Klondike in 1909, the disputes and litigation would grow to the point where they threatened the very existence of his Canadian Klondyke Mining Company.

Boyle's troubles with Yukon Gold began in July 1909 before he returned to the Klondike to take over the Canadian Klondyke company. Using water from their newly-opened Twelve Mile Ditch, Yukon Gold were hydraulicking the White Channel Gravels on Jackson Gulch, overlooking the Klondike valley, and the tailings were gradually spreading onto ground lying within the Boyle Concession. Following an exchange of telegrams, an understanding with the acting manager of Canadian Klondyke was cancelled and the work stopped pending an agreement between the two companies. Later, after Boyle arrived, the two were unable to agree on a price for the ground needed for tailings disposal.

In the spring of 1910 there were new difficulties between the two companies over the Golden Age claim, a quartz claim within the Boyle Concession held by W. O. Smith since 1899. Yukon Gold, anticipating difficulties with Smith over quartz claims he held on Bonanza Creek, put a crew of eight men on the claim to sink shafts to bedrock in an attempt to establish the lode values, if any. Boyle countered with his own eight-man crew, contesting the presence of the rival crew and contending that even if the claim were valid he would still control any placer deposits on it.

The case was before the court in the spring of 1910. Smith's crew, backed by Yukon Gold, were given permission to sink three shafts to bedrock, and as many as they liked through the slide material, but were restrained from making test pannings of any of the material excavated.[19] Litigation would go on for years over the Golden Age claim and the related issue as to whether claims excluded from the Boyle Concession when it was granted became part of the concession when they were abandoned or whether they remained as open ground, available to the would-be staker. Finally, early in 1912, Boyle's appeal to the Supreme Court was dismissed with costs, and it was established that the abandoned claims were indeed open ground.

Yukon Gold, hoping to put together a block of ground for dredging, began staking the abandoned claims on Bear Creek. Next year, in May 1913, Yukon Gold went a step further and staked 19 and 20 Bear, claims that Boyle maintained his company had bought for $60,000 and then allowed to lapse on an understanding with the government that they would revert into the Boyle Concession.[20] The battle continued for years. Eventually Yukon Gold was able to assemble the ground needed for their dredge operation, but 19 and 20 Bear became part of the Boyle Concession.

Over the next few years little was settled, and new differences were added to the Canadian Klondyke-Yukon Gold dispute. From time to time, one side, suffering more at the moment, would make an attempt to settle but the other, too spiteful to give up their current advantage, would either raise the ante or simply stall and the negotiations would collapse once more. At one stage, Boyle appears to have borrowed $50,000 from Daniel Guggenheim and Yukon Gold but, instead of aiding a settlement, it became one more item on the long list of differences.[21] There was growing animosity between Joe Boyle and C. A. Thomas, Yukon Gold's resident manager; they were both physically powerful men accustomed to having their own way. Deadlocked in dealings with Thomas, Boyle turned to direct negotiations with Solomon Guggenheim in New York. Even this failed and, in March 1913, Boyle ended a long letter to Guggenheim:

"In conclusion, I have to say that I cannot reconcile your assurance of a desire to get the matter amicably and fairly settled with your action on the ground, including your trespass and sinking of holes and your prosecution of the Smith case, nor with your later refusal to accept my proposal to arbitrate, and I would now like to have a definite statement from you as to just what you are willing to do in the matter."[22]

One by one, new issues began to appear before the courts. A battle with Yukon Gold over electricity began early in

1913. In a bid to take over the electricity franchise in Dawson using his North Fork power, Boyle had submitted a proposed rate structure (about half the existing rates) to Commissioner Black late in 1912. Boyle had control through a lease of Northern Light, Power and Coal Company. Charlie Boyle, as acting manager, announced that the proposed rates would be put into effect as of the first of March 1913.[23] Yukon Gold had been getting power for their Guggieville shops at the mouth of Bonanza Creek for 7½ cents a kilowatt hour, but now Boyle refused to continue supplying them at that rate or include them in his new rate structure for the city. Instead he offered them power at just over 30 cents per kilowatt hour and they could take it or leave it. On the first of April 1913, C. A. Thomas sought an injunction to compel the utility company to continue supplying them at either the old 7½ cents rate or under the new, lower city rates.[24]

Late in 1913, there was more trouble as Boyle's new Canadian Number 4 ground its way toward the Yukon Gold shops at Guggieville. Apprehensive that the change in drainage resulting from the dredging would divert the spring floods into their shop area, Yukon Gold sought a court injunction to halt the dredging.[25] Their request was denied, but Canadian Klondyke was warned that they would be held responsible for any damage that might result from their actions. Later, the ownership of the ground actually dredged was contested; in a decision more than a year later, Yukon Gold was awarded $11,700.60 in damages.[26] Appeals in the action continued until Yukon Gold won in the Supreme Court of Canada in 1917.[27]

Another new round in the battle began on 8 November 1913 when C. A. Thomas sent a registered letter to Boyle serving notice of cancellation of the power contract between Yukon Gold and Canadian Klondyke Power Company, successor to Granville Power Company.[28] At the time he gave notice, Yukon Gold's operations were shut down for the year, and the Twelve Mile plant could be put back into operation again the following spring. True, Boyle's North Fork plant might be able to start earlier in the season and run much later in the fall, but there was little prospect of increased profits, judging by the 1913 season when Boyle cut off the power to Yukon Gold from 26 to 31 May 1913 and later, in the fall, cut back the power delivered, forcing Yukon Gold's dredges to shut down on 24 October. Boyle's attitude that his dredges came first, regardless of the terms of any contract,

Panorama of Guggieville and Canadian Number 4 dredge, taken from Acklen Farm on 9 September 1913. Tailings in the background are on Yukon Gold's Bonanza Creek operations. Eventually Yukon Gold would win a dispute over ownership of some of the ground worked by Boyle's dredges.

together with all the other disputes, were ample justification for having one's own power plant!

Undoubtedly, many Dawsonites enjoyed the spectacle of Joe Boyle taking on Yukon Gold, or the "Guggs" as they knew them. Yukon Gold and the Guggenheims brought their supplies in from Outside and had little to do with the merchants in town. At times, there had been conflict with the community over working conditions and the importation of contract labor from Outside. Yukon Gold's engineering and office staff formed part of the Ping-pongs, the local name for the Dawson social set that included senior government and bank employees, lawyers and professional men, officers of the Royal North-West Mounted Police and the heads of the big commercial companies.[29] This exclusive group kept up a busy social life, including numerous parties and fancy dress balls, and each of the women had a "day" during the month when she would be "at home" to callers. The Boyles, living at Bear Creek some six miles from the city, were not directly involved. So it was not expected that all of Dawson, Ping-pongs and otherwise, would unite to battle with Joe Boyle over the rates charged by his leased utility companies.

Boyle's management seemed at first to be an improvement. At the first of March 1913, the residential rate for electricity had been reduced to a base rate of twenty cents per kilowatt-hour that could drop as low as eight cents with increasing consumption, down from the previous base rate of forty cents that could only drop to thirty. Boyle's control was still tenuous;

bondholders of Northern Light had refused to approve the lease at a meeting in London in April 1913.[30] Despite this, in late August, there was a proposal from Boyle to install twelve additional hydrants at a price of $900 per month to the city.[31] If approved, the water company's revenue from the hydrants would increase from $16,200 to $27,000 annually. Initially, there was some support for the increased fire protection, despite the cost, but early in October there was consternation when the *Dawson News* began carrying Boyle's advertisement stating that water service would be cut off for the winter on 15 October unless his proposal was accepted. At the same time, he filed a new electrical rate that would increase the charge for the first 100 kilowatt-hours used each month from twenty to thirty-one cents per kilowatt-hour. Exchanges of ultimatums between Boyle and Commissioner Black followed, and all were published in the Dawson paper. A hurriedly called plebiscite on a proposal by Boyle to continue the water service if guaranteed the increased hydrant revenue of $27,000 for the next three years was defeated on 14 October 1913 by a vote of 314 to 211.

Surprisingly, perhaps because both enjoyed a battle, Commissioner Black and Joe Boyle remained friends. Just after the plebiscite Commissioner and Mrs. Black visited the Coal Creek thermal plant as the guests of Mr. and Mrs. Joe Boyle.[32] The trip, made just before ice closed the river for the year, involved a ride of about fifty-five miles down the Yukon River on the steamer *Lightning,* followed by a twelve-mile trip on the narrow-gauge railway from the mouth of Coal Creek to the mine and power plant. The thermal plant operated part of October, in parallel with the North Fork plant, in an attempt to supply the power needed by Boyle's own dredges and the Yukon Gold fleet. Boyle was at the plant, supervising a crew preparing the mine and power plant for operation the following spring. Up to now, despite all the promotion by Northern Light, only about half the equipment delivered to the plant site had been installed and put into service. The Blacks' visit proved more than a social visit: A new proposal was worked out and telephoned back to Dawson.

In Dawson, there was uncertainty over what would happen next, and preparations began for the shutdown. Once again, fire protection for most of the city would depend on the old system of steam-powered fire engines, mounted on scows on the river. The engines, with steam up at all times, would pump water from holes kept open through the river ice. A new city well was started to supply a pipe and hydrant service in the south end of town. Hotels and stores began drilling their own wells or hooking up to old wells that had been out of service for years, but most householders, as in earlier years, would be forced to buy their supply from the water wagons. Shortly after the plebiscite Boyle's crews began draining and blowing out the water lines, and perhaps it was no coincidence that one of the first residences disconnected was that of C. A. Thomas, manager of Yukon Gold.[33] Later in the month, there were threats from Boyle to cut off the light and telephone services for the unprofitable winter months as well.[34]

Unexpectedly, in early November when all seemed lost Boyle began to back down from his stand. First, he announced that he was willing to reopen the water service if customers would guarantee him an additional $5,400 in income and agree to take electricity for the next three years at the average price they had paid over the last three years.[35] Commissioner Black counselled caution, but, less than a week later, Boyle announced that the necessary customers had signed up and water service would be restored. Commissioner Black, in his next letter, wondered why Boyle was so anxious to restore service when he had lost $16,200 in hydrant revenue in return for the possible increase of $5,400 from his other customers. A week later, Boyle announced that the water pressure would not be high enough to operate the hydrants but that his crews had instructions to increase the pressure on a telephone call from the Fire Department.

Boyle's sudden change of heart may have resulted from the realization that his bluff had been called, but a more likely reason was foreknowledge of a legal action started in mid-November 1913 by Oscar Newhouse, an unhappy bond- and stockholder of Northern Light, for an injunction to set aside the lease to Boyle and Canadian Klondyke. Among other things, Newhouse charged that the directors of Northern Light had given all their authority to Boyle, which was inappropriate because he was manager of the lessee company; that the bondholders had refused to approve the lease in a meeting on 14 April 1913; that the Dawson thermal plant had been destroyed by overloading, the result of gross negligence by Boyle; and that Boyle was now threatening to shut off Dawson water supplies and to close the Coal Creek thermal plant. The case dragged on until almost

Christmas, at which time it was put off until June 1914, but, for the moment at least, there was an uneasy truce between Dawsonites and the utility companies.

Canadian Klondyke's mining operations went smoothly in 1913, free from much of the controversy that swirled about the President and General Manager, Joe Boyle. The new dredges mined huge blocks of ground in the Klondike River flats. When the last one shut down on 26 December 1913, they had treated a total of 6,363,000 cubic yards of gravel, recovering 85,899 ounces of gold with a value of $1,331,000; operating expenses were $480,000.[36] The North Fork power plant had worked well aside from the period in late October when slush ice jammed the canal and power production dropped. In addition, Joe Boyle had solved the problem of operating the plant year-round. During the first cold weather the canal was flooded to capacity, and a thick ice coating allowed to form; then the water was dropped to its normal level and kept from freezing by three electric heaters in the canal. It was an important development, even though the problem of generating enough power to keep the dredges operating during the critical freeze-up period would never be completely overcome.[37]

Pleased by its growing status in the Klondike, the Boyle family held a party for Joe on his forty-sixth birthday in November 1913 and a group of his younger employees presented him with a sterling silver loving cup. One of them expressed the feelings of the group:

"Mr. Boyle made history when he came here, and is still doing so, and the scope of his work is widening. He met difficulties in the beginning, and his genius then, as now, asserted itself when the occasion demanded, and only those associated with him closely ever will appreciate his broadmindedness, his capacity for long, laborious and efficient effort, drawing heavily on his marvelously rugged physique without apparent exhaustion. He always has a foundation of clear and logical thinking, and his mind works rapidly in the grasp of detail and general plans. He never fails in the keen appreciation of the human side of things, and he is ever an inspiration to the men under his direction.

"Covering hundreds of square miles in this particular field of operation, and handling investments of millions of dollars, he looks not only to the welfare of the vast material assets, but also to the comfort of the most modest of his employees, and indirectly to the welfare of the army who are supported by his enterprises. He has an abiding faith in young men as well as in the sourdoughs of the land, and scores of college men and school boys have done their first work under his direction. He believes ardently in young recruits. Mr. Boyle knows the value of getting a young man of reliable character and ability, and recognizes talent quickly. Manly, frank and courageous, he sets a splendid example for the youth who join him. He is a true citizen, doing well his part in respect to public progress, in private walks and in every pursuit he undertakes."

Boyle, taken by surprise, took "a little time to get under way in the reply, but before the evening was over he had done his share and, as usual, proved the master raconteur."[38]

Early in 1914, Boyle and his wife again left the Klondike for a trip Outside. This time it was made at a more leisurely pace, with visits to Ireland and Ottawa before the return to Dawson in mid-June. The returning party included Joe and Mrs. Boyle, Joe Jr., and four young men who would be working for Canadian Klondyke. Summer plans included completion of the ditch that Treadgold had started from the Klondike River to Hunker Creek and the installation of two more stripping machines, one a traction shovel and the other a special device with power-operated clamshell buckets. Boyle had no comment on plans for the Coal Creek plant.[39]

Preparations for the 1914 season had gone well under the supervision of Charlie Boyle. A crew of almost 400 was at work by mid-March, and at the end of March Canadian Number 4, the first dredge to get underway in 1914, started up on Coal Creek power. There were still problems over the Dawson utilities. Charlie Boyle had started negotiations for a new rate for hydrant service, and he announced that the higher electricity rates, introduced in the fall of 1913, would remain in effect for the summer. In reaction, a plebiscite authorizing the city to issue $200,000 in debentures to purchase the utilities had been called for late June. Despite the bad feelings over the utilities, Canadian Klondyke made a policy of purchasing its supplies in Dawson and relations with the townspeople were still good. It promised to be another good season.

In late July 1914, the bondholders of Northern Light, Power and Coal Company were successful in having the lease to Boyle declared null and void in the Yukon courts.[40] The same bondholders, gulled into believing their company should be a

"A group at the Old Inn before the place was dredged out. . . .
29 June 1913." The gathering was premature; at the last minute the
building was found to be on ground controlled by Yukon Gold Company,
and Boyle's Canadian Number 4 swung away from it.

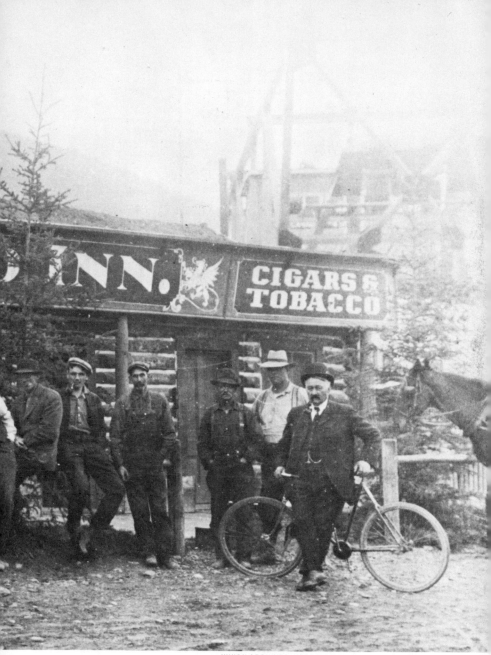

Top—Canadian Number 2 in operation on Christmas Day, 1913.

Bottom—Canadian Number 4 opposite Ogilvie Bridge and working towards Yukon Gold's shops at Guggieville, near the mouth of Bonanza Creek, 18 July 1913. Two years later, Joe Boyle would be involved in a dispute when Canadian Number 3 working upstream in the remaining strip threatened the New North Hotel, just across the bridge.

highly profitable operation, would fight for years to gain control. Boyle, on the other hand, having solved the problem of keeping the North Fork hydroelectric plant operating through the winter, had no real use for power from the Coal Creek thermal plant. Aside from this, the Dawson utilities could be a source of cash through sales of his North Fork power to them. Perhaps out of spite, Joe Boyle continued the battle to control the company and the squabbles were still going on when Boyle left the Yukon in the summer of 1916. Subsequently, in late 1917 and early 1918, the Coal Creek plant, last used in 1914, was dismantled and much of the equipment shipped to Japan.[41] About this time the Gold Fields group acquired control of Northern Light, and the Dawson utilities were destined to be operated by successor dredging companies on a hand-to-mouth basis until the shares were sold to an agency of the Canadian government in 1966.[42] The expected profits never materialized: Total payments to the prior lien bondholders were less than the face value of their bonds; holders of the first mortgage gold bonds and the shares received nothing.

In the summer of 1914, the excitement came from Outside with Britain's declaration of war on the night of 4 August 1914 and her acceptance of Canada's offer of an expeditionary force two days later. Even Dawson, over 7,000 miles and weeks of travel from the battlefields, was drawn in by the excitement and speculation over what might happen next. Joe Boyle, used to thinking in grandiose terms, probably had a better idea than most and, unlike them, was in a position to do something about it. He proposed equipping and sending a fifty-man machine gun battery from the Yukon. On 4 September 1914, Sam Hughes, Minister of Militia and Defence, wired his acceptance of Boyle's offer. There were no delays. Hughes's acceptance was received on Thursday, and by the following Tuesday prospective recruits were being given medical examinations. Since the United States was not at war it was considered best that the group should not be sworn in until they reached Victoria. Meanwhile, the men were not on any payroll; Boyle hit on the idea of giving them work with Canadian Klondyke in the morning and drill sessions in the afternoon. There was little time to be lost if the group was to go Outside by steamer. Once the ice blocked the river there would be a delay of several weeks until travel began over the winter trail. Departure was set for Saturday, the 10th of October, with a final reception and ball to be held the Tuesday before at the AB Hall. There were speeches and musical entertainment but Joe Boyle had only a brief comment: "If I thought myself a better fighter than this bunch I would leave them home and go myself but I am sure they will be a credit to the Yukon and [I am] only too glad to do what I can to aid the cause."⁴³

Fate played a nasty trick on Joe Boyle. It happened early on Saturday morning, 10 October 1914, the day his contingent left. For some reason, Canadian Number 2, the first of his monster dredges, began to take on water, and it soon sank in twenty to thirty-five feet of water opposite the Bear Creek bluff. Boyle, always directly involved in an emergency situation, had spent most of the day at the scene, making sure that everything possible was done to protect the dredge from further damage. Finally, realizing that nothing more could be done for the moment he hurried to Dawson.

"Old Dawson throbbed Saturday night. Under the blaze of lights and with the band playing and the populace shouting the boys of the Boyle Yukon detachment got away for war. It was the first departure in the history of the Northland of a body of men for war and it was made memorable. The tale of the enthusiasm and good cheer will bear repeating for generations and the sailing of the Boyle contingent ever will be a bright page in the history of Yukon.

"No such turnout and enthusiasm have prevailed in Klondike at any other time since the halcyon days when this camp swarmed with tens of thousands of adventurers who came in the first great rush for gold. The streets were black with people from the city and the creeks. The same throng covered the wharf when the troop sailed at midnight. . . .

"When the last whistle blew the boys in khaki were lined up on the forward deck. . . . The band played 'God Save the King' and a more impressive rendition never fell on the ears of the Klondike. The spirit of the occasion seemed to move all, and all stood and sang to the band accompaniment. The lights shone dimly from the wharf but over all spread a glowing effusion of light from the *Lightning's* searchlight and revealed the hundreds of friends occupying every available inch of the wharf. . . .

"The boys proposed three cheers for the people of Dawson and yelled mightily. They gave three ringing cheers and a tiger for Joe Boyle and many more for Joe. . . . The people responded with a tremendous round of cheers and a tiger for the

Canadian Number 2 sank in the Klondike River opposite Boar Creek bluff on 10 October 1914, the day the Boyle-Yukon Contingent left Dawson to fight in World War 1.

boys. The cheering became continuous from both sides: the boat pulled back quietly from her moorings and the space between the Yukon boys and the wharf widened. . . . With the exciting exhaust of steam, the kicking up of a foamy wake by the whirring wheel, the streaming of sparks and a column of smoke into the starry sky, the screaming of the whistle and the jostling of the dancing waves against the shore, the scene was a superb climax to the departure of the pride of the Yukon.

"Standing at the end of the barge, in the shadow of the bulkhead, with bared head during all the excitement as the steamer plowed past the shouting crowd was a silent man who watched the ship and her brave boys until she was out of hailing distance. He stood transfixed, gazing until only the dancing lights were visible on the water. It was Joseph Whiteside Boyle, the man who made it possible for the Yukon contingent to go to the front. Quietly he turned from the place on the barge and marched up the street with the people and soon was happily relating in his characteristic style one of his tales of good cheer from the inexhaustible fund which is his."[44]

There were many delays, and the detachment, now known as the Boyle-Yukon Motor Machine Gun Battery, did not go into action until late in 1916. It fought fiercely and became one of the most decorated units in the Canadian Army. But it paid a terrible price in casualties; by August 1919 only three of the originals had returned to the Klondike.[45]

On the creeks in 1915, Canadian Number 1 dredge, now on Hunker, was the first to start (17 April); Canadian Number 3 was at work a few days later. There was trouble with the water supply to the North Fork power plant at night, so the old Bear Creek steam plant had to be put back into operation. Early in June, the electric pumps installed on Hunker were at work lifting 600 miner's inches of water over 600 feet from the new canal to the Last Chance Hillsides. Up to 150 men were at work repairing Canadian Number 2. It was finally righted early in July, only to have it drop from the posts and pilings supporting it and settle in about four feet of water. One man working inside the hull was drowned but, luckily—the accident occurred between shifts—only three others were injured.[46] Prospects for the 1915 season were poor; the three dredges that were working were all known to be in poor ground, and by now Boyle was paying only those who quit or were discharged.[47]

The legal actions were still going on, but Joe Boyle unexpectedly became involved personally in a new one. Dredging by Canadian Number 4 had already displaced many of the squatters near Ogilvie Bridge, close to the mouth of Bonanza Creek, and now Number 3, having completed work downstream, was preparing to dredge upstream through a narrow strip of gravel that Number 4 had left for her. By mid-July 1915, it was menacing the Golden North Hotel. When Joe Boyle had gone to negotiate with Arthur Moreau, the owner, Moreau had chased Boyle off the property with a revolver, threatening to shoot him if the dredge dug his ground. Boyle laid a complaint and had Moreau arrested for threatening and intimidation. Moreau's counsel, F. T. Congdon, chose trial by jury before the Territorial Court. At the trial, the six-man jury, with Andrew Baird as foreman, possibly more concerned with overall fairness than the specific incident before it, found Moreau not guilty and, in effect, accepted his claim that he had simply bluffed Boyle using a metal spectacle case rather than a revolver. Freed from that charge, Moreau then sued Canadian Klondyke and Boyle for damages, and in a trial the following year he would be awarded $3,000 and costs for a trespass by Number 3.[48]

Troubles continued to plague Boyle's operation. Canadian Number 2 had gone back into service in late September but Number 3 had to be shut down in November after a shipment of new bucket lips was lost in the sinking of a coastal steamer. At Bear Creek, the 400 KW standby steam plant, installed in 1905, was destroyed by fire in late October. Canadian Number 1 shut down at the end of November; 2 and 4 operated until early in 1916.[49] The year 1915 had been a poor one. Gold production was just over $1 million, about the same as 1914 and down more than $200,000 from 1913 when all four dredges had been in full operation. Even more alarming, direct operating costs had increased more than $200,000 during that period.[50]

Preparatory work on Canadian Number 1 and 2 started in late February 1916, after a two-day delay to allow the men to attend a Patriotic Dance held in Dawson by the American Woman's Society. The dance, chaired by Mrs. J.W. Boyle, had been a huge success, filling both the AB and Moose Halls and raising a total of $1,000.75 for the Patriotic Fund. The refreshments were served by "ten Japanese waiters from Canadian Klondyke. . . . Each . . . was attired in snowy linen and moved with the ease and grace of Pullman car specialists."[51] The dance over with, repairs to the dredges got underway. Canadian Number 1 started up in mid-April 1916, the three big dredges shortly after. It was hoped that with all four dredges in operation 1916 would be a better season.

Canadian Klondyke's financial problems were growing worse. Wages for 1915 had not been fully paid and would have to wait until the new gold returns began to come in. The company's suppliers were growing more and more apprehensive over allowing additional credit in the gamble that their ever-increasing accounts could be settled in a good season. In February 1916, there was a story around Dawson that the N.C. Co., apparently caught with a bill for $50,000 run up when Boyle was leasing the utility companies, had refused Mrs. Joe Boyle credit for a dollar's worth of oranges.[52] In late May 1916, Joe Boyle, acting as chairman of a public meeting of the People's Prohibition Movement, spoke out on the situation:

"It has been asserted that the wages of the men have been mortgaged. I will say that if any wages of any workingmen are mortgaged to anybody in any instances it probably is only a few and then to the saloon men. The Canadian Klondyke company last year spent over $600,000 here for wages, and when it came to the close of the season and extra work was required in repairs to one of the dredges, I explained to the men the money market was shut down by reason of the war causing the bank where we had secured loans to stop making loans, but that the men could work if they cared to on bedrock, and I must say to the credit of every man, they all went to work. It is no disgrace to borrow money in a large business, but a common matter, and the other large companies here and almost all companies operate on borrowed money. As far as the report is concerned that the men have to work without pay and cash to meet bills, I want to say that any married man in the company's employ who needs cash for such purposes never fails to get it."[53]

Early in 1916, there was a new round of legal battles with Northern Light, Power and Coal Company. In mid-January 1915, Joe Boyle had signed an agreement with F. W. Corbett, manager for Northern Light since August 1914, covering the sale of power from the North Fork plant to the Dawson utilities. The contract appeared to offer a good source of cash for Boyle with little or no additional cost to his operations. However, in late November 1915, Corbett disconnected the lines from Boyle's Canadian Klondyke Power Company because of fluctuations in the supply, a result of the heavy dredge load. Boyle, in turn, blamed the fluctuation on improper operation of the automatic regulators at Northern Light's Dawson plant and countered Corbett's move by attempting to prevent the acting manager of the Dawson utilities paying for wood supplies delivered to the Dawson thermal plant. Boyle, who had already received almost $59,000 under the agreement, next sought an injunction to compel Northern Light to take power from Canadian Klondyke Power Company rather than generating their own. In late March 1916, his application was refused, and the Dawson utilities were ordered to pay any monies collected in excess of their operating expenses into the court pending a final settlement.[54]

The contest with Yukon Gold continued. Some of the earlier actions had been appealled to higher courts and there was a rash of new ones.

Near the mouth of Bonanza Creek, Yukon Gold's dredge Number 1 was working toward a fraction lying between claims 101 and 102 Below. Boyle claimed the fraction as part of the Boyle Concession and sought an injunction to prevent Yukon Gold from thawing the ground. Yukon Gold responded that the dredge was not expected to reach the ground in question until mid-July 1916 and agreed not to thaw the ground. Boyle's application for an injunction was allowed to stand on the understanding that he could renew it at any time if the occasion arose.[55]

There were other problems on Bear Creek. Yukon Gold was moving their dredge Number 3 onto the claims they had already acquired. Power lines were already in and now a flood of debris was coming down onto claims 19 and 20 Bear from the stripping on 17 and 18. Yukon Gold had built a watercourse to carry away the debris but it had been washed out in a heavy shower in late May, and the new watercourse was obviously incapable of carrying the coarser material. Boyle hadn't fought for inclusion of claims 19 and 20 in the Boyle Concession only to have them buried by Yukon Gold's debris, and he started an action to prevent it. He won the day, and the court issued an order restraining Yukon Gold from releasing anything other than silt and fine sand that could be carried away by the stream.[56] Yukon Gold succeeded in getting dredge Number 3 in operation in 1916 but it was a short-term operation and the dredge was shut down at the close of the 1918 season.

Joe Boyle was growing increasingly restless. Things were going badly in the Klondike and even he, an inveterate optimist and promoter, must have realized that there was little chance of improvement. Even if he won all his legal actions he would be left with a company capable of little more than trading dollars, probably unable to pay off its creditors let alone meet the obligations to Granville Mining. The excitement was now with the war in Europe but Joe, almost forty-nine, was too old to take part in it. His contingent, still training in England, would soon be going to the front without him, and Commissioner Black, only a few years younger at forty-three, had been given permission to organize and lead a Yukon Infantry Company. In early June 1916, Boyle, used to being the centre of attention, had been

BROWN. STEWART. TRITES. MACDONELL. RYLEY. TAYLOR.

FRAME. PEPPARD. ROSS. COOK. GILL. GENTRY.

KELSEY. WADDELL. FORREST. MORGAN. SMALL. JONES. EDELSTAN. ELLIS. KING

HOSKINS. YOUNG. BOUTIN. FALCONER. AKERS. FITSGERALD. JENNINGS CAPT KNOTT. D

The Boyle Yukon Machine Gun Detachment was organized and financed
by Joe Boyle. The men had been formally enlisted and issued uniforms
(and had their picture taken) Outside, rather than in Dawson, because of
the necessity to pass through Alaska on their way to the war.

LIN 7460 MILES.

CHINE GUN DETACHMENT.

BABB. PENDER. CURRY.
MACALPINE. LOBLEY. HANEY. — McKINLEY.
McCAW. BLACK. PATTERSON. FENWICK.
INNON. TULLY. STRONG. MORTON. BLAIKIE. JOHNSTON. TURNER.

Pub. by C. Thomas

relegated to head of the reception committee that welcomed Black on his return to Dawson to take command of his company.[57]

Suddenly, the Klondike must have seemed too small.[58] Boyle slipped out of Dawson quietly in mid-July 1916 accompanied by his private secretary, John Kennalley, and his nephew, Ralph Morgan. The *Dawson News* carried only a brief story on his plans the day he left.[59] About ten days later in Vancouver, he told a newspaper reporter that he was on his way to London to confer with backers on gold dredging on the Lena River in Siberia.[60] If plans materialized, a dredge built of B.C. fir timber would be shipped from Vancouver to Vladivostok and then on the Trans-Siberian Railway. While in England he would be visiting his machine gun battery. In Europe, Boyle was to find the excitement he sought, but that is another story.

Joe Boyle Jr., a mining engineer, was left in charge of Canadian Klondyke. By now, it was little more than a holding operation. All four dredges worked until late in the season, but 1916 was another poor season and production fell to $866,242.71.[61] All four dredges, including Number 2 down for only a short period, were working again by early 1917. But by now the dredges were in poor mechanical condition, unable to operate efficiently, and only Number 4 was mining reasonably good ground. Thirty buckets for the large dredges, promised by the Marion company for early September, had arrived in Seattle in November, too late to ship north. Numbers 2 and 4 had ended the season with many open links in their bucket lines, even though Number 3 had been shut down early and stripped of buckets, ladder rollers, belting and other equipment.[62] Gold production for 1917 dropped slightly to $833,994.45.[63]

By 1917, the action between Yukon Gold and Boyle's companies over Yukon Gold's cancellation of the power contract at the end of the 1913 season was before the Supreme Court of Canada. Boyle's companies were contesting the cancellation and claiming damages of $235,098.32 for having power available. Yukon Gold was claiming $119,960.38 for losses when Boyle had thrown the switches in May 1913 or reduced the power supply to the point that their dredges were unable to operate. Finally, in mid-November 1917, Yukon Gold won the case and was awarded damages of $33,684.58.[64]

At the same time another action was threatening the very existence of the Canadian Klondyke companies. Granville

Joe Boyle, honorary colonel in the Canadian Army, about 1919.

Boyle's son, J. W. Boyle Jr., 1916.

Mining Company had been placed in receivership in England on 1 May 1917, and the receiver, Edward Dexter, had applied for a receivership for Canadian Klondyke Mining Company on the grounds that it had failed to issue the $1,500,000 debenture to Granville. The application was heard on 16 November 1917 with Yukon Gold represented as a judgment creditor. For the moment there was an appointment of a temporary receiver, H. G. Blankman, the court stenographer. He was Outside and planning to winter in California, and any further action was delayed until Joe Boyle Jr. could get a lawyer to represent his companies. C.W.C. Tabor, Boyle's lawyer for many years, had died in a hotel

218

fire the previous February, and the numbers of lawyers practising in Dawson had dwindled to the point that all were already acting in the case. Joe Jr. was able to obtain E. C. Mayers, a Victoria lawyer. There was a wait of almost a month while Mayers, travelling together with Blankman, made the long journey from Outside.[65] First, their steamer, the *Jefferson*, had encountered a violent storm in the Lynn Canal and arrived in Skagway two days late, sheathed in ice from the waves and spray that had lashed it. Next there was a two-day wait for the train to Whitehorse, now running only twice a week, and, at Whitehorse, another two-day delay until the temperature rose to -25 degrees Fahrenheit. Finally they were away on the White Pass stage, an open sleigh drawn by four horses. Temperatures continued to drop for the next few days on the road, and it was down to 60 below when one of the horses gave out halfway between the Minto and Pelly roadhouses. It had taken the driver 9½ hours to urge the remaining horses the dozen or so miles to the Pelly and, once there, the party waited for five days while the temperature hovered around 70 below. Finally, when the temperature rose to 42 below, they were away again, but it proved a false break, and for the final three days on the trail the temperature never rose above 60 below.

The first hearing was held a few days later, and on Christmas Eve, Joe Jr., undaunted by Canadian Klondyke's problems, announced that the company would be at home to its employees on Christmas and invited all to a Christmas dinner to be held at noon in the Bear Creek mess hall. Granville's action was uncontested and, on 5 January 1918, Joe Boyle's Canadian Klondyke Mining Company and other related companies were placed in receivership. Mayers, no longer needed, left immediately by sleigh to catch the White Pass stage south of Indian River. Fortunately, the cold snap had broken and his return trip was easier. His trip, including the three weeks in Dawson, had taken just over two months and, on his safe return to Victoria, he concluded: "The only real asset of a country is the energy of its people. You can have all the natural advantages in the world and do nothing or you can have nothing and do everything."[66]

For Joe Boyle, now somewhere in Eastern Europe, the end had come; his long association with the Klondike was over, and he would never return. Choosing to remain in Europe after the war, Boyle died in April 1923 at the home of Ed Bredenberg, an old friend from Klondike days.

RECEIVERSHIPS, COVERING ALL WITH THEIR BLIGHT 1917-1925

Granville Mining, North West Corporation and the Canadian Klondyke companies were all in receivership but each had different problems and, for the moment at least, consolidation of the three was out of the question. Granville, simply a holding company, would have nothing until one of the other two could establish a profitable operation. North West held vast stretches of placer ground which might prove profitable but as yet there had been no mining. Canadian Klondyke Mining had their four dredges but values in the ground worked were low and the company was hopelessly in debt. Working costs had risen markedly during the latter years of World War 1 and it was questionable whether any management, no matter how efficient, could salvage the company. Granville and North West with their relatively low overheads could be left for the moment but there could be no delays with Canadian Klondyke. F. P. Burrall, the American engineer, was acting as field manager for both Granville Mining and North West on behalf of Edward Dexter, the English receiver for the two companies, but H. G. Blankman, receiver of the Canadian Klondyke companies, had chosen to manage those companies himself.

Later, in a report on his management of the Canadian Klondyke companies during 1918, Blankman described some of the problems he faced when he took over on 5 January 1918:

"(1) Your Receiver took office at the most critical period in the history of gold mining. In all countries gold mines, both quartz and placer, were suspending operations, the purchasing power of the gold dollar having diminished to a point where the average mine could not meet the cost of production. Owing to the world war the prices of dredge repairs (if at all obtainable) were prohibitive; labor scarce and of a low degree of efficiency, the younger men having either enlisted or been drafted to serve their country, with a general feeling of dissatisfaction and unrest which made reorganization extremely difficult.

"(2) Unpaid liabilities in wages alone amounted to the sum of $158,570.00; the total liabilities (excluding the claims of the litigants) aggregating $662,037.78; and the company was entirely without credit either locally or elsewhere.

"(3) Considering the bulk of operations the company appeared to have an exceedingly heavy over-head in superintendence and other administrative and office charges. It was possible to effect a reduction in this excessive 'over-head' within a few weeks which approximated over $30,000.00 per annum.

"(4) The mining operations of the company were done through the medium of one 7 cubic foot bucket dredge and three larger 16 cubic foot bucket dredges. With the exception of necessary spring repair work the condition of the smaller dredge was excellent. Your Receiver had absolutely no means of knowing the exceptionally bad condition of the three larger dredges. It was, of course, apparent that dredge Canadian No. 3 was not in operating conditoin as it had been stripped . . . to supply the other two dredges; the buckets of which were in very bad shape, resulting in many break-downs during the operating season and consequent large loss in efficiency.

"(5) Before the chair of the Receiver was warm he was burdened with wage and other liabilities of the former management (by consent of the litigants and order of the Court) amounting to the sum of $238,659.63, which, in addition to his own necessary expenditures, he was expected to pay from the proceeds of the operations. The evident confidence reposed in the Receiver to do the impossible, although duly appreciated, was not justified by the existing conditions.

"(6) The ground available for dredging for dredges Canadian No. 2 and Canadian No. 4 during the season of 1918 was known from the prospects and data of the company to be of very much lower average values than theretofore dredged.

"(7) No funds were in the treasury of the company to take care of current expenses or necessary spring repair work."[1]

Somehow, Blankman had managed to get things underway. Receiver's Wage Bonds, totalling $158,418.41, bearing 8-percent interest and due 1 February 1920, had been issued to cover wages dating from before 31 October 1917. One wage claim that was disallowed was from Joe Boyle for $80,000.[2] At the last minute, in March 1918, the $70,000 needed for spring repairs was obtained through a first mortgage bond taken by Gold Fields American Development Company. Blankman himself personally guaranteed to pay for provisions and supplies cadged from the N.C. Co. store in Dawson. Canadian Klondyke employees had approved the issue of the Wage Bonds at a meeting in early March 1918 and, once he had the money from Gold Fields, Blankman in turn guaranteed to meet the going minimum wage of 45 cents an hour plus a $2 a day board allowance.[3] Employees trying to exchange their Wage Bonds in the Dawson stores found the bonds would be refused in some, discounted in others, and taken at face value in a few.

Spring repair work had started late, but, on 1 May 1918, Canadian Number 4 was started up, Number 2 was ready to go as soon as there was sufficient water in the power plant ditch, and repairs to Number 1 were almost completed. Number 3 was still stripped, and, for the moment at least, there were no plans to put her back in service. It had been a close call for Number 4. She had been left in the middle of the Klondike River at the close of the season, when no one knew the future of the company; there had just been time for the dredge to dig her way into a hurriedly-thawed patch of ground where she would be protected from the huge ice floes that ground against any obstacle in the channel during the spring run-off.

In addition to inherited problems, Blankman faced a new one when the machine shop at Bear Creek burned to the ground early on the morning of 24 June 1918. The building, about

50 by 200 feet, was built mainly of logs covered by galvanized sheeting and the floor and lower portions of the walls were oil-soaked from the shop operations. Joe Boyle Jr. led the fight to save the nearby buildings and salvage part of the machinery. Rushing out dressed only in an undershirt, trousers and shoes he was soon "drenched to the skin from head to foot looking as if he had just been dragged from the river." Nearby buildings were saved by drenching them with water; the blacksmith shop had been protected by a large sheet of canvas kept saturated with water. A team of horses was hitched up, and autos, motor trucks and wagons were hauled from the blazing building. The electrically-operated pumps were back in service in about thirty minutes, but by then the main shop was gone.[4] Later in the year the shop was rebuilt and the fire-damaged machinery salvaged and repaired. Blankman was particularly proud of the new welding equipment he had added; he predicted that discarded dredge buckets could be rebuilt at a cost of $150 per bucket, about a tenth the landed cost of a new one. One bright spot in the season's operation had been the bumper crop on the sixty-acre farm used to supply produce to the mess hall.

During 1918, Canadian Klondyke's gold returns and other income totalled $487,119.80, leaving a gross profit of $216,963.01 after deduction of direct operating costs of $270,156.79.[5] Other expenses (administration, the camps, power, the fire loss at the machine shop, royalties and mint charges) took most of the profit, and at the end of the year the company had just over $3,000 on hand in the form of gold dust and cash at the bank. There was no money for 1919's spring repairs. Gold Fields offered to extend the $70,000 loan for six months and to consider a further renewal at that time but Blankman, knowing there could be no income by that date, refused the offer and repaid the loan.

Now that the world war was over, some improvement could be expected in the labor and supply problems. But, for the moment, the entire community was still in a state of shock over the sinking of the coastal steamer, *Princess Sophia,* in late October 1918, with the loss of many Klondikers. The ship, en route from Skagway to Vancouver, carried many who had left Dawson on the last river steamer of the season, planning to winter Outside. Included were eighty-eight men, crew members of the White Pass river steamers, laid off for the winter months. Virtually everyone in the Klondike had lost either relatives or friends. Worst of all, the loss had been avoidable. For more than a day after the ship struck a reef in a blinding snowstorm, the captain had refused to transfer his passengers to other ships standing by. Then it became too late, and the ship slipped from the reef and disappeared, with the loss of all 343 persons on board—288 passengers and 55 crew members. Dawson, suffering already from the decline in gold mining, was beginning a long period of decay that would last almost fifteen years until an increase in the price of gold brought a modest revival.

Early in April 1919, Blankman took the unusual step of publishing a detailed receiver's report for 1918. In addition to accounts, he discussed some of his differences with Granville Mining and published correspondence with their representatives, F. P. Burrall and Andrew Baird. Obviously, the Granville group had expected that Blankman, as receiver, would take little part in the day-to-day operation of Canadian Klondyke. Instead he had taken full control, and, just as in the days with Boyle, Granville was little more than a spectator. Blankman's attempt to keep the companies in operation might be best for the Klondike at the moment, but there was no reason why this course had to be Granville's long-term object. There was hope for a change; Blankman concluded his report to the court with the request that he be allowed to resign as soon as his accounts were passed.

Granville Mining held their annual meeting in London on 31 December 1918. With the receivership they were finally learning more of Joe Boyle's operation, much of it carried on using their money. They were not pleased with what they learned. The chairman, F. A. Govett, commented:

"While in the past the gold won has perhaps exceeded the expenditure, these facts seem to answer the question which I have heard asked many times, what Mr. Boyle did with all the gold. He appears to have paid himself a personal salary of $25,000 a year for management, and the rest would seem to have gone in working costs for development and equipment. From the large liabilities disclosed I infer that the explanation is that he did not reveal the true position when we came in in any direction. Generally the position now is this: that we shall shortly have all these companies under control. Our first idea was to amalgamate the lot, but this would involve harmonising so many conflicting interests that it would plainly be impossible to satisfy anyone, and such amalgamation would destroy any possible value of the

Granville shares. As far as one can judge with the diminished prospects of the Canadian Klondyke, and the heavy debt load of Granville obligations which have accumulated, the ordinary shares can be of little, if any value, but it seems that there are some persons who still hold a contrary view, and, therefore, we conclude that it is better to give these more sanguine parties every chance to wait and see if possibly they are right and not sacrifice any of their rights whatever they may be at the present moment."

There had been an attempt to negotiate with Boyle:

"The position is this: when we got to grips, a series of proposals were made to us by Mr. Boyle's son on his behalf, which after a long period ended in a provisional agreement that Granville should buy the whole of Mr. Boyle's interest in the Canadian Klondyke and the Power company for $130,000, all claims on either side being thereby satisfied. With our experience on previous occasions, we insisted that this must be confirmed personally by Mr. Boyle, but we could not get at him, for he had disappeared into the depths of Russia. Whether he was in communication with his son or no, we do not know, but the ratification was not obtainable. We are, however, advised that an order of the court will have the same effect, and subject to this being obtained and the necessary money being found, the troubles with the Canadian Klondyke are possibly at an end."[6]

Canadian Klondyke was back in operation in 1919. Joe Boyle Jr., left in January; he was unpopular with the Granville group. Somehow Blankman had managed to get the money required for spring repairs. During 1918, he had made a settlement with the White Pass over goods that had accumulated on their Dawson dock since 1911. The goods originally cost $154,000; the unpaid freight and storage charges amounted to about $70,000. All of the impounded goods, and they included bucket lips and ladder rollers for the dredges, were hauled from the docks in mid-April 1919 by a triumphal procession lead by a Yuba tractor hauling two large wagons followed by other wagons pulled by two-horse, four-horse and six-horse teams.[7] Canadian Number 4, down for less than a month, was ready to go again in late April 1919. Number 1 followed, but Number 2 was delayed until mid-July while its line of sixty-eight buckets was made up with rebuilt buckets collected where they had been discarded in the creeks. New metal had been built up on the worn spots by means of the newly-acquired welding equipment.[8]

By mid-summer, all was running smoothly; the three dredges and the hydraulic plant on Last Chance hillside were in operation. Expenses had been pared to the bone, and the company showed signs of making a modest profit after current expenses. There was a new problem in mid-September when the Marion Steam Shovel Company and other creditors attempted to seize the assets of Canadian Klondyke as judgment creditors.[9] There was a quick settlement between Granville (as a bondholder), Yukon Gold and the other creditors which was not made public at the time. Finally, at the end of September 1919, Blankman's resignation as receiver was accepted and he was replaced by Andrew Baird, an old antagonist. Soon after, Canadian Klondyke's offices were moved to the N. C. building in Dawson to join those of Granville and North West Corporation.[10] With the obdurate Blankman gone, Burrall, as manager of all three companies, could interweave their activities as he chose.

Burrall, as agent for Gold Fields, had begun settling the outstanding debts of the Canadian Klondyke Mining and Power companies. The final cost would come to just over $280,000; including $174,622.89 paid for seventy-four unsecured debts totalling $292,523.59 (an average of about sixty cents on the dollar) and $107,024.98 paid for the receiver's wage bonds and coupons, purchased at eight-five cents on the dollar. The largest creditor was the Marion company, owed over $140,000, most of it dating from a settlement over the big dredges reached in 1914. Among the other names, principally individuals and suppliers, were Howard Brenner, who supervised the construction of all four dredges, and Boyle's auditors, a Detroit firm; both were owed about $4,000.[11]

Joe Boyle personally had drawn about half a million dollars from his companies between 1904 and 1917. Initially, under the 1904 agreement, he was to receive 25 percent of the gold returns up to a total of $250,000, and he continued this credit after the Detroit group withdrew. Later, the 1912 agreement with Granville Mining called for the issue to Boyle of $300,000 of the 6-percent bonds of the Canadian Klondyke Power Company "provided he shall by then have performed all of his obligations hereunder." Boyle, of course, would also receive at least 51 percent of any profits distributed by Candian Klondyke Mining Company. At the end of 1912, in lieu of a guaranteed payment to Granville Mining he had credited that company with $146,000 in

Canadian Klondyke Mining Company bonds at 90, and, not to be outdone, he credited himself with $152,000 in bonds, in the ratio 49:51 between the two parties. Neither the power company nor the mining company had ever issued their debentures, but Boyle's account with Canadian Klondyke Mining Company was credited with the interest routinely and Boyle drew cash against the credit. In addition, there were credits for dividends declared by Canadian Klondyke Mining in 1908 and 1914 and a distribution of the 1912 capital surplus of Boyle Concessions, Limited. Boyle drew no salary, but later, in February 1917, he instructed his auditor to credit him with $25,000 in salary and $5,000 in expenses for each of the years 1912 to 1916, inclusive. It was never paid, and Boyle's account showed a credit of almost $150,000 when the collapse came at the end of 1917.[12]

North West Corporation's affairs were even more tangled than those of Canadian Klondyke. When F. P. Burrall took over as manager in the summer of 1917, he found that only sketchy field data was available, Treadgold's employees had not been paid for many years, and payments due on many claims had not been met. Considerable stripping had been done, but there were still no blocks of ground properly thawed and ready for dredging. Burrall paid the back wages with the consent of the prior lien debenture holders and then set to work to untangle the company's affairs and establish the value of their holdings.

North West lacked dredges but there was a possibility that the Lubecker chain excavators could be put to work. Excavator Number 1 had been assembled on Dominion Creek, but most of Number 2 had been on the White Pass dock in Dawson since the end of the 1916 season. The White Pass refused to move the remaining eight-five tons from Skagway until they were certain that their freight charges would be paid. En route to Dawson, Burrall had met with Dave Elliott, the excavator mechanic in Vancouver. Elliott had been in charge of assembling Number 1 for Treadgold, and he had been involved in the manufacture of Number 2 in England. Then he had been ordered to wait in Vancouver for additional shipments. In July 1917, almost a year later, Burrall reported to the receiver in London: "He is still there. And entirely out of any Company funds. He asked me for instructions and not knowing if the machines are to be put into service, I could give him none. And your instructions do not allow us to send him funds at present."[13]

To put Number 1 in service, Burrall estimated that some four miles of railroad track would be needed. Possibly this could be obtained from the Klondike Mines Railway, now controlled by Treadgold, but work would have to start immediately to complete everything during the 1917 season. There was another problem: New parts to replace some of the unsuitable parts on Number 1 had not been invoiced separately, and now they were buried somewhere in the 335 tons of equipment forming Number 2. Delay followed delay. Eventually Elliott was paid off and the project forgotten—for 1917 at least.

On 31 December 1918, A. Chester Beatty, Chairman of North West, reported Burrall's progress to a meeting of North West held immediately after a Granville Mining meeting at the registered offices of both at Number 8, Old Jewry, London. Through the sale of receiver's notes, North West had raised £50,000 and another £15,000 had been approved. Stripping operations had been carried on, the more important property payments made, and pressing debts paid. A total of just over five million cubic yards of material had been removed by stripping betwen 1910 and 1918, and now it was proposed to install a dredge on Upper Dominion Creek and the Lubecker excavator on either the Granville Flat or Middle Dominion Creek. The plan would entail a further cost of £125,000. Beatty, disenchanted with receiver's notes, suggested that some other form of financing, preferably one that would involve the owners of North West and Granville securities, should be used.[14]

Treadgold was present at the meeting, and he wanted to know what part Granville would take "in this sound and promising scheme which has been outlined or half promised." Beatty replied that Granville was not in a position to subscribe to any new issue by North West but that its shareholders could be approached directly to assist. Any scheme would have to be underwritten as, in Beatty's experience, many appeals by circular failed to bring in even the cost of the postage. In reply to another questioner, Beatty gave his personal thoughts: "I am not particularly keen about buying the receiver's notes to keep this company from going on the rocks. I have not had a dollar of fees, and I have paid the expenses of taking those diggers up myself, so I should be charmed to have somebody come in and buy these notes. We have come to the point when people who have been buying the notes say, now something must be done. We have steered this company practically into harbour and now it is up to the shareholders, or someone, to finance the company.'' But Beatty had no definite proposal for financing and, after some discussion, a committee of three was elected to work with the board in preparing a plan.

Treadgold, forced out of North West Corporation and drifting towards bankruptcy, was still dreaming of his Klondike consolidation. He refused to turn over the records of test pannings done in the past, saving them until his dreams could be realized. At one point he chided Francis Cunynghame, secretary of North West and acting for the receiver, for paying North West's employees in the Klondike. He claimed they had their own ground to work in off hours; besides every penny would be needed for the consolidation and his employees knew that he would look after them when the time came. Nevertheless, he was pleased that they had been paid; certain that it would make Cunynghame a friend of every man in the Klondike and valuable when the time came for his consolidation.[15]

Burrall spent the entire summer of 1919 in the Klondike. On the North West ground at Upper Dominion and at Granville small crews were at work stripping. Early in September 1919, preparations were underway to install a dredge at 17 Below Lower Discovery on Dominion Creek. Burrall declined to say where the dredge would be obtained; perhaps he preferred to wait until Blankman was gone and control of Canadian Klondyke was secure. Wherever the dredge came from, it would have to be hauled over Hunker Summit on the flank of the Dome. The government road had too many curves for heavy hauling. A crew was put to work clearing out the second growth on an old road along the creek bottom, and plans were made to install an electric winch to haul loads up the last steep pitch to the Fournier roadhouse on the summit.[16]

The dismantling of Canadian dredge Number 1 began early in March 1920. By late that month two-thirds of the material had been delivered to the new site, a distance of about ten miles.[17] At Hunker Summit, the winch hauled up thirteen-ton loads in a scene reminiscent of the Chilkoot Pass in 1898. In late May 1920, the steamer *Canadian* reached Dawson carrying a crew of carpenters to work on the new dredge, together with a load of lumber that had been dropped off at Minto when ice closed the river the previous fall. The rebuilt dredge, now North West

Number 1, started digging on 24 August 1920. It was the first real attempt to mine North West's ground. Initially, steam thawing was used, the boilers fired with spruce logs from the 5,000 cords of wood that had been assembled at the site, but later in the season the company switched to the newly-developed cold water thawing.[18]

Burrall, Outside since November 1919, arrived back in Dawson in late April 1920. Travelling by White Pass stage he was "bronzed by the reflection of the bright spring sun on the snow until he has the tint of a rich old russet apple."[19] While in London he had visited with Treadgold and Tom Patton, formerly Treadgold's agent in the Klondike. On Canadian Klondyke's ground, he planned to operate Canadian Klondyke dredges 2 and 4; spring repairs were already underway. In addition, a drilling program would be carried out ahead of Number 3, which still lay stripped and idle. Numbers 2 and 4 were digging by late May, but, early in June, Number 2 dropped her bucket line into the pond. A diver, wearing a suit brought in when the same dredge sank in 1914, had to search the murky pond for the huge buckets, each weighing 4,600 pounds.[20] Dredges North West Number 1 and Canadian Number 4 shut down in early November 1920; Canadian Number 2 continued a little longer. Cold water thawing had worked well ahead of North West Number 1. The method (developed by John H. Miles at Nome in 1917) cut the cost to about half that of steam thawing. In the future, steam thawing would only be used in the spring when the weather made cold water thawing impractical.

Early in 1921, North West Corporation crews were at work hauling Yukon Gold Number 4, a Marion dredge with seven-cubic foot buckets, over the divide from 62 Below on Hunker Creek to a site on Lower Dominion Creek. Rebuilt as North West Number 2, she was digging by late July 1921.[21] Now, with four dredges operating, two on each side of the Dome, Burrall was finally building a stable operation from the wreckage left by Boyle and Treadgold. Perhaps even Granville Mining might be revived!

In late September 1921, Canadian Klondyke Mining Company, Limited was foreclosed for failure to issue $1,798,000 in debentures and pay interest on them. The company was taken over by Burrall and Baird, Limited, a company incorporated in the Yukon.[22] Later, in March 1922, Canadian Klondyke Power

Company, Limited was also foreclosed, again for failure to issue debentures. A few days later, its assets and those of North West Corporation passed to New North West Corporation Limited, incorporated in Canada and free of receiverships. For the moment, Burrall and Baird with its heavy debt load remained a private company, but New North West Corporation had been refinanced. The new share structure consisted of $1,500,000 in 12½-percent cumulative preferred-A stock, $1,275,000 in 8-percent cumulative preferred-B stock and $4,000,000 in common

Hauling the spud of Canadian Number 1 over Hunker Summit, en route to Dominion Creek, March 1920.

shares. All of the stock had a par value of $1. It was a house of cards. Close to $6,500,000 in stock had been issued to creditors and shareholders of the former North West Corporation, but cash for the new dredges had come from almost $1,500,000 in income notes, redeemable at $130 per $100 from the profits of the new company.[23]

The four dredges operated again in the 1922 season, those for Burrall and Baird handling a total of 3,819,443 cubic yards and the smaller dredges for New North West 955,360 cubic

COURTESY OF C. GLOSLIE

yards.[24] The conflict with Yukon Gold had ended. In mid-October 1922, crews from that company removed a 200-foot section of the siphon across the Klondike valley at Bear Creek to allow Canadian Number 4 to move onto new ground to the east.

There were still dreams of consolidation. In December 1922, Cunynghame, a Gold Fields employee and president of New North West, had partially revealed his hand in a letter to Warren McFarland, assistant manager in the Klondike:

"Now, with regard to the question of reconstruction of the companies. I have, myself, been working at this for some twelve months or more, and you will realize the difficulties with which one is faced because of the tremendous number of various classes of stock in our different companies, and a large number of antagonistic elements, who have at various times been at variance with each other. I venture to flatter myself that I have been able to keep on good terms with all these varying elements, and for this reason it has been possible for me to produce a scheme of reconstruction, which is favorable to all parties. . . .

"I turned, therefore to the only man remaining in England, who has still implicit faith in the future of the Klondike, and that is Mr. Treadgold. Mr. Treadgold, as you may know, is an exceedingly difficult, and I may say, aggravating man to deal with in many ways. He is most unbusinesslike, is essentially a dreamer, and added to everything, has considerably lost his credit owing to the bankruptcy, which was forced on him. Never the less, there are a certain number of financial houses and persons in London who continue still to have great faith in him as a man and as a miner, and I have absolute evidence of certain good people who are still willing to back him and to stand behind a consolidation. . . ."[25]

Early in 1923, Burrall resigned to manage a family business and was replaced by his assistant, McFarland, who had been an engineer for Yukon Gold for fifteen years before joining Burrall the year before. The four dredges were in operation again and, in addition, a crew for Burrall and Baird were driving an adit (a nearly horizontal tunnel) to test the values in the White Channel Gravels on Lovett Hill near the mouth of Bonanza Creek.[26] McFarland's plans involved extensive thawing for New North West and, once again, the three parties who had financed Granville Mining and, later, North West were asked to take more income notes of New North West in the proportion Gold Fields 60 percent, the Govett companies 25 percent and A. Chester Beatty 15 percent.[27] About this time, there was a note from the past when Treadgold's Lubecker excavator Number 2, forgotten since it had been rushed to Dawson at the end of the 1916 season, had to be moved from the White Pass dock—which it was slowly collapsing with its weight—to a fenced-in spot near the old coal bunkers of Northern Light, Power and Coal Company. The excavator was still in bond, custom duties unpaid.[28]

McFarland continued his program for the two companies in 1924. In addition to the dredging, the Vulcan shovel brought in by Treadgold in 1911 was moved from Granville to Quartz Creek in preparation for a stripping program. The distance was twenty miles and sixteen teams of horses were involved in the move.[29] But there were setbacks. First, early in the morning of 1 April 1924, the Bear Creek machine and forging shops were lost in a fire that started from creosote in the main smokestack. The rear of the structure was saved, and teams of frightened horses had been kept under control long enough to drag a lathe and a shaper from the building. Then in mid-May 1924, Canadian Number 4 sank in its pond just as spring repairs were completed. Three large pumps had been rushed to the dredge as soon as the leak was noticed but it was no use. No attempt was made to refloat Number 4 and, once again, the future of the entire operation hung by a thread.[30] The two dredges on New North West ground ran until October and Canadian Number 2 until almost the end of November 1924.

Unexpectedly in late April 1925, McFarland resigned, Andrew Baird was appointed acting manager and there was word that Treadgold would arrive on the first boat in the spring.[31] Somehow, Treadgold had regained control of the companies and one of his first actions was to cable that the "yeasty top" would have to go.[32] A few days later, Baird was ordered to cease making weekly reports and, from now on, Treadgold's backers would learn only what he chose to tell them of their operation.[33]

TREADGOLD
IS KING!
AT LAST!
1925-1930

Treadgold, still an undischarged bankrupt, had
acquired operating control of all the elements of the original
Granville consolidation plus the holdings of The Northern Light,
Power and Coal Company. This time it was all his and there was
no Joe Boyle to share it with! The financial legerdemain which
had made all this possible was still going on and would not be
revealed until it became the subject of investigation and litigation
some five years in the future. There had been rumours of
consolidation for years and, in May 1923, the *Canada Gazette* had
carried a notice of the formation of The Yukon Consolidated
Gold Corporation Limited with the object of acquiring the
securities of Burrall and Baird, New North West Corporation,
Canadian Klondyke Power and a number of smaller companies
originally incorporated by Treadgold. The *Dawson News* in
reporting it commented: "The application is . . . made over the
names of a number of Ottawa lawyers, who are mentioned as
agents in the matter."[1] For the moment, the consolidation was
known as the "Treadgold Company" or the "Treadgold

Holdings''; the name Yukon Consolidated, usually written YCGC and pronounced "wye-cee-gee-cee," would not come into common use until 1928.

"Mr. Treadgold," as he would always be known to his employees, returned to Dawson by river steamer in early July 1925.[2] It was a triumphal occasion. He was bubbling over with enthusiasm for his new dreams, and the local people, having watched the struggle of the operating companies under receivership, were certain that better days lay ahead. At Bear Creek, he recognized all the old-timers who had worked with him in the past and greeted each one by name as if only a few days had elapsed since he left the Klondike in 1912. A few days later, on a visit to the North Fork hydroelectric plant he behaved like an excited schoolboy, running up and down the steep penstock and later confiding to the operator: "And to think that I lost the whole thing for fifteen years!"[3]

Treadgold managed his field operations personally and refused to have superintendents interposed between himself and the man on the job. He seemed to be everywhere that season, and his employees could do little more than shrug their shoulders and do their best to carry out orders that often changed from day to day. Dressed in old clothes that looked like—and sometimes were—others' castoffs, he might appear at any time of day or night in a Ford runabout, usually driven by Ed Hickey. In addition, there were calls over the high-tension telephone, a device that necessitated the user's standing on a carefully insulated glass plate. He was constantly on the move; the time of day or night, meals, sleep or his employee's personal obligations meant little to him. What possible difference could time make when there would be almost continuous daylight until mid-August? Still, there was none to be wasted and, out of the car, he moved crouched over and at a half-run. In excellent physical condition, he appeared to take a perverse delight in wearing out those accompanying him and then deserting them far from the car.

Three pieces of equipment usually accompanied him in the car: his butterfly net, a short T-handled shovel, and the "skewer," a piece of steel rod about five feet long having a point at one end and a wooden handle at the other, used to probe for frozen ground. The shovel had many uses, including filling a hole in the road, opening a culvert or ditch, or sampling the gravels in an open cut. Often Treadgold would use it to pry loose one of the tussocks of sphagnum moss (up to several feet in diameter) that carpeted the frozen ground. Holding the offending clump over his head, the tiny Englishman would exclaim: "These, these are the enemy!" before pitching it as far as he could into the muskeg.[4]

His memory was incredible. He seemed to know the name of every miner he had encountered since 1898, and he had the details of hundreds of claims at his fingertips. He would know who the owners of a claim had been, how much it had sold for, where the paystreak lay, the amount and fineness of gold that had been mined and the location of the claim posts. If the posts had been destroyed in later mining operations, he could pick their locations from features he remembered on the hillsides.

He was pleasant enough in his dealings with most of his employees, but he often vented his spleen on Edward Bredenberg, an associate since 1898. Bredenberg, away from the Klondike since 1907, had returned as Treadgold's secretary. He was expected to be with Treadgold at all times, and attempts to slip away and visit at one of the homes at Bear Creek would be followed by a call on the high-tension telephone and a querulous: "Edward?" Finally, Bredenberg caught the last boat out in October 1925, abandoning Treadgold to his own devices.

Treadgold had three dredges, Canadian Number 2 and North West numbers 1 and 2, in operation during the 1925 season. Two of Boyle's big dredges were still not in service: Canadian Number 4, sunk the year before, had not been raised and Number 3, cannibalized for parts in 1917, had never been reequipped. Treadgold, still critical of dredges, took little interest in them and begrudged every penny spent on their upkeep, choosing to ignore the fact that they were the only important source of income. Once again, he was interested in replacing them. The Lubecker chain excavator had been a failure and was forgotten; his new scheme would make use of electric shovels.

In July 1925 a new Marion electric shovel with a 1¾-cubic-yard bucket, brought in early in the season, began work on Hill 78, a rich hillside at 78 Below Lower Discovery on Dominion Creek. Initial results were discouraging but Treadgold, unconcerned over these early reports or finances, ordered three additional shovels for immediate delivery.[5] It was a frantic rush. Canadian Pacific Railway in Vancouver was persuaded to advance the sailing of their *Princess Ena* by four days, and the ship left port on September 16th with 100 tons of freight for

Treadgold, the shovels included. There were no delays, and the river steamer, *Whitehorse,* delivered everything to Dawson at the end of September, well ahead of the river closing. Andrew Baird telephoned news of their arrival to Treadgold, who was at Fraser's store on Dominion Creek.

"Mr. Treadgold, there are three more of your damned shovels here on the dock."

"I am quite aware of it, Andrew."

"But Mr. Treadgold, we can't pay for them."

"I am not asking you to pay for them, Andrew, but when I do you will pay for them."

Turning to the members of his crew with him at the store, Treadgold grinned: "You know, Andrew is just a small shopkeeper."[6]

Finally, in late November 1925, Treadgold's field work was finished for the season and it was time to move on to company business Outside. Treadgold, together with Billy Rendell, Vic Moquin and Ed Hickey as driver, left Bear Creek in the Ford runabout, the latter now complete with a special low gear installed for the trip over the winter road. There were some problems but the party reached Yukon Crossing in five days. Actual travelling time had been thirty-seven hours at an average speed of 5½ miles per hour. The ice on the Stewart River had been alarmingly thin, but it had held. On the Pelly River, the travellers were forced to work their way a mile and a half downstream to where the river was frozen right across and then, once across, creep back up to the road over the shore ice along the opposite shore. At Yukon Crossing, Treadgold caught the mail truck, now operating on a regular basis between there and Whitehorse.[7]

Some aspects of the consolidation could be handled by others, and, in mid-December 1925, Andrew Baird called meetings of the Dominion, Big Creek, Sulphur, Dago Hill, Calder, Burrall and Baird, and Deep Vale companies for 30 December to approve lay agreements that Treadgold had signed on 11 November 1925 as acting trustee for YCGC. Obviously no problems were anticipated; the seven meetings were scheduled at ten minute intervals.[8]

Treadgold had been careful to keep his activities in the Klondike and in England separated. His associates in the Klondike (with the possible exception of Andrew Baird) knew next to nothing of his promoting and financing activities Outside, and those in England were dependent on Treadgold for reports of the Klondike mining activity. For a brief period after Treadgold returned to the Klondike, the English group had continued to receive reports from an informant in the Klondike. Throughout the receivership, his letters to Treadgold had been highly critical of Burrall and McFarland; now they were equally critical of Treadgold. But the informant had drowned in August 1925 and there was no one to replace him.[9]

Disputes over his business dealings followed Treadgold as relentlessly as he would have pursued a moth with his net. Early in February 1926, Francis Cunynghame (instrumental in Treadgold's consolidation), Raleigh Smallman (Treadgold's solicitor) and others started an action against Treadgold and the trustees of The Northern Light, Power and Coal Company. At issue was $233,000 in Northern Light bonds that Treadgold had transferred to YCGC using a power of attorney granted him by Cunynghame and Smallman. An injunction was granted to restrain a distribution of $83,000 planned by the trustees.[10]

Treadgold, back in London in March 1926, brought YCGC shares with him to be exchanged for the shares of the older companies. The two main parties to be dealt with were Francis Govett and A. Chester Beatty, who together with Gold Fields had been involved in the Granville Mining Company financing and the later bond issues, in the proportion Gold Fields, 60 percent; Govett, 25 percent; and Beatty, 15 percent. Treadgold delivered the agreed numbers of YCGC shares to Govett and Beatty but they both stalled in turning over their old shares, probably concerned over the value, if any, of YCGC shares as long as Treadgold ran the company without technical management or an effective board of directors. Despite this setback, Treadgold set to work collecting securities of the old companies, acting through a committee of two friends, W. E. Martyn and William Trask.[11]

Treadgold, busy in London, did not return to the Klondike in 1926; Andrew Baird was left in charge of operations. As in 1925, three dredges were operated, but there were problems. Treadgold had halted the thawing operation ahead of Canadian Number 2 in late 1925, and the dredge, worked into a pocket surrounded by frozen gravel, had been unable to start up until the beginning of July 1926.[12] North West Number 1, on Dominion Creek, had started up on 20 June 1926, but two days later the clevis of a guy holding the stacker in place broke, and the stacker

Andrew Baird, wearing the regalia of President of the Grand Lodge, Yukon Order of Pioneers, on Discovery Day, 17 August 1953. First associated with Treadgold in 1909, Baird was with many of the operating companies and, in later years, was accountant for YCGC. This composite photo, placing Baird in front of Pioneer Hall, was created by Western Miner Press.

swung around, canting the dredge until it shipped water over the deck and sank in sixteen feet of water. Fortunately, the pond the dredge had wintered in was still intact, and it took less than two weeks to pump out the pond, right the dredge and put it back in service.[13] One of the new Marion shovels was still mining on 78 Below Lower Discovery on Dominion Creek and the other two were at work relocating the road in the Quigley Gulch area of the Boyle Concession, preparatory for dredging. With the delays, it had not been a good year, especially for Burrall and Baird, where operating costs alone exceeded the gold returns by almost $20,000.[14] Treadgold, immersed in the problems of the consolidation until early 1927, dealt with the Klondike situation in an exchange of telegrams with Andrew Baird. His thoughts were expressed within the fifty-word message allowed by the rate structure, with any punctuation left to the recipient's imagination:

OTTAWA, 2 MARCH 1927

YOURS TODAY UNINTELLIGIBLE HERE
ACCOUNT FOR CASH RECOVERED FROM
TOTAL GOLD AND OTHER SOURCES IF ANY
DURING TWENTY SIX WHERE IS IT PAY
NOTHING [M]ORE WITHOUT GETTING
EXPENDITURE SANCTIONED FIRST IF UNABLE
TO EXPRESS NEEDS LIKE OTHER PEOPLE
SUBMIT IT QUICKLY AM HOLDING YOU
LIABLE ALL UNSANCTIONED EXPENDITURE
SHOW RENDELL
                    ANC TREADGOLD

OTTAWA, 11 MARCH 1927

YOUR ALTERATION OF POWER RATE TO
LIGHT AND CONTRACTS BACK AND FORWARD
FOR WOOD TALLY EXACTLY WITH YOUR
FOOLISH DEALING FOR A YEAR WITHOUT
REFERENCE TO MYSELF YOU ARE NOW
APPOINTEE TO CARRY OUT MY POLICY WHICH
YOU HAVE FRUSTRATED OR EVADED IN
IMPORTANT RESPECTS WHOM YOU ARE
FOLLOWING QUICK
                    ANC TREADGOLD

DAWSON, 12 MARCH 1927

BEING YOUR APPOINTEE HAVE ACTED
SOLELY IN YOUR INTERESTS IN CARRYING
ON OPERATIONS ALL COMPANIES POWER
CONTRACT FLAT RATE WINTER INCREASE
CONSUMPTION DOES NOT CARRY INCREASE
EARNINGS LIGHT ONLY SOURCE WINTER
REVENUE SINCE YOU APPEAR TO HAVE
FAULT TO FIND WITH MY ACTIONS AGAIN
CHEERFULLY SUBMIT RESIGNATION AS
YOUR MANAGER
                    ANDREW BAIRD

OTTAWA, 14 MARCH 1927

YOUR RESIGNATION AS APPOINTEE
GUARDIAN DESPOT MANAGER AND VARIOUS
OTHER USELESS CAPACITIES IS HEREBY
ACCEPTED BUT IF YOU REALLY DESIRE TO
LEND YOUR USEFULNESS TO ME FOR
CONSTITUTIONAL EMPLOYMENT SAY SO
QUICKLY AND I WILL CONSIDER SINCE YOU
COMMENCED MESSING ABOUT AND DEFYING
INSTRUCTION YOUR TELEGRAMS ARE
FREQUENTLY UNINTELLIGIBLE
                    ·   ANC TREADGOLD

OTTAWA, 22 MARCH 1927

YOU ARE NOT ACCOUNTANT MANAGER OR
ANYTHING IN MINING OR UTILITY COMPANIES
IN ANY CAPACITY FROM MARCH FIFTEENTH
YOU ARE NOT TRUSTEES SERVANT MINE
FIFTEENTH INSTEAD OF HASTENING YOUR
COMPLIANCE AND REGRET LONG OVERDUE
STARTED AFRESH YOUR IMPUDENT MEDDLING
AND DEFIANCE OF ORDINARY DISCIPLINE
LEAVE THE OFFICE FOR GOOD FORTHWITH
                    ANC TREADGOLD
                    PRESIDENT AND GENERAL
                    MANAGER

Andrew Baird was replaced as manager by W. J. Rendell, the company surveyor, who like many senior company employees had first arrived in the Klondike in 1898. A mild-mannered man and no match for Baird, Rendell nonetheless followed Treadgold's order to lock Baird out of the Dawson office. It was done over the lunch hour. Rendell and the secretary,[15] waiting inside, made no comment when Baird broke down the back door with an axe from the electrical shop and returned to his desk. Predictably, Treadgold was soon finding fault with Rendell; in mid-May 1927, Treadgold filled out the allowed fifty words of a telegram to Rendell with the admonition:

YOU ARE LOSING PRICELESS TIME
WAKE UP [16]

Early in April 1927, YCGC acquired Yukon Gold Company's remaining assets in the Klondike. Treadgold planned hydraulic operations on Lovett and Jackson gulches, on opposite faces of the ridge between Bonanza Creek and the Klondike River valley, and water would be brought to the workings by the Twelve Mile Ditch, last used by Yukon Gold in the 1925 season. In mid-April 1927, F. M. Fenton, Yukon Gold's former hydraulic supervisor, returned to manage the operation, and the crews left for the camps along the ditchline a few days later. It was a dry season and, with the ditch in poor condition, it was mid-August before the first Twelve Mile water reached Lovett Gulch.[17]

Work to raise Canadian Number 4 started in late March 1927. The pond was pumped dry, and workers quarried out the huge mass of ice filling the hull of the dredge. This done, the hull was repaired and the pond allowed to refill. The dredge was floating by early May, but the refitting took time, and the dredge was not put back into service until mid-November 1927.[18]

Treadgold, accompanied by Edward Bredenberg, arrived back in the Klondike in late June 1927 and the frantic pace of the 1925 season resumed. Despite the repairs underway to Canadian Number 4, Treadgold was still seeking a new mining method that would replace the dredges. This season his schemes involved a shovel operation on Quartz Creek and a cableway or high-line system installed near the Granville settlement on Lower Dominion Creek. The cableway, strung between two tall steel towers and controlled by an operator perched in a cage halfway up one of the towers, was intended to move huge buckets filled with barren overburden between shovels working in the open cut and the bank. Installation of the equipment took about six weeks and the crew had unexpected difficulties with permafrost in sinking the deadmen required to anchor the guy cables for the towers.[19] The system was tested the following spring after a shovel had been walked to the site; it proved capable of moving gravel but the crews were unable to cope with the huge piles of waste that grew close to one of the towers where the buckets dumped their loads. Soon the piles blocked further operations and, even worse, it was obvious to all that as soon as mining advanced the towers would have to be moved and the laborious assembly, including sinking the deadmen, repeated each time. After a few hours of testing, the cableway shared the fate of the Lubecker excavators and was forgotten. Later, in 1933, one of the towers was dismantled and moved to the nearby hillside so that North West Number 2 could dredge the ground, but the other tower remained standing for many years, another monument to Treadgold's attempts to do away with the dredges.

Other new equipment purchased by Treadgold included two Caterpillar tractors that arrived in late July 1927 and were soon at work freighting to the Quartz Creek shovel operation. There was an unusual problem; an estimated 60,000 caribou, migrating into the Klondike from an area west of the White River, were interfering with traffic on the roads and getting caught in man-made obstacles such as abandoned telephone lines. The tractors had no problem forcing the animals aside, but the machines lacked bulldozer blades and there were many delays while the crews rolled away the rocks the animals had knocked onto the road in their frantic scramble to escape up the steep slopes.[20]

This season there were two Ford runabouts. Treadgold had lent the original to an employee on an afternoon when none of the other company vehicles were serviceable and then, impatient to go somewhere, simply phoned into Dawson, bought another and had it rushed to Bear Creek. For the rest of the season, Treadgold alternated vehicles and drivers.

One evening near midnight as his car was crossing Eldorado Summit, Treadgold caught sight of a strange butterfly and he and an unwilling companion were away in hot pursuit. The chase led almost to the Indian River and when the butterfly was

Treadgold at a test of his cableway and electric shovel in the summer of 1928.

finally netted it proved to be identical to a specimen he had already collected. More important though, the chase had been successful, and when Treadgold arrived back at the car at 6:00 a.m. he was ready for another day in the field.[21]

Under Treadgold's management everything had to be done his way, no matter how inefficient or impractical this might seem to those attempting to carry out his orders. Employees who questioned or offended him were seldom fired; instead, the common punishment was to be banished to an obscure corner of the company's operations. Once, when the pole line crew fell from grace, they, plus a small supply of grub, were dropped off on Gold Run Creek and ordered to pick up sections of an old telephone line abandoned by Yukon Gold. Other company employees were forbidden to go near them until finally, after serving two weeks on Gold Run, the bedraggled crew was moved back into one of the company camps.

Treadgold's memory was excellent. In the very early years in the Klondike he had met a Jimmy McCrank, a blacksmith, and without revealing his identity asked him what he thought of this fellow Treadgold. The reply had been "He's some kind of a freak who's been going around buying up claims." McCrank was now working as a blacksmith at Bear Creek, and he had not seen Treadgold for almost thirty years. Treadgold, standing talking to a group of his employees, spotted McCrank as he looked out of the blacksmith shop and called over: "Hey Jimmy—the freak's back!"[22]

Three dredges operated in the 1927 season; Treadgold still balked at spending money on their upkeep. When the dredgemaster of Canadian Number 2 pleaded for a new belt for the tailings stacker, Treadgold refused to buy it and nearly drove the dredgemaster to distraction by sending him pieces of discarded belting picked up in his travels along the creeks. Because of the continual stops to splice in the scraps of belting, the dredge was down much of the season, and the production dropped accordingly. At a meeting of his dredgemasters at the end of the season, Treadgold chided the harried dredgemaster: "See, you didn't need one after all."

In mid-November 1927, Treadgold, as president, called meetings of seven of his subsidiary companies for the end of the month. Once again, the meetings would be held at ten-minute intervals, and if a minority stockholder had any questions to ask,

Treadgold would not be there to answer them. He had left the Klondike on Thursday morning, 24 November 1927, in a dash to catch the *Princess Mary* due to sail from Skagway on Monday night. This time there were two cars. En route, at Pelly Summit, they passed a Yukon Airways airplane forced down by engine trouble on a flight from Whitehorse to Mayo. Treadgold telegraphed from Yukon Crossing that the pilot and his passenger were safe and had walked into Mayo. Treadgold arrived in Whitehorse just after noon on Sunday. He made his connection, but only because the White Pass train from Whitehorse to Skagway had been held for him from Saturday until Monday and the boat had been held for one day.[23]

In 1928, YCGC had four dredges in operation and planned repairs on Canadian Number 3, neglected since 1917. Hydraulic operations were underway again on Jackson and Lovett gulches, and two shovel operations were planned, one on Quartz Creek and the other on Gold Run Creek. In addition, Treadgold planned a new ditch—the South Fork Ditch, about 16 miles long—to bring water from the main Klondike River to the North Fork intake. The additional water would allow the power plant to generate more power, and it would perhaps overcome the problems encountered each fall when slush ice jammed the existing ditch.

Early in April 1928, two shovels, one of Treadgold's new electric models and an old one from Bear Creek, were moved to the new project. Treadgold himself was back in late June to superintend his widespread operations. The dredges operated all summer, with the last closing in early December. Work on the new ditch had gone well, and at last the shovels were being used on a task they were well suited to. In places, the shovels had even proved capable of excavating right to the grade of the new ditch. Treadgold, still dreaming of the future, was probably more interested in the progress of the new ditch than the dredge operations. Just before leaving for Outside, he put on a special inspection trip to show off his new project to Gold Commissioner MacLean, now the senior government officer in the Yukon.[24]

This year there was a larger group on the mid-winter trip to Whitehorse. Treadgold had brought in an English crew, chiefly shovel operators, and on 10 December 1928, fourteen of them were away for Whitehorse on two sleighs drawn by a two-ton tractor. One sleigh had a shanty on it, so that the men were able to escape the worst of the cold. Fortunately, temperatures were around zero Fahrenheit or a few degrees below, unseasonably high for the time of year. Treadgold was part of a smaller group that started out in the two Ford cars the following evening, planning to catch the slower tractor along the winter road.

Despite Treadgold's apparent unconcern, YCGC and the partially consolidated companies were drifting towards financial disaster. Both employees and suppliers were reluctant to start the 1929 season without some assurances of payment. True, the 1928 gold returns had gone up—because Canadian Number 4 was back in service and because the use of water from the Twelve Mile ditch had increased production from the hydraulic operations—but costs had risen, too, leaving Burrall and Baird with an operating loss of nearly $5,000. Almost all the revenue had come from the dredges. The cableway, the shovels, the hydraulic operations, and the other smaller projects that Treadgold had started up and later abandoned had been producing heavy losses for several years. The new power ditch, no matter how important to future operations, could not be expected to produce any new revenue for the moment. In the Klondike, Rendell struggled to get the 1929 operations underway:

DAWSON, 11 JUNE 1929

TREADGOLD, LONDON

COMMERCIAL* HAS NOTIFIED WILL SUE
IMMEDIATELY ENFORCE PAYMENT THEIR
SOLICITORS HERE NOT ENOUGH PROVISIONS
FOR TWO DAYS MEAT FEED GROCERIES. . . .
PLEASE GIVE THIS MATTER YOUR
IMMEDIATE ATTENTION THE SITUATION IS
BECOMING MUCH MORE SERIOUS CREDITORS
BECOMING IMPATIENT INCLUDING WORKMEN
COMMERICAL ACTION WILL MEAN A CRISIS
NO AUTHORITY HAS BEEN GIVEN TO ANYONE
HERE TO DEAL WITH SITUATION
RENDELL

---

*Northern Commercial Company, or N.C. Co., a Dawson supplier.

                    DAWSON, 12 JUNE 1929
LCO TREADGOLD, LONDON

UNLESS GROCERIES BOUGHT TOMORROW BEAR
MUST SHUT DOWN FREIGHT PAID TENTH YOURS
TWELFTH MUTILATED ARE HAVING REPEATED
COMMERCIAL HAS SUPPLIES PRESENT
REQUIREMENTS MONEY OUR SOLE NEED
                    RENDELL

                    LONDON, 12 JUNE 1929
MCLEOD, DAWSON, YUKON

PAYING COMMERCIAL PART WITHIN
FORTNIGHT ANYHOW USELESS THEM SUING
WOULD DELAY THEM GETTING PAID WOULD
MERELY FORCE YUKON CONSOLIDATED TO
ASSERT ITS PRIORITIES AGAINST BURRALL
BAIRD AND ALL SUBSIDIARIES BOTH
WATERSHEDS CONSOLIDATED WILL LIQUIDATE
THEM ALL THIS SUMMER ANYHOW BUT
IF FORCED BY COMMERCIAL WILL COMMENCE
FORTHWITH TRUST COMMERCIAL CAN
COOPERATE
                    TREADGOLD, LONDON

                    DAWSON, 13 JUNE 1929
TREADGOLD, LONDON

COMMERCIAL DEFERRING ACTION UNTIL
AFTER PAYDAY ASK IF WE WILL PAY TWENTY
THOUSAND INSIDE TWO WEEKS
                    MCLEOD [25]

     Once again, the emergency had been deferred. YCGC
shareholders had received even less attention. A circular from
Treadgold in late January 1929 said that only two of the four
dredges were operating on the paystreak; the circular touted the
success of the shovel and hydraulic operations and the cableway.
Treadgold expected to complete the power canal in September
1929 and promised: "When the power supply is thus assured, we
shall be able to carry on all our digging operations and pumping
operations at our discretion. . . . Other consequences also, of far-

reaching importance, of which you will in due course hear, flow from the command of an all-the-year continuous power supply." Later, in July 1929, a balance sheet for 1928 had been sent out, but it was so abbreviated that perhaps the sole piece of useful information was YCGC's bank balance of $839.79 as of 31 December 1928.[26]

Treadgold and Andrew Baird, now restored to grace and coming to replace Rendell, arrived back in the Klondike at the end of July 1929. Dealings over the consolidation in Ottawa had taken longer than anticipated, and their train reached Winnipeg the day the *Princess Louise*[27] was scheduled to leave Vancouver for Skagway. Treadgold, unperturbed, simply telegraphed the CPR's Vancouver office:

> HOLD THE BOAT I AM COMING
> ANC TREADGOLD

and the CPR obliged, obviously preferring to inconvenience all of Treadgold's fellow passengers rather than deal with Treadgold. A group of sixty high-school boys were aboard the *Princess Louise,* travelling to Atlin. When Baird came on deck the first morning of the trip, he found Treadgold doing forward and backward handsprings, surrounded by the boys. Treadgold, by now almost sixty-six, captivated the group. On his habitual late arrival in the ship's dining room the boys would rise and stand at attention until he was seated. Baird, deeply impressed, concluded that "One who could arouse such a measure of affection in the hearts of sixty strange boys in the course of a few days must have what it takes."[28]

Five dredges were operated in the 1929 season (including Canadian Number 3, which had been inactive since 1917), but gold returns dropped about $28,000 from the year before because of poor ground and the deteriorating condition of the dredges.

Treadgold was still obsessed with completing the new power canal but neither banks nor merchants had the slightest interest in advancing credit on a project that offered no prospect of an immediate cash return. Treadgold turned to subterfuge. When the manager of N.C. Company's Dawson store telephoned and asked to see him about the mounting bills for provisions, Treadgold made an appointment to meet him at Bear Creek that afternoon and then slipped away to the North Fork power plant, leaving the manager to wait around the Bear Creek yard most of the afternoon. Wages were postponed, but the crew on the new ditch still had to be fed if the work was to go ahead. Early one morning, the cook at Bear Creek came in to start breakfast and found that every food item in his kitchen had disappeared overnight, appropriated for the South Fork Ditch project.[29]

Desperate for cash needed to keep the operation going, Treadgold had little interest in paying regular wages, and his employees were reduced to pleading for small amounts urgently needed for food or other expenses. If one could talk persuasively enough these could often be obtained. At a conference with a group of his employees, Treadgold's suggestion that he pay wages once a year and avoid interest charges met with the rejoinder: "Mr. Treadgold, I think that an excellent idea provided you pay them at the beginning of the year."[30]

Early in December 1929, Treadgold's caravan, this year numbering about forty men, left Bear Creek. Temperatures were about 50 below zero Fahrenheit and many of the men were cheechakos, inadequately dressed for the cold in sweaters and mackinaws. At one point, pressed for time to catch the *Princess Norah* from Skagway, the sleighs had swayed along for twenty-seven hours without a halt. Once again, Treadgold followed the main party by car. Aircraft were coming into more common use each year and, about the time the Treadgold party was battling the winter road, another pioneer from Keno Hill had flown from Mayo to Whitehorse in just under two hours.[31]

Treadgold's new empire was collapsing. True, the consolidation had been put through, but most of the groups involved had been alienated. Gradually, those who had dealt with Treadgold began to compare notes on the treatment they had received, and ultimately they would combine to defeat Treadgold. All involved had their own interests but a common bond was the fear that any value their holdings still had would be lost if Treadgold continued to manage YCGC. Treadgold, soon involved in a struggle to retain his control, would never return to the Klondike.

DEPOSED
BY THE
CONSPIRACY
1930-1933

Treadgold had exercised operating control of the Klondike activities since 1925, but in mid-July 1929, just before he started on his last trip to the Klondike, he was still assembling securities of the various companies involved. There had been many delays and problems, due in large part to Treadgold's furtive business methods. As he had so often told Cunynghame: "I have my own ways of doing things. They may be slow, but my ways are always best in the end." Cunynghame, after years of dealing with him, had concluded that Treadgold had a fixed policy of never allowing any of his friends to meet one another, if it could possibly be avoided, in the belief that it takes two to make a conspiracy. For the moment, only Treadgold knew the complete story of the consolidation, but his opponents, dubbed "the Conspiracy" by Cunynghame, were gradually fitting the pieces together.[1]

There had been demands for Treadgold's resignation as early as 1925, but now that most of the assets were held by YCGC, it was possible to act against that company. Initially, YCGC had been capitalized at 500,000 preferred shares (par value $1 and convertible into common shares) and 5,500,000 common shares (par value $1). By the summer of 1929, about 5 million shares appeared to have been issued, and almost half of them were held by Treadgold and his nominees.

One of the early court actions against YCGC began when J. T. Patton, a former employee of Treadgold's, got an injunction to restrain a special meeting of the company called for 27 November 1930 and the annual meeting called for 30 December 1930 until the company's books were produced and financial information supplied. The injunction was dissolved about a week after it was granted when Patton was unable to produce a complete list of shareholders. However, Patton was successful in obtaining an injunction against the voting of Treadgold's shares at the meetings. Soon after, there was a compromise, and the two vacant positions on the board of YCGC were filled by J. W. Hughson, a nominee of Patton, and Senator N. A. Belcourt, a nominee of Treadgold. J. B. Watson, deceased, a director and Secretary-Treasurer of YCGC, was replaced in his post by G. R. F. Troop, a chartered accountant and a partner in the Ottawa firm of Clarkson, Gordon, Dilworth and Nash.[2]

Patton had also petitioned the Secretary of State of Canada to investigate the affairs of the company (this procedure was authorized in a statute passed in 1902 but not yet used). He asserted that the investigation would help his group decide whether to litigate or not. A writ for the investigation was issued on 22 December 1930; G. T. Clarkson, a principal of Troop's firm, was chosen to conduct it.

J. T. "Tom" Patton, a Canadian, had first come to the Klondike in 1898 and had spent many years mining on Sulphur Creek. (The exception was the winter of 1902-1903, when he returned to school teaching, his former profession.) He had first met Treadgold in 1908 when the latter was beginning to consolidate claims on Sulphur Creek. Later, between 1912 and 1916, he had acted as agent for Granville Mining and North West Corporation. During the lean years when Treadgold was gone from the Klondike, Patton had done his best to stave off creditors and preserve the consolidation. A teetotaller, he was well known in the Yukon as the leader of the Peoples' Prohibition Movement who, with the help of strong temperance support from midwestern U.S.A., had conducted a campaign to bring prohibition to the Yukon in the summer of 1916. It had ended when the Yukon voted 874 to 871 to remain wet, and an application for a recount was refused. Patton, unpaid for many years, left Dawson for London in late December 1916 determined to collect directly from the companies.[3]

In London, there were countless delays. Treadgold had refused to support Patton's claim for $10,000 per year between 1912 and 1916. In May 1917 Granville had been placed in receivership followed soon after by North West. Patton refused an offer of $10,000 from the receiver to settle the claim almost two years later. In 1921, Patton and the American subsidiary of Gold Fields agreed to a settlement.[4] With money from the settlement, Patton had purchased the Anderson Concession (Hydraulic Lease Number 1) for $10,000; the annual rental was $500[5] Patton, too, had been interested in a consolidation in the Klondike. As early as 1917 he had sounded out Francis Cunynghame, then a Gold Fields' employee, about forming a new company—under Patton's leadership and backed by the three parties who had supported Treadgold.[6]

Despite his differences with Treadgold, Patton had been associated with him in the beginnings of the new consolidation. After July 1924, when Treadgold moved into Cunynghame's office at 8 Queen Street in London, Patton together with Bredenberg, Corbett and others were frequent visitors at what one witness would later agree was "a sort of bear garden or snuggery for people interested in Yukon consolidation."[7] At one point, Patton had offered his Anderson Concession and other interests to Treadgold for $100,000 cash, but later, in December 1924, he had transferred them to Cunynghame and Smallman, both acting for Treadgold, in return for £15,000 ($75,000) cash and 75,000 preferred shares of YCGC. Surprisingly, Patton had promptly put half of the cash back into YCGC with the stipulation that it was to be paid out at Treadgold's direction and repaid to himself within twelve months.[8] For the moment, the consolidation was Treadgold's, but later, when difficulties had arisen, Patton had become one of the leaders of the Conspiracy against Treadgold. He had only his £7,500 ($37,500) to lose and the value of his YCGC shares to protect, but Patton was a dangerous opponent. Not only was he familiar with the actual ground in the Klondike, but over the years he had kept track of both the mining operations and Treadgold's incredibly complex business dealings.

The Conspiracy did not wait until Clarkson had completed his investigation of YCGC. They filed an action by Patton *et al* against Treadgold and YCGC in Ottawa in late 1931. Claiming that they sued on behalf of themselves and *all* other shareholders, the plaintiffs asked that Treadgold be considered a promoter without personal interest in the consolidation and that there be an accounting of both share and cash transactions between YCGC and Treadgold, either directly or through his wholly-controlled North Fork Power Company.

Treadgold was in London when the action was filed, and he contacted Cunynghame, who had broken with him four years before, tired of Treadgold's difficult ways and the endless rows and bickerings. Treadgold and about a dozen shareholders prepared a circular and sent out proxy forms for an informal shareholders' meeting to be held in late August 1931. Some 513 of the 1,329 shareholders of YCGC were present at the meeting or sent in proxies in favour of the committee. Not all at the meeting supported Treadgold. One, Chester Beatty's solicitor, and not a shareholder, spoke through the courtesy of the chairman and having done so put on his hat and walked out.

A Shareholders' Committee was formed with Cunynghame as secretary.[9] The Committee reoccupied the former office at 8 Queen Street and busied itself contacting shareholders. By late September 1931 it counted on the support of 620 shareholders representing 1,538,198 shares of a total (exclusive of Treadgold's own holdings) of 3,469,900 on the register. Cunynghame contacted members of the Conspiracy who were in England at the time but none of them were prepared to negotiate, being suspicious that the Committee was a front for Treadgold.

The Committee was more successful with Treadgold and nagged him into giving them a letter listing his share obligations to various individuals and parties. Delivery of the shares listed would leave Treadgold with just over a million of the 2,419,000 shares held in his or a nominee's name. Obtaining the list was a victory of sorts, but Treadgold refused to transfer the shares to the listed owners, claiming that in doing so he would create potential enemies who could vote against him. By now, YCGC shareholders were receiving circulars from the Committee, from Treadgold and from an opposition group supporting Morrell, one of the leaders of the Conspiracy.

Early in 1932, a near-compromise had been reached

between the Committee and the Conspiracy calling for a five-man board, consisting of Treadgold and two representatives from each faction. Sir William Nicholson and J. H. Fawcett would represent the Committee, G. Goldthorp Hay and F. W. Corbett, the Conspiracy. Francis Cunynghame would be secretary, but not a board member. A draft copy of the settlement had already been initialled and the Committee was preparing to give Corbett authority to represent them at a special general meeting of YCGC to be held in Ottawa on the condition that he would support the proposed board. Suddenly, there was a cable from Tom Patton in Ottawa:

> MAKE NO SETTLEMENT WITH TREADGOLD
> THE CLARKSON REPORT IS EXPECTED THIS
> WEEK AND THIS WILL FINISH TREADGOLD[10]

The Clarkson report was issued in late February 1932 and, as anticipated, it proved damaging to Treadgold. Treadgold's equipment purchases and mining practices aside, Clarkson found many other things to criticize in the management of the company. Between 1925 and the summer of 1930 (when he was relieved of active management of the company, Treadgold had run YCGC on his own initiative without referring important matters to his Board of Directors. (He claimed they were too far away and lacking in technical background.) There had been an overissue of 213,319 common shares more than the number authorized by the board. Share records of the company had not been adequately maintained. Accounts had not been presented to the shareholders in the proper manner, and there was no separate accounting of substantial sums paid to or withdrawn by Treadgold from YCGC or the subsidiary companies. In addition, specific questions were raised which Clarkson thought might form grounds for litigation. More important, though, is in assembling his evidence Clarkson had dealt in detail with many of Treadgold's transactions, and now others in addition to Treadgold would know how the enterprise was run and how their own dealings fitted in.[11]

The court action initiated by Patton *et al* in late 1931 began in Ottawa in early March 1932 before Mr. Justice Raney. Treadgold was represented by Senator N. A. Belcourt, an old associate in the Anderson Concession and other dealings.

Treadgold, in a defiant mood throughout the trial, clashed repeatedly with both the judge and counsel. The trial lasted several weeks and considered in detail the complicated manner in which the older companies had been assimilated by YCGC. The judgment, in contrast, was simple, and it was not concerned with the rights and wrongs of particular transactions. Treadgold had acted as a promoter; he had failed to disclose his interest in the transactions either to his codirectors of YCGC or in the statement in lieu of a prospectus filed with the Secretary of State of Canada on 19 February 1925. The penalty for nondisclosure was the cancellation of all Treadgold's shares of YCGC, whether held in his name or that of a nominee. Involved were 225,030 preferred and 2,366,919 common shares of a total of about 5,200,000 issued by YCGC. In addition, an accounting was ordered of all dealings between Treadgold and YCGC, whether in shares or in money.[12] Treadgold was stunned by the judgment, his reaction so terrible that Belcourt's partner stayed with him in his hotel room until three in the morning, afraid to leave.[13]

Less than a week after the judgment was handed down, Treadgold, no longer a shareholder of YCGC, was removed from the Board of Directors and replaced as President and Director by Patton. At the same meeting, in late March 1932, Senator Belcourt withdrew as a director and was replaced by C. E. McLeod, a Dawson lawyer who had acted for the subsidiary companies for many years. F. H. Chrysler and his son, both members of the 1925 Board, were still there, but by now they too had turned against Treadgold.

Treadgold's foes were in full control, confident that the company could be put on a proper footing at last! The Klondike operations were still managed by Andrew Baird, but Patton; Troop, the Secretary-Treasurer; and G. Goldthorp Hay, of the Govett companies, arrived in Dawson on an inspection trip in late July 1932. Patton remained for most of the summer. The company engaged E. H. Dawson, a consulting engineer and placer expert from New York, to examine their reserves and operations. Thanks to Treadgold's consolidation, YCGC now held most of the placer ground in the Klondike together with the power plant and dredges.

Treadgold entered an appeal against the Raney judgment and attacked the Conspiracy in letters to the shareholders. In one letter dated 6 January 1933 he wrote:

"But certain friends of the Plaintiffs were not, are not, willing to share success; they must have it all; minority though they are, they wish to elevate their, at most, 40 per cent interest into sole ownership and control; and with that aim, they embark on this ruthless campaign against myself, introducing into what should be clean English business the nastiness of American and Canadian politics. I believe that my friends will discern that the stream of vilification, which commenced at Ottawa last February, is merely evidence into what unfit hands the management has been put by the Plaintiffs and their friends."[14]

In a letter dated 19 January 1933, he added:

"Men have been put into power, who are not qualified to bring the enterprise into the enjoyment of the advantages planned for it; there has been no advance since 1929; we are still digging at about the same rate of yards per month as was then reached. Instead of sitting round the table in London to help one another to build up a splendid business by overcoming the physical difficulties, which some of us can measure and deal with, we are torturing our Shareholders and one another with legal complications emanating from men of narrow vision and distorted purpose. The Shareholders have a right to know—and they surely can find out—what is the cause of the diseased condition. My opinion is that, if the financial backers of the Plaintiffs would show themselves opposed to the absurd claim of Mr. Patton that I was not financially interested in the Consolidation, the remedy would at once be found and a meeting, otherwise useless, could be turned to account for all of us. . . .

"Your shares are among those cancelled or declared 'illegally issued' by this Judgment, which only the Appeal Court can alter. The Board cannot restore the status of your shares. You should therefore assist the Securities Committee to prosecute the Appeal by sending to it your *pro rata* contribution of twopence per share. . . ."[15]

261

In addition to his letters to shareholders, Treadgold was writing personal letters to some shareholders, including a clergyman in Somerset who was in desperate need of cash.

"I am afraid in your great need you are failing to see that shortly your Yukon Shares will be your best asset. You are hoping, no wonder, to hear me say *when* they will be. I only wish I could for your sake; but I can't. No man can. The Plaintiffs are full of humbug and the accounts are fakes written in expectation of more libel suits as if two . . . were not more than enough.

"Fight? of course you should fight. In such cases usually relief comes when least expected. The enemy are being pounded hard not only by the Committee but by shareholders on their own who can't afford to lose their money.

"Fight on! do your best and keep your courage up.

Yours sincerely,
A.N.C. Treadgold."[16]

Treadgold's hope for "relief" proved prophetic. Before his appeal could be heard the court stenographer died, leaving only shorthand notes that had not been transcribed and that proved to be indecipherable. The court ruled that an appeal could not be heard without the evidence and ordered a retrial. Jubilant, Treadgold added a personal note on the form letter to the clergyman:

"Cheer up! This is the turning of the tide. We shall have justice now and already those cancellations are wiped out and it is unlikely that we shall again get a foolish judgment. I am expecting to be back [in England] by the end of the month."[17]

YCGC's Klondike operation had limped along, almost forgotten during the struggle for control of the company. At the beginning of the 1930 season, the supplies needed to start operations had been obtained on the personal guarantees of Andrew Baird and Vic Moquin, the stripping foreman. Only four dredges were operated. Canadian Number 2 had finished the 1929 season with the bucket lips worn out, fifteen of the buckets ready for the scrap heap and many replacement parts needed. The $30,000 needed to recondition the dredge was simply not available.[18] Then, in the summer of 1930, an English supplier obtained a judgment against the company and commenced proceedings for the appointment of a receiver. On 13 August 1930, the YCGC Board of Directors, consisting of Treadgold and three members of the Chrysler law firm of Ottawa, authorized Baird to manage the Klondike operations as if he were a receiver and to make no payments other than those required for actual mining operations without specific authority from the board.[19] Revenue for the 1930 season was just over $630,000, down slightly from 1929, and at 31 December 1930 the company had $174.08 in cash and bank accounts and were carrying almost $30,000 in liabilities on the Dawson books, the latter down from $77,000 the year before.

The situation improved in 1931. With the consent of the employees, wages from February to May, inclusive, were deferred until June 15th and a supplier agreed to wait until September 15th for goods delivered in April and May. Five dredges, Canadian numbers 2, 3 and 4 and North West numbers 1 and 2, plus a hydraulic plant were operated, employing about 240 men. By year-end nearly all known obligations had been met and there was a cash balance of just under $140,000. Revenue for the year was $771,764.66, comprised of $749,928.95 in gold returns from the dredges and hydraulics and $21,835.71 from the sale of power.[20]

The free-spending days of Treadgold's management were over, and some who had benefited from it resented the new austerity imposed by Andrew Baird. After a meeting of the ladies of the camp at which the situation was discussed, the wife of a dredgemaster wrote in warning:

> "However, Mr. Baird, I took your part. I
> admitted that you are a tightwad and a skinflint but as
> long as you are in charge the employees know that their
> wages will be paid promptly."[21]

In 1932, the company operated the five dredges and the hydraulic plants on Jackson and Lovett gulches, handling a total of about 5.7 million cubic yards of gravel and producing just over

$685,000 in gold.[22] Operations were no longer on a hand-to-mouth basis and once the legal questions were resolved there was a possibility that new equipment could be added.

The new trial was held in Toronto in late May 1933. Originally scheduled for Ottawa, it had been transferred after two of the Ottawa justices became ill, disrupting an already crowded session. By mid-May, both sides were encamped in rival hotels planning their strategy.[23]

This time, Treadgold had engaged I. F. Hellmuth as his counsel. Hellmuth, almost eighty years of age, had a reputation for tenacity and quickness of wit; he never made notes during a case, relying instead on a first class memory. He refused to meet and consult with Treadgold, having found, like so many others, that it was impossible to get a straight answer from him. Instead, the brief he was to present would be prepared by Treadgold's solicitors, Stuart Brown and W. L. Wallace. But Treadgold's habit of retaining information and his insistence on preparing the brief himself proved too much and at one point Wallace refused to work with him. Cunynghame and others persuaded Hellmuth to speak to Treadgold and insist that the documents be handed over. He received them less than a week before the trial. Hellmuth did not believe that all Treadgold's shares could be cancelled for nondisclosure as had happened in the previous Raney decision.

Patton *et al* submitted a detailed statement of claim asserting: that they sued on behalf of themselves and all other shareholders; that Treadgold had no financial interest in the Klondike properties; that Treadgold had assumed complete control of YCGC from 1925 on, resulting in great loss and damage to the company; that Treadgold had obtained large numbers of YCGC shares illegally; and that there had been no proper accounting of either money or securities. They asked: that Treadgold be found a promoter with no personal interest; that 1,788,900 YCGC shares held by Treadgold or a nominee be cancelled; and that there be a complete accounting of all monies, shares and properties.[24]

Treadgold's response was a complete denial of all allegations and a charge that the action was a conspiracy to defraud him of the results of his consolidation. Patton *et al* had benefited from Treadgold's generosity and the only shares they held were shares obtained from him.

The trial, held before Mr. Justice Davis, began on

29 May 1933 and continued until 23 June with a long parade of witnesses giving their understanding of the complex dealings that had taken place. There were 251 exhibits, made up of agreements, letters, cables, telegrams, documents, minute books and transfer books together with charts prepared by both Treadgold and Troop showing the interrelationship between the many companies, both old and new, involved in the action. There was an unusual aspect to the trial in that Mr. Justice Davis, in addition to urging the two sides to reach a settlement, made a personal attempt to find an acceptable compromise. Shortly before the court adjourned to Ottawa to hear evidence from F. H. Chrysler, a former director of YCGC who was by then over ninety and unable to travel, the judge asked Stuart Brown, Treadgold's solicitor, to sound out his clients for terms of a possible settlement. On the six-hour train journey to Ottawa, the judge sat with Brown and discussed the terms over drinks and on the return trip he did the same with D. M. McCarthy, counsel for the plaintiffs. His attempt failed as had all the others.[25]

Mr. Justice Davis gave his judgment orally on the final day of the trial, stating: "If I do not understand or appreciate the facts to-day, I will never understand them better at a later date." Tracing the dealings in some detail, he found no evidence that Treadgold, still a bankrupt, had put any of his own money into the consolidation. Further, as a promoter who had not fully disclosed his interest either to his board or in the statement filed in lieu of a prospectus, he was not entitled to retain any profit from the transactions. Treadgold was ordered to deliver up all share certificates held either in his name or in trust, totalling 2,129,997 ordinary shares and 15,500 preferred, and he and North Fork Power Company were restrained from any dealings in the shares of YCGC in their possession or under their control. Costs were awarded to the plaintiffs. No provision was made for the issue of shares to any of the persons named in the listing of share liabilities that Treadgold had given to the Shareholders' Committee in his letter of 7 October 1931.[26]

It was over. Treadgold, onetime King of the Klondike, had lost everything. He would receive nothing other than out of pocket expenses for the years spent in consolidating the old companies into YCGC. Even worse, there would not even be one YCGC share to show for the money, both his and that of his friends, that had been put into Granville Mining and North West

Corporation before their collapse. The incredibly complex story of his YCGC consolidation, traced in so much detail during the trial, became almost irrelevant in the face of the complete loss of all his interests for nondisclosure.[27]

Large sums of money had been involved in some of the transactions, but Davis found no evidence that Treadgold personally had put either money or securities into YCGC. The money he used had come either from the various companies acquired or as the purchase price of YCGC shares.

But the paramount question was the nondisclosure of information that was evident in the statement in lieu of a prospectus filed with the Secretary of State on 19 February 1925. The statement was drawn on the printed form of LaFleur, McDougall, the Montreal legal firm that had incorporated YCGC for Francis Cunynghame two years earlier. Honourable Adrian Knatchbull-Hugessen, the junior partner who drew up the document for Treadgold, testified he had typed the word "Nil" opposite questions dealing with any interest the directors might have in proposed agreements or contracts. Before signing, Treadgold had considered these questions very carefully and Knatchbull-Hugessen, impatient at the delay, commented that it was unlikely to be contested. "Oh, yes, but it will be contested," Treadgold had replied, and as Knatchbull-Hugessen added in his evidence: "He was a better prophet than I was."

There were long delays over the cancellation of Treadgold's shares. Some 350,000 of the shares were registered in the name of E. M. Williamson, a New York stockbroker. Although Williamson had testified at the trial that he had not known the shares were in his name and that he made no claim to them, by then the shares had been transferred to others who considered themselves entitled to them. Finally, in May 1936, a judgment in the English High Court returned the last 200,000 shares of what had been the Williamson block to the company.[28]

But now there was additional litigation over the shares registered in Treadgold's name. In February 1934, V. W. Worsdale called on Troop and Patton, then in London, asking them to register 1,750,000 shares that Treadgold had transferred to him in the summer of 1930.[29] It was a totally unexpected development: Worsdale's name had not been mentioned in either the Raney or the Davis trial. On investigation, it was learned that Worsdale, then living in Sussex, was a bankrupt and that he had been involved in dealings with Treadgold. In November 1934, L. C. Clark, as trustee for Worsdale, brought an action to force registration of the shares in question. The share certificates, bearing transfers dated 10 July 1930, were produced in court and there was an attempt, only partially successful, to learn more about the dealings between Treadgold and Worsdale. Worsdale testified that he had been advised that it would not be necessary to produce letters or memos to prove his claim, and none were forthcoming. A judgment in the Canadian courts early in 1936 dismissed the action with costs, but the litigation did not end until December 1938 when a final appeal to the Privy Council in London was dismissed.[30]

Treadgold was back in Canada for the appeal against the Davis judgment heard in the Ontario Court of Appeals in late March 1934. This time there was no battery of expensive lawyers; Treadgold appeared without counsel. He was given a week to submit a written statement and the court later heard a reply by the company counsel. Treadgold's appeal was dismissed with costs.[31] Over the next ten years other appeals to the Canadian courts were either dismissed or refused.

But YCGC had a London office; in 1945 Treadgold began an action before the English courts. At last he was free of the Canadian courts he mistrusted so much. He fared no better. His first action was struck out and less than three months later an appeal against this was dismissed. The last action he brought was started in London in March 1950 against YCGC and the North Fork Power Company. It was to obtain:

1. An order to ascertain the proceeds and benefits accruing under the two agreements of 16 July 1929 and the conveyance of same to Treadgold.

2. A declaration that the properties passed to Yukon, and all proceeds and benefits from the properties, are held in trust for Treadgold.

3. A declaration by Yukon Consolidated and the North Fork Power Company of their trusteeship for Treadgold.[32]

YCGC entered a plea for the action to be struck out as *res judicata* (a thing adjudicated; a case that has been decided).

When the action came up in July 1950 the judge declared that the intended action was not *res judicata* but frivolous and ordered it stricken out. An appeal was dismissed.

One more step remained for Treadgold in England: an appeal to the House of Lords. After that it was his intention to go to Canada to try and effect registration of the cancelled shares. Of the 1,390,000 shares he had claimed he was holding for others in his letter to the Shareholders' Committee of 7 October 1931, over 350,000 had already been reregistered to Canadian and American owners as the result of a threatened lawsuit. Why should the English holders be deprived of theirs?[33] The company he had worked so hard to put together was now profitable and had paid thirty cents a share in dividends between 1940 and 1947.

On his return to England after the trials in Canada, Treadgold returned to his old lodgings at a house in Oxford. He had been separated from his wife for many years. During World War 2 and just after, Francis Cunynghame lived nearby and made a point of visiting the old man once a week. Invariably, he would find Treadgold at work writing long memoranda analysing the judgment of 1933, filling reams of foolscap with the closely written matter. His single room was so crowded with his possessions that there was barely space to move around, and it stank of camphor and naphthalene. Collecting moths and butterflies were still his main hobby and he spent many hours setting them in the hundreds of boxes that cluttered the room. At times, he dealt in them, and more than once a sale had provided him with desperately needed cash.[34]

At one time he had a London office in an underground storeroom in the Mansion House Chambers, a block of offices close to the Bank of England. The office, reached by a difficult wooden staircase and a maze of passages, contained his Klondike specimens, both gold nuggets and moths, and piles of wooden packing cases full of papers and data from the Klondike, including test data from the creeks. But all this, together with the diaries which he had kept from 1898 to 1940, was lost in the London Blitz of May 1941.[35]

Treadgold still had his persuasive powers and, now that his old friends and relatives were gone, he borrowed from others on the strength of his case. Once YCGC was forced to reinstate his shares, his backers should have a bonus of YCGC shares plus their money back or an option to take more shares.[36] In the last five years of his life he borrowed more than £20,000, mostly from women. Asked how he managed it he replied: "Quite simply, get them up to London, take them out to lunch and show them the fine profit they will make—and the rest is easy."[37] If people were willing to lend to him why should he refuse?

The first step in his plan to return to Canada and have the cancelled shares reregistered took place when Treadgold was

Received from Christopher Bredenberg fifteen pounds, which sum, though applicable on the rent (£22) due from Edward Bredenberg to the Public Trustee next Tuesday, is to be counted as a charge against myself and is to share in the security of the deed given by me as security for the funds provided for the Defence against the Patton action

A. N. C. Treadgold
26 July 1933

Promissory note given to Christopher Bredenberg, son of Edward Bredenberg, when the former visited Treadgold in an unsuccessful attempt to raise money for the rent. No money changed hands at the time.

dicharged as a bankrupt in late June 1950. He appeared in the London court dressed for a prospecting trip in the Klondike complete to a haversack slung across his shoulder. He told the court that he was fit and ready to go back to work on his return to the Yukon.[38]

But there were new problems. He had borrowed money and insurance shares from a woman in Norfolk in exchange for shares standing in his name in YCGC—valid only if he could win his action. A daughter became alarmed and the family's solicitors advised the receiver in bankruptcy of the transaction. The receiver ordered that the insurance shares, now held by a bank as security for a loan to Treadgold, be sold and the balance returned to the woman. The bank was ordered to close Treadgold's account and deny him further banking privileges. His discharge as a bankrupt, so recently granted, was suspended for two years.[39]

Despite the setback, Treadgold once again secured funds for his personal needs and was contemplating collecting fresh funds to finance his appeal to the House of Lords when he fell from a London bus, fracturing his thigh and shoulder. He was taken to St. Bartholomew's Hospital, where he proved a difficult patient. Treadgold kept the whole ward awake and in a state of uproar until he was moved to a separate room. When Cunynghame saw him three days later, "He was shouting for the nurses and demanding instant attention."[40] The fractures were set, but Treadgold was old and worn out, and his condition gradually deteriorated. Cunynghame had contacted Treadgold's family and Mary Treadgold visited him in the hospital, the first time she had seen the great-uncle who had lost so much of the family money in the Klondike. Ed Bredenberg, now living in Kent, (never a member of the Conspiracy although he too had been broken by Treadgold) wrote:

> "I am sorry to hear that Treadgold is so ill; he has had a hard life and made it hard for others, but I forgive him.
> "I came to my wits' end and was about to be put out in the street, so I went to Mr. Chester Beatty and he gave me a little cottage to live in and paid my expenses to move down here and allowed me £5 a month to live on for some time, but now I have my old-age pension and keep myself without help.

"If you see Treadgold tell him that he and I
won't go rocking for gold on Bonanza that he dreamed
about and told me about in the long ago.
"I parted from Treadgold without ill feeling.
We never came to words, and I never wrote him,
thinking to bury the past."

Treadgold woke up to hear Cunynghame's news of Bredenberg. "Thank God," he said, "that one good man is still alive. That letter you have just read me is like gentle rain from Heaven."[41] Then he dozed off again.

Treadgold's condition grew worse, and he died on the evening of 23 March 1951, aged 87 years and 7 months.

By 1932, YCGC was controlled by the Conspiracy. The company had extensive holdings of placer ground, was equipped with an efficient power plant and five dredges and was relatively debt-free, with the exception of about $425,000 in New North West Income Notes held by the public. Treadgold by then had no control over YCGC's Klondike operations, but major expenditures would have to be deferred until Treadgold's ouster had been confirmed by the courts and there was no possibility of a further appeal. Even then, changes would probably have to be made gradually, paying their own way.

Originally, much of the money used to build the enterprise had come from the English stock- and debenture-holders of Granville Mining, North West Corporation and later New North West Corporation, all now left with little to show for their investment in Klondike placers. To achieve the consolidation, Treadgold and his Securities Committee had given shares of YCGC in exchange for the securities of the old companies. The offers made varied with the standing of the securities in the old company. In the case of Granville, the offers ranged from forty-five shares of YCGC for every £10 of receivers certificates down to one share of YCGC for 100 common shares of Granville (both stocks were £1 par value).[1] Once control of the companies had been acquired, Treadgold had been able to manipulate them as he chose. It was Treadgold, the promoter, who had produced the consolidation and Treadgold, the operator, who had almost destroyed it. Possibly the consolidation could have been handled differently, with more fairness to all concerned, but that was past and irreversible. The present problem was to build a stable operation from YCGC's Klondike holdings.

The first step was to estimate the potential value of the miles of creek claims held by the company. E. H. Dawson, a consultant, began the task in 1932. He found there was scanty, if any, data for much of the ground he was attempting to evaluate, and hence little of the gravel could be included in proven reserves. If Treadgold had more data it was not forthcoming, a problem Burrall had faced some fifteen years before. Using the information available, Dawson estimated that the YCGC ground might contain 268 million cubic yards of gravel with about $54½ million in gold, based on a price of $20.67 US per ounce. On the Klondike River side of the Dome there might be 127 million cubic yards of dredging ground, enough to keep the three big dredges digging for over twenty-three years, and, on the Indian River side, more than 74 million cubic yards of dredging ground, enough to last the two small dredges at work there more than fifty years.[2] Clearly, if the drilling which would have to be done confirmed Dawson's estimate, there was ample room for more dredges on the Indian River side.

E. A. Austin was appointed manager of YCGC in April 1933.[3] Formerly an engineer with Yukon Gold, he was now manager of four companies operating in the Fairbanks area and, for the moment at least, his time would be divided between the two placer camps. Austin arrived in Dawson in late June, travelling by steamer from the Lower Yukon. It was a two-week visit and he returned again in late September, travelling from Fairbanks by plane. During the summer, the operation had been managed by his assistant, R. E. Franklin, formerly Yukon Gold's electrical engineer. Early in December, Austin and his wife left on a business trip to Ottawa and London, expecting to return to their

Bear Creek home in the spring of 1934. Plans changed when he fell seriously ill on the trip and later resigned in July 1934 without returning to the Yukon.[4] His replacement was Warren McFarland, the former Yukon Gold engineer who had done so much to put Burrall and Baird and New North West Corporation on a sound footing before being summarily fired by Treadgold in 1925. Like Austin, McFarland was also managing an operation in

W. H. S. McFarland, who first came to the Klondike as a young engineer for Yukon Gold in 1908 and, after 1934, built a profitable operation from the wreckage of Treadgold's consolidation.

the Fairbanks area and once again his time would be divided between the two goldfields.

With their managers shuttling back and forth, YCGC had built an airplane landing strip, 1,500 feet long, on hydraulic tailings washed from the hillsides into the Klondike River valley, about two miles from the mouth. Landing instructions were spelled out: "If aviators wishing to land will make the same known by circling the field, two . . . employees will drive immediately to the field by auto and start a fire at the lower end of the field; and should the plane arrive at dusk, an automobile will be placed at the lower end of the field, with its headlights throwing a beam of light up the landing field."[5]

Early January 1934 brought problems for the North Fork power plant. It began with a long period of extremely cold weather at the same time that the water in the North Fork dropped so low there was barely enough to operate the plant. Then the ditch burst, shutting down the plant completely. The Dawson thermal plant was put back in operation but, even when operated for only a few hours, it burned twenty-four cords of wood a day and there was only a small supply on hand. The weather turned warm for a few days but then cold again, and the wood crew—working sixteen hours a day in temperatures down to 66 below—were barely able to keep the plant supplied. Repairing the ditch was out of the question until late February, and it was mid-April before the North Fork power plant was back in operation.[6]

Changes began gradually as they could be afforded. The Twelve Mile Ditch, no longer economic, was abandoned at the end of 1933. Badly in need of extensive repairs, it had deteriorated to the point where it would carry only 1,000 miner's inches of water instead of the 5,000 it had been designed for.[7] The drilling, stripping and thawing ahead of the dredges was put on a more systematic basis, and production crept up to $857,984.28 in the 1933 season. Much of the increase was due to the rising price of gold, up from about twenty-five dollars at the end of March 1933 to close to thirty-five dollars in 1934.[8] In June 1934, Tom Patton reported to the annual meeting:

"Your three largest dredges operate in the Valley of the Klondyke River, an area where gold values are low and scattered, and where it is often difficult for a dredge to do more than meet operating costs. These large dredges nevertheless employ 75 percent of the Company's total labour force and from every point of view they must be kept in operation if at all possible.

"Even while the operations in the Klondyke Valley do not yield a large profit they none the less absorb a substantial portion of the overhead costs. The results of last year's prospecting in the Klondyke Valley taken with the present price of gold promise a solution to what has been one of our most serious operating problems."[9]

It had taken almost twenty years but once again the big dredges were showing some of the potential they had seemed to promise when everything was new and Joe Boyle was King of the Klondike.

Production in 1934 was $959,463.83, up for all the dredges with the exception of North West Number 1, which was down about $100,000. Shareholders were told something of the problems with that dredge in a letter of 24 December 1934:

"The decreased recoveries from Dredge North West One are owing to the sinking of the dredge on July 31st, 1934. It was raised and recommenced operations on September 1st. It sank again on September 13th and was again raised and restarted on October 1st. On October 20th this dredge was put into winter quarters. The sinking appears to have been due to lack of buoyancy. The necessary reconditioning of the hull will be taken care of next spring."[10]

The dredge had ample cause to be temperamental. Now working for her thirtieth consecutive season, she was worn out and nearing the end of her working life.

In 1935, new dredges were under construction, and the existing ones were renumbered:

Yukon Number 1 was formerly North West Number 1. It was built by Marion with seven-cubic-foot buckets, and was mining on Upper Dominion Creek.

Yukon Number 2 was formerly Canadian Number 2. It was built by Marion with sixteen-cubic-foot buckets, and was mining in the Klondike Valley.

Yukon Number 3 was formerly Canadian Number 3. It was built by Marion with sixteen-cubic-foot buckets, and was mining in the Lower Bonanza area.

Yukon Number 4 was formerly Canadian Number 4. It was built by Marion with sixteen-cubic-foot buckets, and was mining in the Arlington area of the Klondike Valley.

Yukon Number 5 was formerly North West Number 2. It was built by Marion with seven-cubic-foot buckets, and was mining in the Lower Dominion area.

Yukon Number 6 was rebuilt from Yukon Gold Number 6, abandoned on Gold Run Creek. It was built by Bucyrus with seven-cubic-foot buckets, and began mining on Lower Sulphur Creek in June 1936.

Yukon Number 7 was rebuilt from Yukon Gold Number 1, closed down at Guggieville in 1919. It was built by Bucyrus with five-cubic-foot buckets, and began mining on Lower Quartz Creek in August 1935.[11]

Later, the term "Yukon" would be dropped and the dredges simply referred to by number.

The operation expanded each year. In 1935, the new South Fork Ditch, from the main Klondike River to the North Fork intake, was finally completed. This was the project that Treadgold had been obsessed with in 1928 and 1929. Now there was an immediate need for the additional power that could be developed. Another 5,000-hp turbine was added to the North Fork power plant, bringing the generating capacity to about 10,700 KVA.[12] Extensive prospecting and drilling were done on the Indian River side at the Granville flats, on Sulphur Creek upstream to Discovery, and for a mile on Dominion Creek downstream from 17 Below Lower Discovery, the point where North West Number 1 had started in 1921. A total of 5,224,144 cubic yards of gravel was handled by the six dredges operating in 1935; the production was valued at $912,566.45.[13]

During 1935, the financial structure of YCGC was changed to complete the consolidation and permit a debenture issue. The preferred shares of YCGC were exchanged for common shares on the basis of 130 common shares for 100 preferred. The income notes of New North West Corporation, originally redeemable at $130 for each $100 held, had been purchased for 130 common shares of YCGC for each $100 held. This done, the expansion could be financed by $1,500,000 in 6-percent convertible debentures, authorized in 1935 and early 1936, and these, convertible into 1,500,000 common shares at $1 par, carried options to subscribe for an additional 750,000 shares at the same price. Authorized capital stock of YCGC was increased to 8 million common shares to allow for the conversion. Despite their unhappy experiences in the Klondike, New Consolidated

Gold Fields had sufficient faith in McFarland's program to take the bulk of the new debentures. At the annual meeting in July 1936, J. A. Agnew, Chairman of Gold Fields' parent company, was elected a director of YCGC; at a director's meeting held later the same day, he was elected President of YCGC.[14] J. T. Patton, a leader of the Conspiracy that deposed Treadgold, remained a director until the following year, when he declined to stand for reelection.

In 1936, preparations were underway to dredge Sulphur Creek. Because the creek did not provide enough water for the stripping and thawing operations planned, work began on a complex ditch system, about fifteen miles long, to bring 1,500 miner's inches of water from Australia Creek, south of Indian River. The water would be brought by almost five miles of ditch to a crossing of Dominion Creek; it would cross the creek in an inverted steel siphon and be lifted to the hillside above Sulphur Creek by a 1,600-hp pumping unit, from where a ditch 10.7 miles long would carry it to the new operations. Extensive drilling was done during the season which included work on Black Hills Creek, about fifteen miles south of Granville, drilled and later abandoned. During the season, the seven dredges, now including Number 6 put into service in late June, treated a total of 7,957,108 cubic yards of gravel with a production of $1,456,423.77. About 470 men were employed during the three summer months.[15]

In 1937, the expansion program continued. Another new dredge, Number 8, a Yuba machine with seven-cubic-foot buckets, was under construction in the Middle Sulphur Creek area. The ditch system between Australia and Sulphur creeks was completed in mid-August and considerable work was done to widen and strengthen the ditches carrying water to the North Fork power plant. During the season, the dredges handled 7,443,785 cubic yards of gravel and recovered gold valued at $1,287,723.05. An average of just over 500 men were employed during the operating season.[16]

In 1938, nine dredges were in operation. Number 9 was a Bucyrus machine with five-cubic-foot buckets; it began digging on Upper Sulphur Creek on 15 September. The dredge had been rebuilt from Yukon Gold's Number 3, abandoned on Bear Creek. And a new dredge was under construction at 10 Below Lower Discovery on Dominion Creek; Number 10 was a Yuba machine with seven-cubic-foot buckets. Dredge Number 1, her useful life over, was dismantled and abandoned at the end of her thirty-fourth season. Prospect drilling had not been continued because a total of 92 million cubic yards of gravel reserves—enough for the estimated lives of the dredges—had already been proved. It would contain about $40 million in gold.

During the season, there had been some anxious moments with Number 4, which was being hurried ahead to reach rich ground in the Arlington area near the mouth of Hunker Creek.[17]

"What might have been a serious disaster occurred on June 10th when Dredge Yukon 4 at Arlington suddenly sprang a leak in the forward part of the hull and sank in three minutes. Most fortunately for us the dredge remained on an even keel while settling in the dredge pond, and did not turn over on its side. Pumps were quickly assembled, the pond pumped out and the leak located. Repairs were then made to the hull and the dredge refloated and cleaned. The whole operation was most speedily and skilfully carried out, with the result that the dredge was digging again by June 18th, a loss of time of only eight days. . . .

"Risks of sinking are unavoidable when we are working with old dredges. Dredge Yukon 4 was built in 1912, so that her hull is now twenty-seven years old. Her operating life is expected to finish in 1940, when she completes the digging-out of the Arlington area. The cost of building a new hull would, at this stage, be prohibitive, and we are forced to carry on with full knowledge of the risks involved."[18]

During the 1938 season, the dredges had handled 8,550,652 cubic yards of gravel and recovered gold valued at $2,127,103. An average of 606 men were employed during the operating season.

In 1939, ten dredges were operated. The new dredge, Number 11, was built over the spring and summer of 1939 at 57 Below on Middle Hunker Creek. Like 10, it was a Yuba machine with seven-cubic-foot buckets. The bucket line and some other parts had been salvaged from Number 1. The gamble on Number 4's hull had been won; working in the rich Arlington area she had recovered $941,236 in gold (about one-third of the total production) at a cost of $248,956. Enough ground remained to keep the dredge working until July 1940, after which it was planned to rebuild her on Bonanza Creek. Weather conditions

Bulldozer sluicing plant in operation on Dominion Creek in 1961. Water supplied by a hydraulic monitor is directed at the gravel that the bulldozer is pushing into the dump box. The method is often used by individual miners; it is well suited to the mining of benches and other areas inaccessible to dredges.

had been favorable, other than a cold snap in early November that forced the shutdown of several dredges, and numbers 3 and 5 had been able to operate until almost mid-January 1940. During the year, the dredges had handled 10,090,182 cubic yards of gravel and recovered gold valued at $2,735,730. An average of 566 men were employed during the operating season. Early in 1940, YCGC paid its first dividend of 8 cents per share.[19]

By 1939, McFarland's expansion program was essentially complete. Ample ground had been proved ahead of the dredges, and no additional major expenditures were planned. By now, prospecting and preparation of new ground had become routine. The first step involved scout drilling using Keystone drills, essentially a simple type of churn drill. Techniques had changed. Frozen ground, once considered almost impossible to drill, now became an advantage. Instead of attempting to thaw the ground and finishing with the drill at the bottom of a crater that resembled a monstrous shell hole, the hard, frozen ground was now used as the wall of the hole. Drilled without casing, the actual volume of the hole in the pay zone was determined by adding a measured amount of water to the hole and determining the rise by means of a tape and float. Gold values in the hole were obtained by sluicing the drill cuttings followed by careful panning and weighing of the gold recovered. If dredging was being considered, the drilling was generally done on cross-section lines 500 feet apart with the holes along the line spaced from 50 to 300 feet apart, depending on the width of the pay-streak. Using the drill sections, calculations were made of the "amount of muck," the "dredging section" (gravel plus pay bedrock) and the gold content. [20]

Stripping was done two years in advance of thawing and the thawing at least a year and a half ahead of the dredging; when the thawing was well done the ground tended to improve over the waiting period.

The first stage of the stripping operation involved clearing away brush, old buildings and abandoned machinery. Then hydraulic monitors operating at pressures of 50 to 120 pounds per square inch were used to push the thawed muck into prepared drains that would carry it from the area. With the thick, insulating blanket of sphagnum moss removed, the underlying muck thawed to a foul-smelling mass that could be swept away by the streams of water from the monitors. It was composed of partly decomposed plant material, silt, fine sand and perhaps thirty percent ice. A number of monitors were connected to each water line and the operator worked each in turn, clearing away the muck that had been thawed by the sun and by standing water during the idle period. Water for stripping came either from ditches or from the local stream; it was delivered under pressure from portable electric pumps.

Thawing was done using cold water points spaced at the corners of equilateral triangles with 16-foot sides. A unit of about 600 points was fed from a network of pipes, ranging from 11 inches in diameter at the gate valve of the pump, through header pipes of 6 and 4 inches and from crossheads on these to rubber hoses, 1 inch in diameter, leading to the points. Most of the points were made of extra-heavy ¾-inch pipe with a tip of high-carbon steel. Points were driven to bedrock by men known as point drivers using a slotted driving weight to hammer on an anvil attached to the point. The points could be driven as the ground beneath them thawed; the usual advance on a group of points was two to fifteen feet per man-hour. Once the points reached

Top—YCGC's cold water thawing plant on lower Dominion Creek, about 1936. Thawing is done by water forced through slender steel points; point drivers keep the points driven down as the gravels beneath them thaw.

Bottom—Muck is stripped off with a hydraulic monitor before cold water thawing is begun. Gravel in the background is from an old underground working.

bedrock, they were taken over by men known as point doctors, who made sure that the ground between the points was properly thawed. Particular care had to be taken in areas with old underground workings, because the latter tended to provide channels for the water and leave islands of frozen ground between. Additional points would have to be driven to thaw these islands. Stripping and thawing were carried out from early May to late September, but there were several weeks of work in addition to that, getting ready in the spring and cleaning up in the fall.

McFarland estimated that the use of stripping and cold water thawing had reduced dredging costs to between sixteen and twenty cents per cubic yard of ground dredged, in contrast to costs of between thirty-five and forty cents per cubic yard for steam thawing in partially frozen ground. Not only that, but when half the volume was removed by stripping the muck, the values in the remaining gravel dredged were nearly double those obtained if both thawed muck and gravel were handled by the dredge.

In contrast to stripping and thawing, the actual dredging had changed very little from that done by Yukon Gold and Canadian Klondyke. To a great extent, the yardage handled and gold recovery still depended on the skill of the dredgemaster. Those who operated dredges 2, 3 and 4 had to be careful not to damage the rapidly-deteriorating hulls and, in the event of trouble, be ready to make speedy jury-repairs to keep the dredge afloat. The dredging season was still controlled by the availability of power from the North Fork plant. Uusally, there would be enough power for all the dredges by mid-May, and they would operate until about the first of November, when decreasing power and cold weather would start the shutdown, beginning with the dredges on the smaller creeks.

In the 1940 season, ten dredges were operated. In early July, Number 4 completed her work in the Arlington area, and the move to 65 Below on Bonanza began. The practicality of reworking the ground already dredged by Yukon Gold had been well demonstrated by Number 3, which had worked up Bonanza Creek until the fan of White Channel Gravels spreading out from Lovett Gulch grew too deep to handle. The larger dredges could dig deeper and tear out several feet of bedrock undisturbed in the earlier dredging. In places, Yukon Gold's steam thawing had not been complete and now almost all the tailings were completely thawed. During the year, the dredges had handled 10,480,799

Members of a YCGC stripping crew assembling one of the hydraulic monitors.

GEORGE HUNTER

cubic yards and recovered $2,617,227 down slightly from 1939. An average of 625 men had been employed in the operating season.[21]

As World War 2 progressed, YCGC had increasing difficulty in obtaining labour and supplies. Growth of the company had taken place during the Great Depression, when jobs were hard to get. The working conditions were often difficult. Despite protective clothing, the men on the stripping and thawing crews would be wet much of the day in temperatures that were often close to zero Fahrenheit towards the end of the season. Most shifts were ten hours long, seven days a week, all paid at the going hourly rate without overtime. All employees were required to produce. Any unable to meet the company's expectations, whether for physical or other reasons, were replaced immediately. The camps were spread out along the creeks, up to fifty miles from Dawson. Even though new buildings had been added, the camps were often crowded and lacked many amenities, such as adequate washing facilities. There were many complaints over the food. Now, with better-paying wartime jobs available Outside, the crews began to expect more.

In late July 1941, after their request for a one-dollar-a-day cost-of-living bonus was refused, the crews in the camps left their jobs and walked into Dawson. The men arrived over a two-day period, those from the Granville camp having walked close to fifty miles. The townspeople of Dawson grew apprehensive as the 500-odd men streamed into town, but their leaders kept them in order and there was neither picketing nor violence. At the outset, the company, already hurt by wartime costs and shortages, offered a profit-sharing bonus at the end of the season, soon withdrawn in favour of an additional fifty cents a day. It wasn't enough.

The men were refusing to call their action a strike; they were simply unwilling to return to work on the company's terms. Finally, company officials and leaders of the walkout met in a midnight session with a federal government conciliator who had been flown to Dawson to aid in the negotiations, and hammered out an agreement. Under it the men received a cost of living bonus of 62½ cents per shift, certain grievances were to be corrected, and the right to form an "employees' council" and negotiate with the company recognized. The stoppage had shut down the company's operation for nine days.[22]

The walkout was just the beginning of YCGC's wartime problems. Over the next few years the 700-man crew needed to keep the company in full operation were not available, and management was forced to concentrate on keeping the operation together until there could be a return to full production. Gold returns from the operation fluctuated:

1941	$2,336,708	
1942	2,834,631	crew 400 average
1943	1,353,147	crew 197 at peak
1944	616,229	crew 172 at peak
1945	918,442	crew 186 at peak
1946	1,364,664	crew 406 at peak

The main objects had been achieved. The debentures had been retired in 1945, the equipment maintained in good condition and most of the key employees were still with the company. When the time came, YCGC would be ready to rebuild their operation. In both 1944 and 1945, only three dredges had operated, and two others were gone: Number 2 was dismantled in 1942 and Number 5, temporarily idle, was destroyed in July 1943 by a fire started by a lightning strike. Six dredges were operated in 1946 and 1947, seven in 1948 and all eight in 1949, when Number 9 on Upper Sulphur Creek was put back in service. By now, gold returns were edging up towards those of the pre-war years. At the end of 1947, W. H. S. McFarland, General Manager since 1935, gave up active management of the company he had done so much to build. He continued as Consulting Engineer and later as a director until the end of 1961.[23]

It became obvious that YCGC was trapped. Wage rates continued to climb and the price of gold remained at $35 US an ounce (plus a small supplement paid by the Canadian government). The company's methods of stripping and thawing were based on the use of cheap labor that no longer existed. And gravel reserves had dropped so much—eithert through mining, or because increased working costs had eliminated some deposits from use—that there was not enough ground left to justify the purchase of new equipment or the development of new methods. As the equipment deteriorated, the cost of working with it grew, both in man-hours and in total cost. The crews might be skilful in making temporary repairs to pipe and other equipment that

Winchman Art Fry at the controls of YCGC Number 3 in 1950. This is one of the dredges with 16-cubic-foot buckets; she was built by Joe Boyle as Canadian Number 3 in 1912.

should have been discarded, but it was gradually becoming a makeshift operation. Highly skilled men were still needed as superintendents, dredgemasters and foremen, and many of them stayed with the company until mining ended in 1966. But the quality and efficiency of the unskilled labor tended to drop each year as better jobs became available Outside. In later years, many of these men were brought in from Outside, with the expectation that most of them would quit before the time came to cut back in the fall.

Dawson and the Klondike were changing, and many of the differences that set the community apart had already disappeared. Nickels and dimes, always rejected by the business community as too insignificant to bother with, came into more common use in June 1936, after the younger and more sympathetic of the town's two bank managers was persuaded to bring in a small shipment for use at a street fair sponsored by the Graduate Nurses Association.[24] Gone, too, were the easy-going days of the early 1940s when another bank manager could leave gold bricks worth over a quarter of a million dollars unguarded in a vault that had been haywired shut because the door of the frost-heaved structure refused to close.[25]

The excitement of the war years had passed them by and now there was a long, demoralizing decline as YCGC's activities began to slow down. Even the government was abandoning them. In 1953, after a period of uncertainty and delay, Whitehorse, now a growing transportation centre on the Alaska Highway, had replaced Dawson as the capital of the Yukon Territory.[26] The same year, an all-weather road linked Dawson to the Whitehorse-Mayo road completed a few years earlier, and the river traffic ended. As transportation improved, the barrier separating Dawson from the Outside began to crumble, and Dawson, once the largest centre west of Winnipeg, became a near-ghost town at the end of a long dusty road.

Dawson and YCGC were drawing apart. Company operations were centered at Bear Creek and, with the highway, there were few ties with the merchants still remaining in Dawson. Most of the permanent employees lived at Bear Creek, and almost all of the temporary employees went Outside by air or highway as soon as they drew their final pay. The permanent residents tried to keep the town going. YCGC's manager still lived in the best-kept house in Dawson, and company crews were involved in a never-ending struggle to keep the rundown utilities in operation. It was difficult, because the occupied houses the utilities were attempting to serve were scattered through a townsite intended for ten times the population.

Unless the price of gold increased there was little chance of YCGC extending their placer operations in the Klondike. Other creeks and areas had been tested in the 1930s and, to a lesser extent, later, but they had been considered uneconomical then and operating costs had increased steadily since. A new method of open cut mining, using bulldozers to push the gravels into the sluice boxes, had been developed by others in the late 1930s. It was particularly suited to small areas missed by or inaccessible to the dredges. From 1957 on, YCGC used the method to a limited extent on the low benches above Dominion Creek but, used to operating on a much larger scale, they were never able to equal the efficiency of individual operators who worked alone or with very small crews. A modest hydraulic plant had been operated on Paradise Hill, overlooking Hunker Creek, between 1952 and 1960, using water pumped from Hunker Creek.

The company began to prepare itself for the eventual shutdown, and uniformity became the watchword. Originally, it involved machinery and equipment, working methods and building design but, towards the end, it affected even the field management of the company. To the casual observer the most obvious signs were the buildings and dredges, all painted the same battleship-grey with white trim, and the many dark green, near-vintage, Ford pickups seen along the roads between the scattered operations. The outstanding exception, perhaps a silent protest, were the brilliant floral displays that brightened the yards of many company houses during the almost continuous daylight of the summer months.

The end came slowly. Dredge Number 1 had been abandoned in 1938, Number 2 in 1942, Number 5 in 1943, and now the others began to follow as their ground ran out: Number 7 in 1950, Number 3 in 1952, Number 4 in 1959, Number 10 in 1964, Number 12 in 1965 and finally Numbers 6, 8, 9 and 11 in 1966. Number 12 was a smaller dredge with 2½-cubic-foot buckets. It had been installed on the Dominion Creek benches in 1953 and shut down in 1960, but in 1962 it was moved to a left limit bench on Dominion Creek, about 1½ miles above the mouth of Jensen Creek, and operated there until 1965. When the end

The remains of YCGC Number 3, formerly Canadian Number 3, in July 1976. The bucket line and much of the heavy machinery were removed after the dredge was shut down on 19 August 1953.

came in 1966, Number 9 was shut down in mid-October to free what crew remained for the other dredges. The last three, Numbers 6, 8 and 11, operated until mid-November, when a cold spell with temperatures of 40 below zero Fahrenheit brought everything to a standstill. [27]

The operation had been profitable. Following the initial dividend early in 1940, there had been annual dividends until 1965, with the exception of 1942, 1943, 1945, 1946, 1948 and 1949. A total of $7,383,924 had been paid,amounting to $1.26 on each $1 par share. When the dredging ended, investments and cash were worth about fifty cents per share, and YCGC was involved in the financing of a lode mining venture, far from the Klondike, that seemed certain to assure the future of the company. In the period 1932 to 1966, some 205,433,920 cubic yards of gravel had been treated and $58,767,368 in gold produced. [28] Between 1935 and 1963, total dredging costs, including stripping and thawing write-offs, had averaged 18.75 cents per cubic yard; recovery had been 27.26 cents. [29] Proven reserves remaining at the conclusion of operations were reported as 2,187,680 cubic yards with an average value of 35.95 cents or a total of $786,656 at $35 per ounce. On Gold Run Creek there were an additional 10,052,642 cubic yards of virgin ground and tailings estimated to contain a total of just under $3.7 million in gold.

With the closing, YCGC's Klondike assets were grouped into four categories and each written down to a nominal one dollar. The company still held two concessions, the Anderson (Number 1) and the Boyle (Number 18) and 299 claims, many of them under lease to independent miners. Shares of the three Dawson utility companies were sold to a government agency. A few items, such as copper wire from the transmission lines, were sold, but there was no immediate market for the dredges, mining equipment or buildings. Only two employees remained in the Klondike; once there had been more than 700. [30]

After 1966, a number of small, independent operations remained. The mining was done by bulldozer sluicing and by hydraulic methods, the latter little changed in seventy years. With the rapid increase in the price of gold in 1973, there has been renewed interest in the area and a marked increase in the limited gold production. Placer gold still holds the fascination that it has for thousands of years, and men still dream, but, in the Klondike at least, their dreams now are only a tattered remnant of the glittering and, in part, unreal prize that tempted Big Alex McDonald, Joe Boyle and Treadgold, the Guggenheim and YCGC engineers, and a host of others whose names have been forgotten. Now, long sections of the creeks are silent and deserted. Most of the old cabins are gone, either crumbled or pulled down for firewood. The few that remain are ransacked each summer by tourists searching for Klondike souvenirs.

Few tourists can comprehend that the old-timers who lived in the simple cabins had an untold wealth in character and experience. Many of the owners were old men content to live out the last few years of their lives along the creeks that had been their home for more than fifty years. A few continued to hand-mine tiny patches of ground, either overlooked by the dredges or considered not worth mining when the creeks were booming.

Much of the old-timers' history was verbal, and only a tiny fragment of it has been preserved. Even the physical evidence of their search for gold is disappearing. Their cuts and shafts have sloughed in; their boilers and machinery, remnants that until a few years ago littered the second growth everywhere, have been collected and hauled away as scrap metal. In contrast, the large-scale mining by Yukon Gold, Canadian Klondyke and YCGC has left permanent scars in the huge fans of White Channel Gravels spreading into the valleys from the old hydraulic workings above the creeks and in the crescent mounds of dredge tailings filling the valley bottoms. But even these are softening as the second growth spreads slowly across the barren debris.

Appendix 1: Chronology

1896

AUGUST 16—George Carmack and party stake Discovery group of claims on Rabbit (later Bonanza) Creek.

1897

JULY—Klondike rush begins when ships *Excelsior* and *Portland* arrive with gold at San Francisco and Seattle, respectively.

AUGUST—J. W. "Joe" Boyle and Frank Slavin reach Dawson.

DECEMBER 1—Slavin applies to the Gold Commissioner for a concession covering placer ground in the Klondike River Valley between the mouths of Hunker and Bonanza creeks.

1898

JANUARY 2—A.N.C. Treadgold sails from England, en route to the Klondike as a Special Correspondent for *The Manchester Guardian* and *The Mining Journal*.

JANUARY 12—Anderson Concession on lower Hunker Creek is granted by Clifford Sifton, Minister of Interior.

MAY—Treadgold, in Ottawa, meets Sifton and begins negotiations for an interest in the Anderson Concession and other pending applications.

JUNE—Treadgold arrives in the Klondike and remains until early August.

1899

MAY—Treadgold, back in Canada, negotiates with Clifford Sifton for a concession covering the water supply to Klondike mining claims.

1900

NOVEMBER 5—Boyle Concession (Lease Number 18) covering the Klondike valley is issued to Joe Boyle.

1901

JUNE 12—The Treadgold Concession, giving control of the water supply for mining, is approved after three years of lobbying.

JULY 30—First protest meeting over the Treadgold Concession is held in Dawson.

SEPTEMBER 6—Sifton modifies his interpretation of the Treadgold Concession, and ordinary miners are again permitted to stake claims within its boundaries.

DECEMBER 7—New Order in Council is passed: all abandoned claims are to revert to Treadgold after 1 January 1902.

1902

FEBRUARY—More protest meetings when text of new Order in Council is posted in Dawson.

APRIL 21—Another Order in Council is passed after a delegation from the Yukon confers with Commissioner Ross and Sifton in Ottawa.

1903

JANUARY 17—News of the Tanana (Fairbanks) Gold Field reaches Dawson, and the campaign against the Treadgold Concession is revitalized as miners begin to leave for the new discovery.

1903

MAY 12—Treadgold Concession is debated in the Yukon Council and in the House of Commons at Ottawa.

JULY 30—Britton Commission is appointed by the federal government to inquire into the Treadgold and other concessions.

AUGUST 17—Britton Commission begins hearings in Dawson.

SEPTEMBER 7—Britton Commission hearings end abruptly. Britton leaves Dawson the same afternoon.

1904

JUNE 22—Treadgold Concession is rescinded when the English backers withdraw. Other concessions, including the Boyle Concession, remain in force.

1905

AUGUST 13—Canadian Klondyke Mining Company dredge, Canadian Number 1, is started up on Bear Creek near the Boyle Concession, the latter now controlled by Detroit money.

1906

MARCH 19—C. A. Thomas and six engineers arrive in Dawson to begin development of Treadgold's interests, reportedly for the Guggenheims.

AUGUST—Daniel and Solomon Guggenheim and their wives visit the Klondike.

1907

MAY 29—Twelve Mile power plant put in operation and three Guggenheim dredges started up. Work continues on the Twelve Mile Ditch.

1908

MARCH—Thomas W. Lawson attempts to float 700,000 shares of the Guggenheims' Yukon Gold Company on the New York curb market.

1909

MAY—Joe Boyle gains control of Canadian Klondyke Mining Company in an agreed settlement following a lengthy court battle.

JUNE 4—Water from the Twelve Mile Ditch flows to the hydraulic operations on Lovett Hill. Yukon Gold is now operating seven dredges.

1910

MARCH—Treadgold, no longer with the Guggenheims, starts work on a power plant on the North Fork of the Klondike River, and he is believed to be consolidating ground on the Indian River watershed.

NOVEMBER 4—The world's largest dredge, Boyle's Canadian Number 2, is started up at Bear Creek.

1911

MAY 8—Treadgold's North Fork power plant is put in operation.

AUGUST—Formation of the Granville Mining Company is announced. It is to be financed by Consolidated Gold Fields, A. C. Beatty and H. C. Hoover, and managed by Treadgold.

1912

MARCH—Amalgamation of the Granville and Canadian Klondyke mining companies is revealed. Boyle is to control everything north of the Dome and Treadgold everything to the south.

1913

MAY—Boyle's Canadian Number 3 and 4 dredges start up. Sister ships to Number 2, they were built with money advanced by Granville.

SEPTEMBER—Granville Mining, faced with an uncertain income, becomes a holding company, and Treadgold's operations south of the Dome are refinanced as North West Corporation.

1914

OCTOBER 10—Boyle's Canadian Number 2 dredge sinks in the Klondike River. Boyle-Yukon Contingent leaves Dawson to fight in the world war.

1915

JULY—The first of Treadgold's Lubecker excavators, intended to supplant the dredges, arrives in Dawson.

SEPTEMBER 23—Boyle's Canadian Number 2 dredge is put back in service, nearly a year after it sank.

1916

JULY 17—Joe Boyle leaves Dawson for Europe and new adventures. His Canadian Klondike companies, in default on payments to Granville Mining, are paying only those employees who quit or are discharged.

1917

APRIL—Granville Mining, left without income from either Boyle's or Treadgold's operations, goes into receivership, followed by North West Corporation.

1918

JANUARY 5—Boyle's Canadian Klondyke Mining Company is placed in receivership. H. G. Blankman, appointed receiver by the court at Dawson, operates three of the four dredges during the 1918 season.

1919

SEPTEMBER—Blankman's resignation as receiver is accepted. F. P. Burrall, agent for Gold Fields, assumes control of the operating companies and begins to negotiate settlement of the outstanding debts and judgments.

1920

FEBRUARY 26—Treadgold, living in England, is adjudicated a bankrupt, with liabilities totalling £446,134 ($2,230,670).

AUGUST 24—Canadian Number 1 dredge, dismantled, is hauled over Hunker Summit and rebuilt on Dominion Creek as North West Number 1. Begins digging in the first serious attempt to mine North West's ground.

1921

SEPTEMBER—Canadian Klondyke Mining Company is foreclosed for failure to issue and pay interest on $1,798,000 in debentures, and is taken over by Burrall and Baird, Limited, a private company.

1922

MARCH—Canadian Klondyke Power Company is foreclosed for failure to issue debentures. Its assets and those of North West Corporation are passed to New North West Corporation Limited, incorporated in Canada and free of receiverships.

1923

MAY—The Yukon Consolidated Gold Corporation Limited is formed with the object of acquiring the securities of the operating companies in the Klondike.

1924

APRIL AND MAY—Following the loss of the Bear Creek shops in a fire and the sinking of Canadian Number 4 dredge in its pond, the future of Burrall and Baird hangs in the balance. Only Number 2 dredge remains in operation.

1925

APRIL—Treadgold, still an undischarged bankrupt, gains control of the operating companies in the Klondike and dismisses Warren McFarland, the engineer who has been rebuilding the operation.

JULY 7—Treadgold, after being away from the Klondike since 1912, returns in triumph to manage his new empire.

1926

DECEMBER—Treadgold purchases Yukon Gold Company's Klondike assets for $100,000.

1927 to 1929

Mining operations, personally supervised by Treadgold, drift towards disaster.

1930

AUGUST 13—Pressured by creditors, the board of YCGC relieves Treadgold of active management.

DECEMBER 22—The Secretary of State of Canada orders an investigation of the affairs of YCGC.

1931

Under Andrew Baird's management, YCGC operates five dredges, meets nearly all known obligations and ends the year with a substantial cash balance.

1932

MARCH 18—In a court action, all of Treadgold's shares of YCGC are ordered cancelled for Treadgold's failure to disclose his interest as a promoter in dealings with the company.

1933

FEBRUARY—A new trial is ordered when the court stenographer dies before transcribing his notes of the 1932 trial.

JUNE 23—Treadgold's shares are ordered cancelled in the new judgment. Treadgold continues legal actions but fails to have his shares reinstated.

1934

JULY—McFarland returns as manager of YCGC and begins to build a profitable operation.

1935 to 1939

An expansion program, financed principally by the Consolidated Gold Fields group, is completed with ten dredges in operation.

1940

MARCH 30—An initial dividend of eight cents per share is paid.

1941 to 1945

Beset by labour and material shortages during World War 2, operations are gradually cut back until only three dredges remain in service.

1946 to 1949

Operations are expanded until eight dredges are in operation. Gold returns approach those of prewar years.

1950

JUNE—Treadgold is discharged as a bankrupt. He tells the London court that he is fit and ready to go to work on his return to the Klondike.

1951

MARCH 23—Treadgold dies in London. He had kept up his battle against YCGC until his brief final illness.

1952 to 1965

Trapped by increasing labour costs, shrinking gravel reserves and the fixed price of gold, YCGC prepares for the inevitable end of dredge operations.

1966

NOVEMBER 15—The last of the four dredges operated in 1966 is shut down, ending YCGC's mining operations in the Klondike.

Appendix 2: The Gold Dredges

Gold dredges used in the Klondike compare well in both size and capacity with any heavy equipment in use today. Canadian Klondyke's big Marion dredges with their 16-cubic-foot buckets had an operating weight of about 2,000 tons and a daily capacity of up to 16,000 cubic yards of gravel and bedrock, weighing close to 30,000 tons. Operating weight of the dredges with 7-cubic-foot buckets varied from about 535 tons for Canadian Klondyke Number 1, with a wooden hull, to about 770 tons for Yukon Gold Number 8, with a steel hull. Both types had a daily capacity of about 5,000 cubic yards of gravel and bedrock. Dredges with 5-cubic-foot buckets, proportionately lighter, had a capacity of about 3,500 cubic yards.

MANUFACTURERS

A number of companies supplied dredge machinery and hull designs. In some cases construction of the hull and installation of machinery were done under the supervision of a company representative.

ALLIS-CHALMERS MANUFACTURING COMPANY, Milwaukee, Wisconsin. Bonanza Basin dredge, 1905.

BUCYRUS MANUFACTURING COMPANY, South Milwaukee, Wisconsin. Yukon Gold Numbers 1, 2, 3, 5, 6, 8, 9, between 1906 and 1911.

MARION STEAM SHOVEL COMPANY, Marion, Ohio: Canadian Klondyke Numbers 1, 2, 3 and 4 and Yukon Gold Numbers 4 and 7, between 1905 and 1913.

RISDON IRON WORKS, San Francisco, California. Risdon built the Lewes River dredge, 1898.

YUBA MANUFACTURING COMPANY, San Francisco, California. YCGC Numbers 8, 10 and 11, 1938 and 1939.

DREDGING COMPANIES

Bonanza Basin Gold Dredging Company (1906-1909)

The company operated one dredge, an Allis-Chalmers with 6½-cubic-foot buckets, on ground near the mouth of the Klondike River. The machine, first started up in May 1906, was initially steam-powered with a side discharge but was later modified to electrically-operated with a conventional tailings stacker. Despite many changes it proved incapable of handling the ground effectively and was operated intermittently until the 1909 season. Treadgold acquired control of the company soon after. Later, in May 1912, Joe Boyle began construction of dredges Canadian Numbers 3 and 4 on the ground.

Burrall and Baird, Limited (1921-1933)

A private company, originally controlled by the Gold Fields, Govett and Beatty interests, that took over the assets of Canadian Klondyke Mining Company when that company was foreclosed in September 1921 and operated dredges Canadian Numbers 2, 3 and 4. After February 1925, Burrall and Baird was controlled by A.N.C. Treadgold through The Yukon Consolidated Gold Corporation and was finally consolidated into that company in 1933. For total production of these dredges see YCGC Numbers 2, 3 and 4.

Canadian Klondyke Mining Company, Limited (1905-1921)

Canadian Klondyke operated four Marion dredges; three with 16-cubic-foot buckets were the largest in the Klondike River valley. The company was foreclosed in September 1921, and the three large dredges were taken over by Burrall and Baird, Limited. For total production of these dredges, see YCGC Numbers 1, 2, 3 and 4.

CANADIAN NUMBER 1. 7-cubic-foot buckets; Marion Steam Shovel Company. Built in 1905 near the mouth of Bear Creek. Moved in 1913 to 21 Below on Hunker Creek. Moved in 1920 to 17 Below Lower Discovery on Dominion Creek, where it operated until it was abandoned in 1938. Became North West Number 1 in 1920, YCGC Number 1 in 1935. Some of its machinery was salvaged for use in YCGC Number 11.

CANADIAN NUMBER 2. 15-cubic-foot buckets, soon modified to 16; Marion Steam Shovel Company. Built in 1910 near Bear Creek and operated in the Klondike River valley until 1942. Became YCGC Number 2 in 1935.

CANADIAN NUMBER 3. 16-cubic-foot buckets; Marion Steam Shovel Company. Built in 1912-1913 near the mouth of the Klondike River. Operated in the Klondike River valley from 1913 to 1917 and from 1929 to 1952, except that from 1936 to 1939 it was on Lower Bonanza Creek.

CANADIAN NUMBER 4. 16-cubic-foot buckets; Marion Steam Shovel Company. Built in 1912-1913 near the mouth of the Klondike River. Operated in the Klondike River valley from 1913 to 1940 (except May 1924 to November 1927, when she was left sunk in the dredge pond). Became YCGC Number 4 in 1935. Rebuilt in 1941 on Lower Bonanza Creek and dredged upstream until 1959.

Lewes River Mining and Dredging Company (1901-1908)

DISCOVERY DREDGE. 3¼-cubic-foot buckets and steam-operated; Risdon Iron Works. Assembled in September 1898 at Cassiar Bar on the Yukon River, about 75 miles north of Whitehorse. Brought to Dawson in 1901 and installed at 42 Below on Bonanza Creek. Moved to Discovery group of claims in 1903 and to 6 and 7 Below in 1907; operated until the 1908 season and perhaps even longer. The dredge was brought to Dawson in September 1911 and shipped downriver to the Circle district, Alaska.

North West Corporation, Limited (1920-1921)

Formed in 1913 and for a brief period from 1920 on operated two dredges, originally built for other companies, that had been rebuilt on Dominion Creek ground. Assets of the company passed to New North West Corporation late in 1921. For total production of the two dredges see YCGC Numbers 1 and 5.

New North West Corporation, Limited (1921-1936)

Formed in 1921 to take over the assets of North West Corporation and, in March 1922, those of Canadian Klondyke Power Company. Originally controlled by the Gold Fields, Govett and Beatty interests, but after February 1925, by A.N.C. Treadgold through The Yukon Consolidated Gold Corporation.

Between 1922 and 1935, New North West operated dredges North West Numbers 1 and 2, two Marion dredges that had been built for predecessor companies and were later passed on to successor companies. For total production of these dredges see YCGC Numbers 1 and 5.

NORTH WEST NUMBER 1. 7-cubic-foot buckets; Marion Steam Shovel Company. Built in 1905 as Canadian Number 1. Rebuilt in 1920 as North West Number 1 at 17 Below Lower Discovery on Dominion Creek. Known only briefly as New North West Number 1, it was designated YCGC Number 1 in 1935.

NORTH WEST NUMBER 2. 7-cubic-foot buckets; Marion Steam Shovel Company. Built in 1908 as Yukon Gold Number 4. Rebuilt in 1921 as North West Number 2 at 249 Below Lower Discovery on Dominion Creek. Known only briefly as New North West Number 2, it was designated YCGC Number 5 in 1935.

The Yukon Consolidated Gold Corporation Limited (1925-1966)

YCGC, incorporated in 1923, took over control of Burrall and Baird, Limited and New North West Corporation, Limited in February 1925 although these companies were not consolidated into it until 1933 and 1936, respectively. From 1925 until 1966, when dredging ended, the company operated 12 dredges, although not all at one time. Eight dredges, those numbered 1 through 7 and Number 9, came from predecessor companies. Three were built new in 1938 and 1939. One was bought used in 1953.

YCGC Number 1. 7-cubic-foot buckets; Marion Steam Shovel Company. Formerly Canadian Number 1 and North West Number 1; some of its machinery was later used in YCGC Number 11. Built in 1905 near the mouth of Bear Creek. Moved in 1913 to 21 Below on Hunker Creek. Moved in 1920 to 17 Below Lower Discovery on Dominion Creek, where it dredged upstream until it was abandoned in 1938. In its 34 seasons, from 1905 to 1938, it dredged 15,447,289 cubic yards of ground and recovered $6,549,599 in gold.

YCGC Number 2. 16-cubic-foot buckets; Marion Steam Shovel Company. Formerly Canadian Number 2. Built in 1910 near Bear Creek and operated in the Klondike River valley until 1942. Designated YCGC Number 2 in 1935. From 1910 to 1942, it dredged 48,855,501 cubic yards of ground and recovered $5,135,793 in gold.

YCGC Number 3. 16-cubic-foot buckets; Marion Steam Shovel Company. Formerly Canadian Number 3. Built in 1912-1913 near the mouth of the Klondike River; operated from 1913 to 1917 and from 1929 to 1952. Designated YCGC Number 3 in 1935. It dredged 48,266,723 cubic yards of ground and recovered $6,591,474 in gold.

YCGC Number 4. 16-cubic-foot buckets; Marion Steam Shovel Company. Formerly Canadian Number 4. Built in 1912-1913 near the mouth of the Klondike River. Operated in the Klondike River valley from 1913 to 1940 (except May 1924 to November 1927, when it was left sunk in the dredge pond). Rebuilt in 1941 on Lower Bonanza Creek and dredged upstream until 1959.

Designated YCGC Number 4 in 1935. It dredged 65,559,475 cubic yards of ground and recovered $8,603,553 in gold.

YCGC Number 5. 7-cubic-foot buckets; Marion Steam Shovel Company. Formerly Yukon Gold Number 4 and North West Number 2. Built in 1908 on the Anderson Concession. Moved in 1910 to 41 Below on Hunker Creek. Beginning late in the 1920 season it was moved over Hunker Summit to 249 Below Lower Discovery on Dominion Creek and rebuilt in 1921 as North West Number 2. Designated YCGC Number 5 in 1935. The dredge, idled at the end of the 1942 season by the wartime labor shortage, was destroyed by fire from a lightning strike in 1943. On Dominion Creek, between 1921 and 1942, it dredged 13,700,754 cubic yards of ground and recovered $3,780,891 in gold. Its total production, from 1908 to 1942, was 21,318,880 cubic yards and $6,665,161.

YCGC Number 6. 7-cubic-foot buckets; Bucyrus Manufacturing Company. Formerly Yukon Gold Number 6. Built in 1908 at 90 Below on Bonanza Creek. Moved in 1913 to Gold Run Creek, where it operated until 1923. Rebuilt on Lower Sulphur Creek as YCGC Number 6 in 1936 and operated there until 1966. On Sulphur Creek, between 1936 and 1966, it dredged 22,325,177 cubic yards of ground and recovered $5,703,235 in gold. Its total production, from 1908 to 1966, was 31,903,398 cubic yards and $10,211,001.

YCGC Number 7. 5-cubic-foot buckets; Bucyrus Manufacturing Company. Formerly Yukon Gold Number 1. Built in 1906 on Lower Bonanza Creek. Shut down in 1919. Rebuilt on Quartz Creek as YCGC Number 7 in 1935 and operated there until 1950. On Quartz Creek, between 1935 and 1950, it dredged 7,217,137 cubic yards of ground and recovered $2,725,567 in gold. Its total production, from 1906 to 1950, was 13,326,518 cubic yards and $4,651,837.

YCGC Number 8. 7-cubic-foot buckets; Yuba Manufacturing Company. Built in 1938 at 49 Below on Sulphur Creek and operated on the creek until 1966. It dredged 19,578,477 cubic yards of ground and recovered $8,132,117 in gold.

YCGC Number 9. 5-cubic-foot buckets; Bucyrus Manufacturing Company. Formerly Yukon Gold Number 3. Built in 1906 on Lower Bonanza Creek. Moved to Bear Creek in 1916 and operated until the end of the 1918 season, when it was shut down. Rebuilt on Upper Sulphur Creek in 1938 as YCGC Number 9 and operated on the creek until 1966. On Sulphur Creek, between 1938 and 1966, it dredged 10,274,915 cubic yards of ground and recovered $4,353,175 in gold. Its total production, from 1906 to 1966, was 14,766,476 cubic yards and $7,040,768.

YCGC Number 10. 7-cubic-foot buckets; Yuba Manufacturing Company. Built in 1938-1939 at 10 Below Lower Discovery on Dominion Creek and dredged downstream until the end of the 1964 season. It dredged 18,604,366 cubic yards of ground and recovered $6,837,850 in gold.

YCGC Number 11. 7-cubic-foot buckets; Yuba Manufacturing Company. Built in 1939 at 59 Below on Hunker Creek; some of the machinery from YCGC Number 1 (formerly Canadian Number 1 and then North West Number 1) was used in its construction. It operated on Hunker Creek until 1966. It dredged 21,921,063 cubic yards of ground and recovered $9,598,769 in gold.

YCGC Number 12. 2½-cubic-foot buckets; pontoon-type dredge purchased used in 1953. Operated on Dominion Creek benches from 1954 to 1960 and on another site from 1963 to 1965. It dredged 1,881,200 cubic yards of ground and recovered $1,071,556 in gold.

Yukon Gold Company (1907-1925)

The company and its predecessors operated in the Klondike from 1906 to 1925. Late in 1926, its remaining assets in the Klondike were sold to A.N.C. Treadgold, although the company remained active elsewhere, principally in Malaya. Yukon Gold operated nine dredges. Three were Bucyrus dredges with 5-cubic-foot buckets; the remaining dredges, two by Marion and four by Bucyrus, had 7-cubic-foot buckets. Four of the dredges were dismantled and shipped to Yukon Gold operations in Malaya and elsewhere and four ended up with YCGC.

YUKON GOLD NUMBER 1. 5-cubic-foot buckets; Bucyrus Manufacturing Company. Built in 1906 on Lower Bonanza Creek. Shut down in 1919 after dredging 6,109,381 cubic yards of ground and recovering $1,924,270 in gold. Later, in 1935, it was rebuilt on Quartz Creek as YCGC Number 7 and operated until 1950.

YUKON GOLD NUMBER 2. 5-cubic-foot buckets; Bucyrus Manufacturing Company. Built in 1906 on Lower Bonanza Creek and operated there from 1907 to 1918. It dredged 5,747,219 cubic yards of ground and recovered $3,906,918 in gold. Some of its machinery was later used in a dredge on Highet Creek in the Mayo district of the Yukon.

YUKON GOLD NUMBER 3. 5-cubic-foot buckets; Bucyrus Manufacturing Company. Built in 1906 on Lower Bonanza Creek. Moved in 1916 to Bear Creek and operated there until the end of the 1918 season. In that period it dredged 4,491,561 cubic yards of ground and recovered $2,687,593 in gold. Later, in 1938, it was rebuilt on Upper Sulphur Creek as YCGC Number 9 and operated until 1966.

YUKON GOLD NUMBER 4. 7-cubic-foot buckets; Marion Steam Shovel Company. Built in 1908 on the Anderson Concession. Moved in 1910 to 41 Below on Hunker Creek and operated until 1920, dredging a total of 7,618,126 cubic yards of ground and recovering $2,884,270 in gold during this period. After the 1920 season, it was moved over Hunker Summit to 249 Below Lower Discovery on Dominion Creek and rebuilt as North West Number 2. Designated YCGC Number 5 in 1935; destroyed by fire from a lightning strike in 1943.

YUKON GOLD NUMBER 5. 7-cubic-foot buckets; Bucyrus Manufacturing Company. Built in 1908 on the Anderson Concession. Moved in 1910 to 31 Below on Bonanza Creek; by the end of the 1917 season had dredged upstream to 7 Eldorado Creek. From 1909 to 1917 it dredged 6,714,922 cubic yards of ground and recovered $3,299,814 in gold. Some of its machinery was shipped to Malaya in 1919.

YUKON GOLD NUMBER 6. 7-cubic-foot buckets; Bucyrus Manufacturing Company. Built in 1908 at 90 Below on Bonanza Creek. Moved in 1913 to Gold Run Creek, where it operated until 1923. From 1908 to 1923 it dredged 9,578,221 cubic yards of ground and recovered $4,507,766 in gold. In 1936 it was rebuilt on Lower Sulphur Creek as YCGC Number 6 and operated there until 1966.

YUKON GOLD NUMBER 7. 7-cubic-foot buckets; Marion Steam Shovel Company. Built in 1908 at 36 Below on Hunker Creek and operated until the end of the 1911 season, dredging 1,546,533 cubic yards of ground and recovering $856,460 in gold. Early in 1912 it was dismantled and shipped to a Yukon Gold operation at Iditarod, Alaska.

YUKON GOLD NUMBER 8. 7-cubic-foot buckets and a steel hull; Bucyrus Manufacturing Company. Built in 1911 at 4 Above on Bonanza Creek and operated until the end of the 1917 season when it had worked out its ground. It dredged 4,688,302 cubic yards of ground and recovered $3,365,911 in gold. In 1919, it was dismantled and shipped to the company's operation in Malaya.

YUKON GOLD NUMBER 9. 7-cubic-foot buckets and a steel hull; Bucyrus Manufacturing Company. Built in 1911 at 7 Eldorado Creek; halted in 1915 on 26 Eldorado by a property dispute. It dredged 2,420,066 cubic yards of ground and recovered $1,694,945 in gold. In the winter of 1916-1917 the dredge was dismantled for shipment to a Yukon Gold operation at Murray, Idaho.

Notes

Preface
1. Watt to Newhouse, 22 November 1915, Papers of N. A. Watt, Yukon Archives, Whitehorse.

Chapter One
1. Leroy N. McQuesten, *Recollections of Life in the Yukon*, p. 5, and Allen A. Wright, *Prelude to Bonanza*, p. 127.
2. *Ibid.*, p. 10.
3. R. G. McConnell, "Report on an Exploration in the Yukon and Mackenzie Basins 1887-1888," reprinted in part in *Report 629*, Geological Survey of Canada, p. 243.
4. L. H. Green, *Geology of Nash Creek, Larsen Creek, and Dawson Map-Areas, Yukon Territory*, p. 127.
5. William Ogilvie, *Early Days on the Yukon and the Story of its Gold Finds*, p. 130-131.
6. *Ibid.*, pp. 131-132, 160-161.
7. *Dawson News,* 9 September 1922.
8. Ogilvie, *Early Days*, pp. 160-174.
9. *Ibid.*, p. 213.
10. Pierre Berton, *Klondike*, p. 154.
11. Green, p. 5.
12. Art Downs, *Paddlewheels on the Frontier* Vol. 2, p. 71.
13. Canada, Department of Interior, *The Yukon Territory, 1907*, p. 96.
14. *Klondike Nugget*, 30 September 1899.
15. *Ibid.*, 26 September 1901.
16. David R. Morrison, *The Politics of the Yukon Territory, 1898-1909*, p. 10.
17. Canada, *Sessional Papers*, Number 87 (1899), "Report of the Ogilvie Commission of Inquiry."
18. R. G. McConnell, "Report on the Klondike Gold Fields," *Geological Survey of Canada Annual Report*, pp. 31B-33B.
19. *Dawson News,* 9 and 19 January 1909.
20. Andrew Baird, *Sixty Years on the Klondike*, p. 24.
21. *Ibid.*
22. Ogilvie, *Early Days*, pp. 233-235. T. A. Rickard, "Dredging in the Yukon," *Mining and Scientific Press* 97(1908):290-293, 354-357.

23. Canada, *Sessional Papers,* Number 142 (1904), "Report of the Britton Commission on an Inquiry Into the Treadgold and Other Concessions in the Yukon Territory," p. 34.
24. Jeremiah Lynch, *Three Years in the Klondike*, pp. 181-183.
25. Canada, Department of Interior, *The Yukon Territory, 1907*, p. 18.
26. Francis Cunynghame, *Lost Trail*, p. 36.

Chapter Two
1. David R. Morrison, *The Politics of the Yukon Territory, 1898-1909*, p. 14.
2. *Klondike Nugget,* 15 November 1899.
3. Privy Council, Number 22, 12 January 1898.
4. Canada, *Sessional Papers.* Number 142 (1904) "Report of the Britton Commission on an Inquiry Into the Treadgold and Other Concessions in the Yukon Territory," p. 30.
5. *Ibid.*, p. 17.
6. Francis Cunynghame, *Lost Trail,* pp. 14-17 and p. 24.
7. *Yukon World, 24 July 1907. Dawson News, 2 September 1903.*
8. Treadgold to Sifton, 9 May 1898, Papers of Sir Clifford Sifton, vol. 54, p. 37034, Public Archives of Canada, Ottawa.
9. One article, dated Dawson, 5 August 1898, is credited to Treadgold in *The Manchester Guardian* of 20 September 1898 and also in *The Mining Journal* of 1 October 1898. Other articles that appear to be Treadgold's are one, dated Lake Bennett 8 June 1898, in the *Guardian* of 11 August 1898 and another dated Dawson 10 August 1898, in *The Mining Journal* of 8 October 1898. Both publications carry other reports on the Klondike, but some of the reports, at least, seem to be by other correspondents.
10. R. G. McConnell and J. B. Tyrrell, "Preliminary Note on the Gold Deposits and Gold Mining in the Klondike Region," *Geological Survey of Canada Annual Report,* vol. 11

(1898) part A, p. 40A.
11. J. B. Tyrrell, "Dalton Trail, from Haines, Alaska, to Carmacks, on Lewes River, and Exploration of Nisling River," *Geological Survey of Canada Annual Report,* vol. 11 (1898) part A, p. 41A.
12. *The Mining Journal,* 5 November 1898.
13. Treadgold to Smart, 13 October 1898, Sifton Papers, vol. 54, p. 37035.
14. *Toronto Globe,* 31 October 1898.
15. Morrison, p. 15.
16. Treadgold to Sifton, 26 December 1898, Sifton Papers, vol. 54, pp. 37037-37041.
17. Treadgold to Sifton, 30 May 1899, Sifton Papers, vol. 73, pp. 54569-54570. The period ending the first sentence (". . . Klondike itself.") was not in the original.
18. Treadgold to Sifton, 17 and 27 September 1899, Sifton Papers, vol. 73, pp. 54571-54582.
19. Barwick to Sifton, 17 October 1899, Sifton Papers, vol. 56, pp. 39509-39510.
20. Treadgold to Sifton, 2 February 1900, Sifton Papers, vol. 90, pp. 70028-70029.
21. Treadgold to Sifton, 17 July 1900, Sifton Papers, vol. 90, p. 70030.
22. Sutherland to Sifton, 29 September 1900, Sifton Papers, vol. 89, p. 69846.
23. Treadgold to Sifton, 9 June 1903, Sifton Papers, vol. 151, p. 121081.
24. Canada, *Sessional Papers,* Number 63 (1903), "Correspondence, Orders in Council or Applications Relating to or Concerning the Grant or Concessions to A.N.C. Treadgold, or to the Hydraulic Mining Syndicate, . . ." p. 1. Emphasis added.

Chapter Three
1. Canada, *Sessional Papers,* Number 63 (1903), "Correspondence, Orders in Council or Applications Relating to or Concerning the Grant or Concessions to A.N.C. Treadgold, or to the Hydraulic Mining Syndicate . . . ." p. 3.

2. *Klondike Nugget,* 3 August 1901.
3. Canada, *Sessional Papers,* Number 63 (1903), pp. 4-5.
4. *Klondike Nugget,* 25 September 1901.
5. *Ibid.,* 16 and 17 October 1901.
6. *Ibid.,* 12 February 1902.
7. Canada, *Sessional Papers,* Number 63 (1903) pp. 5-7.
8. *Klondike Nugget,* 14 February 1902.
9. *Yukon Sun,* 16 February 1902. In Canada *Sessional Papers,* Number 63 (1903), p. 17.
10. Canada, *Sessional Papers,* Number 63 (1903), pp. 18-19.
11. *Klondike Nugget,* 18 February 1902.
12. *Ibid.,* 20 February 1902.
13. *Ibid.,* 22 February 1902.
14. *Ibid.,* 24 February 1902.
15. *Ibid.,* 27 February 1902.
16. *Ibid.,* 1 March 1902.
17. *Ibid.,* 3 March 1902.
18. *Ibid.,* 19, 24 and 25 March 1902.
19. Canada *Sessional Papers,* Number 63 (1903), p. 20.
20. *Klondike Nugget,* 17 and 18 April 1902.
21. *Ibid.,* 18 April 1902.
22. *Yukon Sun,* 22 April 1902.
23. *Klondike Nugget* and *Dawson News,* 22 April 1902.
24. *Yukon Sun,* 1 May 1902.
25. *Dawson News,* 18 April 1902.
26. *Klondike Nugget,* 1 May 1902.
27. *Dawson News,* 1 May 1902.
28. *Ibid.,* 6 May 1902.
29. *Ibid.,* 19 May 1902.
30. *Ibid.,* 4 June 1902.
31. *Ibid.,* 24 June 1902.
32. *Ibid.,* 27 August 1902. *Klondike Nugget,* 28 August 1902.
33. *Dawson News,* 11 October 1902.
34. *Ibid.,* 2 September 1902.
35. *Ibid.,* 10 September 1902.
36. Smart to Sifton, 15 September 1902, Papers of Sir Clifford Sifton, vol. 133, p. 10621, Public Archives of Canada, Ottawa.
37. *Dawson News,* 11 October 1902.
38. *Ibid.,* 22 October 1902.
39. *Yukon Sun,* 28 November 1902.
40. *Dawson News,* 21 May 1902.

Chapter Four
1. *Klondike Nugget,* 6 March 1903.
2. *Ibid.,* 9 March 1903.
3. *Ibid.*
4. *Ibid.,* 11 March 1903.
5. *Ibid.,* 20 March 1903.
6. *Ibid.,* 24 March 1903.
7. *Yukon Sun,* 22 March 1903.
8. *Klondike Nugget,* 6 April 1903.
9. Canada, House of Commons, *Debates,* 12 May 1903, col. 2822.
10. *Ibid.,* col. 2847.
11. *Klondike Nugget,* 9 April 1903.
12. *Dawson News,* 1 April 1903.
13. *Ibid.,* 10-18 April 1903.
14. *Klondike Nugget,* 13 April 1903.
15. *Ibid.,* 21 April 1903.
16. *Yukon Sun,* 13 May 1903.
17. *Ibid.*
18. Canada, House of Commons, *Debates,* 12 May 1903, cols. 2826 to 2915.
19. Treadgold to Sifton, 27 May 1903, Papers of Sir Clifford Sifton, vol. 151, pp. 121075-121076, Public Archives of Canada, Ottawa.
20. Orr Ewing, Treadgold and Collinson to Laurier, 2 June 1903, Sifton Papers, vol. 151, p. 121078.
21. Laurier to Treadgold et al, Sifton Papers, vol. 151, p. 121098.
22. Treadgold et al to Sifton, 9 June 1903, Sifton Papers, vol. 151, pp. 121080-121103.
23. Canada, House of Commons, *Debates,* 11 June 1903, col. 4541.
24. *Klondike Nugget,* 28 May 1903.
25. *Dawson News,* 4 October 1904.
26. Canada, *Sessional Papers,* Number 142 (1904), "Report of the Britton Commission on an Inquiry Into the Treadgold and Other Concessions in the Yukon Territory," p. 5.
27. *Yukon Sun,* 23 August 1903 .
28. *Ibid.*
29. *Dawson Record,* 23 August 1903.
30. *Dawson News,* 23 August 1903.
31. *Ibid.,* 23 November 1905.
32. *Ibid.*
33. *Ibid.,* 29 August 1903.
34. R. G. McConnell, and J. B. Tyrrell, "Preliminary Note on the Gold Deposits and Gold Mining in the Klondike Region," *Geological Survey of Canada Annual Report,* vol. 11

(1898) part A, p. 57A.
35. *Dawson News,* 28 August 1903.
36. *Ibid.,* 27 August 1903.
37. *Ibid.,* 2 September 1903.
38. *Ibid.,* 4 September 1903.
39. *Dawson Record,* 9 September 1903.
40. *Yukon Sun,* 12 September 1903.
41. Canada, House of Commons, *Debates,* 11 September 1903, col. 11078.
42. *Ibid.,* col. 11077.
43. *Dawson News,* 22 September 1903.
44. *Ibid.,* 24 March 1904.
45. *Yukon Sun,* 25 September 1903.
46. *Dawson News,* 24 September 1903.
47. *Dawson Record,* 20 September 1903.
48. *Dawson News,* 18 July 1904.
49. Canada, House of Commons, *Debates,* 29 June 1904, col. 5762.
50. *Dawson News,* 9 July 1904.
51. Canada, *Sessional Papers,* Number 142 (1904).

Chapter Five
1. *Yukon World,* 26 August 1904.
2. *Dawson News,* 28 March 1905.
3. *Dawson News* 18 May 1903. *Dawson Record,* 18 October 1903. *Dawson News,* 12 August 1904.
4. *Dawson News,* 8 March 1905.
5. *Ibid.,* 1 October 1904.
6. *Klondike Nugget,* 27 February 1902.
7. *Dawson News,* 22 July 1905.
8. *Ibid.,* 29 August 1905.
9. *Ibid.,* 1 November 1905.
10. *Ibid.,* 19 March 1906.
11. *Ibid.,* 3 April 1906.
12. *Ibid.,* 30 March and 3 April 1906.
13. *Ibid.,* 28 June 1906.
14. *Ibid.,* 24 July 1906.
15. *Ibid.,* 24 April 1906.
16. Canada, Department of Interior, *The Yukon Territory, 1907,* p. 55.
17. *Dawson News,* 6 October 1906.
18. *Ibid.,* 8 August 1906.
19. *Ibid.,* 11 August 1906.
20. *Ibid.,* 19 November 1906.
21. *Ibid.,* 28 November 1906.
22. *Yukon World,* 25 April 1907.
23. *Dawson News,* 16 August 1907.
24. *Ibid.,* 14 March 1908.
25. *Yukon World,* 11 May 1907.
26. *Ibid.,* 30 May 1907.

27. T. A. Rickard, "Dredging in the Yukon," *Mining and Scientific Press* 97(1908):290-293, 354-357.
28. *Ibid.* Also: E. E. McCarthy, "Stripping Frozen Gravel," *The Mining Magazine* 10(1914):289-295. Henry M. Payne, "The Development and Problem of the Yukon," *Transactions of the Canadian Mining Institute* 16(1913):228-240, and "Further Notes on Yukon Mining Problems," *Transactions of the Canadian Mining Institute* 20(1917):188-206. O. B. Perry, "Development of Dredging in the Yukon Territory," *Transaction of the Canadian Mining Institute* 18(1915): 26-44.
29. *Ibid.*
30. Canada, Department of Interior, *The Yukon Territory, 1907,* pp.57-58.
31. T. A. Rickard, "Mechanical Elevator," *Mining and Scientific Press* 98(1909):415-418.
32. *Dawson News,* 21 June 1907, 3 April 1908.
33. *Ibid.,* 20 July 1907.
34. *Ibid.,* 19 November 1907.
35. *Ibid.,* 23 December 1907.
36. *Ibid.,* 14 July 1905.
37. *Ibid.,* 6 February 1908.
38. *New York Times,* 24 March 1908.
39. *Ibid.,* 25 March 1908.
40. *Ibid.,* 26 March 1908.
41. *Ibid.,* 27 March 1908.
42. *Ibid.*
43. *Ibid.,* 29 March 1908.
44. *Ibid.,* 30 March 1908.
45. *Dawson News,* 1 April 1908.
46. *New York Times,* 1 April 1908.
47. *Wall Street Journal,* in Edwin P. Hoyt Jr., *The Guggenheims and the American Dream,* p. 190.
48. *New York Times,* 6 and 7 April 1908.
49. *Ibid.,* 4 August 1908.
50. *Dawson News,* 23 and 30 June, 6 July and 21 August 1908.
51. *Ibid.,* 25 July 1919.
52. T. A. Rickard, "The Yukon Ditch," *Mining and Scientific Press* 98(1909):117-120, 148-152.
53. *Dawson News,* 29 September 1908.
54. *Ibid.,* 10 October 1908.
55. *Ibid., Yukon World,* 23 and 24 July 1907.
56. *Yukon World,* 8 August 1907.
57. *Dawson News,* 18 September 1907.
58. *Ibid.,* 12 and 14 January and 4 and 24 March 1909.
59. *Ibid.,* 7, 10 and 12 May 1909.
60. *Ibid.,* 21 September 1909.
61. *Ibid.,* 5 January 1910.
62. *Ibid.,* 27 April 1911.
63. *Ibid.,* 24 and 27 February 1913.
64. Eudora Bundy Ferry, *Yukon Gold,* pp. 125-129. *Dawson News,* 16-25 July 1913.
65. Andrew Baird, *Sixty Years on the Klondike,* pp. 71-72. *Dawson News,* 21 March 1912.
66. Baird, p. 72. *Dawson News,* 30 December 1916.
67. Baird, pp. 71-72. *Dawson News,* 30 April and 7 August 1918 and 27 August 1919.
68. Baird, p. 71. *Dawson News,* 7 August 1918.
69. Canadian Klondyke Mining Company, Reports, Letters, Options etc., 1918, Records of the Yukon Consolidated Gold Corporation Limited, vol. 60, Public Archives of Canada, Ottawa.
70. *Dawson News,* 14 October 1922 .
71. *Ibid.,* 15 October 1918.
72. Baird, p. 70. *Dawson News,* 22 September 1919.
73. Baird, p. 71. *Dawson News,* 21 September 1920.
74. *Dawson News,* 22 December 1925.
75. *Ibid.,* 11 March and 15 April 1926.
76. *Ibid.,* 5 April 1927.
77. Baird, p. 25. Yukon Gold Company *Annual Reports.*

Chapter Six

1. *Dawson News, Dawson Record,* and *Yukon Sun,* 1 and 2 September 1903.
2. *Dawson Record,* 2 September 1903.
3. Sutherland to Sifton, 9 March 1898, Papers of Sir Clifford Sifton, vol. 53, p. 36641, Public Archives of Canada, Ottawa.
4. Boyle to Guerin, 18 April 1898, Sifton Papers, vol. 39, pp. 25944-25946.
5. Guerin to Boyle, 22 April 1898, Sifton Papers, vol. 43, p. 28947.

6. Boyle to Sifton, 22 April 1898, Sifton Papers, vol. 39, pp. 25947-25950.
7. *Dawson Record,* 2 September 1903.
8. *Ibid. Yukon Sun,* 2 September 1903.
9. *Klondike Nugget,* 24 May 1899. *Yukon Sun,* 2 September 1903.
10. *Dawson Record,* 26 September 1903.
11. Boyle to Sifton, 13 August 1898, Sifton Papers, vol. 39, pp. 25951-25953. On McGiverin's stationery. McGiverin to Sifton, 13 August 1898, Sifton papers, vol. 48, p. 32262. Sutherland to Sifton, 12 August 1898, Sifton Papers, vol. 53, pp. 36653-36655.
12. *Dawson News,* 7-8 December 1905. Canada, *Sessional Papers,* Number 142 (1904), "Report of the Britton Commission on an Inquiry Into the Treadgold and Other Concessions in the Yukon Territory," pp. 23-25.
13. *Yukon Sun,* 1 September 1903.
14. *Ibid.,* 30 August 1903.
15. Martha Louise Black, *My Ninety Years* (c1976), p. 117. Mrs. George Black, *My Seventy Years* (c1938), pp. 258-259. *Dawson News,* 17 July 1903 and 5 July 1904.
16. *Klondike Nugget,* 25 November 1899 and 28 June 1901.
17. Smart to Sifton, 15 September 1902, Sifton Papers, vol. 133, p. 106198.
18. Treadgold to Sifton, 26 July 1902, Sifton Papers, vol. 135, p. 107362.
19. Smart to Sifton, 15 September 1902, Sifton Papers, vol. 133, p. 106198.
20. Welch letter, *Dawson News,* 8 August 1904.
21. *Dawson News,* March to May 1904.
22. *Ibid.,* 16 June 1904.
23. Tancred to Sifton, 4 December 1903, Sifton Papers, vol. 151, pp. 120892-120901.
24. *Dawson News,* 21 June 1904.
25. *Whitehorse Star,* 26 July 1904. Picked up in *Dawson News,* 2 August 1904.
26. *Dawson News,* 9 July 1904.
27. Treadgold to Sifton, 23 November 1904, Sifton Papers, vol. 174, pp. 141614-141618.
28. Treadgold to Sifton, 4 December 1904, Sifton Papers, vol. 174,

pp. 141622-141624.
29. Corporate Records, Secretary of State, Canada, 5 October 1904, no. 46, lib. 182, fol. 181, Public Archives of Canada, Ottawa.
30. *Dawson News,* 11 November 1907.
31. *Ibid.,* 12 December 1904; 12, 14, 17 and 28 January, 7 and 12 February, 4 March and 18 April 1905.
32. *Ibid.,* 12 April 1905.
33. *Ibid.,* 12 and 14 August 1905.
34. *Ibid.,* 3 September 1908.
35. *Ibid.,* 10 April 1906.
36. *Ibid.,* 27 July and 9 September 1906.
37. *Ibid.,* 11 May and 2 July 1906.
38. *Ibid.,* 3 April 1907.
39. *Ibid.,* 16 and 17 July 1907.
40. *Ibid.,* 7 October 1907. Burrall and Baird, Balance Sheets 1905-1931, Records of The Yukon Consolidated Gold Corporation Limited, vol. 58, Public Archives of Canada, Ottawa.
41. *Dawson News,* 11 November 1907.
42. *Ibid.,* 25 November 1907.
43. *Ibid.,* 27 March 1908.
44. *Ibid.,* 30 March 1908.
45. *Ibid.,* 2 June 1908.
46. *Ibid.,* 12 June 1908.
47. *Ibid.,* 4 May 1909.
48. *Ibid.,* 18 June 1909.
49. *Ibid.,* 21 September 1909.
50. *Ibid.,* 24 September 1909.
51. *Ibid.,* 1 and 16 November 1909.
52. *Ibid.,* 25 November 1909.
53. *Ibid.,* 22 December 1909.
54. *Ibid.,* 19 March 1910.
55. *Ibid.,* 29 August 1910.
56. *Ibid.,* 5 November 1910.
57. Burrall and Baird, Balance Sheets for 1905-1931, Records of YCGC, vol. 58, Public Archives of Canada, Ottawa.
58. *Ibid.*
59. *Dawson News,* 22 August 1910.

Chapter Seven
1. Andrew Baird, *Sixty Years on the Klondike,* p. 86. Francis Cunynghame, *Lost Trail,* p. 62.
2. *Yukon World,* 24 July 1907. Treadgold to Sifton, 23 November 1904, Papers of Sir Clifford Sifton, vol. 174, pp. 141614-141618, Public Archives of Canada, Ottawa.

3. *Dawson News,* 23 and 25 November 1914.
4. *Ibid.,* 11 November 1909.
5. *Ibid.,* 1 April 1910.
6. *Ibid.,* 15 September 1909.
7. *Ibid.,* 5 September 1910.
8. *Ibid.,* 29 April 1910.
9. *Ibid.,* 24 September 1910.
10. *Ibid.,* 24 November 1910.
11. *Ibid.,* 17 February 1911.
12. *Ibid.,* 8 May 1911.
13. *Mining Magazine* 5 (1911):88 and 165.
14. *Dawson News,* 6 September 1911.
15. *Ibid.,* 4 August 1911.
16. *Ibid.,* 22 December 1911.
17. *Ibid.,* 30 March 1912.
18. *Ibid.,* 3 September 1912.
19. *Ibid.*
20. Granville Mining Company, Granville Mining versus Canadian Klondyke Mining, Exhibits 1904-1917, Records of The Yukon Consolidated Gold Corporation Limited, vol. 63, Public Archives of Canada, Ottawa.
21. *Dawson News,* 6 July 1912.
22. *Ibid.,* 17 and 24 August 1912.
23. *Ibid.,* 31 May 1912.
24. *Ibid.,* 6 September 1912.
25. *Ibid.,* 14 September 1912.
26. *Ibid.,* 22 October 1912.
27. *Ibid.*
28. *Ibid.,* 22 May 1913.
29. *Ibid.,* 11 September 1912.
30. *Ibid.,* 13 July 1912.
31. Granville Mining Company, Granville Mining versus Canadian Klondyke Mining, Exhibits 1904-1917, Records of YCGC, vol. 63.
32. Cunynghame, p. 70.
33. *Dawson News,* 15 November and 23 December 1913.
34. *Mining Magazine* 9 (1913):240.
35. Cunynghame, p. 71.
36. *Dawson News,* 12 September 1913.
37. *Ibid.,* 15 November 1913.
38. *Ibid.,* 17 March 1914.
39. *Ibid.,* 20 January 1915.
40. *Ibid.,* 11 July 1914.
41. *Ibid.,* 11 March 1915.
42. North West Corporation, *Report of Proceedings,* First Annual General Meeting, 1 July 1915.
43. *Dawson News,* 11 July 1914, 31 July 1915 and 17 August 1917.
44. *Ibid.,* 1 December 1915.
45. *Ibid.,* 17 October 1916.
46. Granville Mining Company, Letters etc., 1917, Records of YCGC, vol. 63.
47. Cunynghame, p. 74.
48. *Ibid.,* p. 77.

Chapter Eight

1. Burrall and Baird, Balance Sheets 1905-1931, Records of The Yukon Consolidated Gold Corporation Limited, vol. 58, Public Archives of Canada, Ottawa.
2. Corporate Records, Secretary of State, Canada, no. 48, lib. 223, fol. 75, Public Archives of Canada, Ottawa.
3. *Ibid.,* no. 24, lib. 232, fol. 4.
4. *Ibid.,* no. 21, lib. 213, fol. 264.
5. *Dawson News,* 28 May 1912.
6. *Ibid.,* 12 July 1912.
7. *Ibid.,* 3 and 17 August 1912.
8. The South Fork Ditch might more accurately be called the "Klondike Ditch," because it draws water from the main branch of the Klondike River, well west of the region where it is known as the South Fork. However, the old-timers call the ditch the South Fork Ditch, and the name is also used in reports on the Canadian Klondike companies.
9. *Dawson News,* 30 August 1912.
10. *Ibid.,* 11 September 1912.
11. *Whitehorse Star,* 27 December 1912.
12. *Dawson News,* 2 January 1913.
13. *Ibid.,* 15 February 1913.
14. *Ibid.,* 25 August 1910.
15. *Ibid.,* 25 April 1913.
16. *Ibid.,* 5 May 1913.
17. *Ibid.,* 10 May 1913.
18. *Ibid.,* 20 May 1913.
19. *Ibid.,* 23 and 28 June 1910.
20. *Ibid.,* 6 May 1913.
21. Yukon Gold Company, Reports, Letters etc., 1914, Records of YCGC, vol. 67.
22. Yukon Gold Company, Reports, Letters etc., 1913, Boyle to S. R. Guggenheim, 20 March 1913, Records of YCGC, vol. 67.
23. *Dawson News,* 28 February 1913.
24. *Ibid.,* 1 April 1913.

25. *Ibid.,* 13 November 1913.
26. *Ibid.,* 23 and 24 November 1914.
27. *Ibid.,* 5 May 1917.
28. *Ibid.,* 19 November 1917.
29. Laura Beatrice Berton, *I Married the Klondike,* pp. 42-46. Eudora Bundy Ferry, *Yukon Gold,* pp. 20-21.
30. Letter from R. J. Shrimpton to bondholders of Northern Light, Power and Coal Company at a meeting at London, 12 November 1914. Author's collection.
31. *Dawson News,* 29 August 1913.
32. *Ibid.,* 17 and 18 October 1913.
33. *Ibid.,* 18 October 1913.
34. *Ibid.,* 30 October 1913.
35. *Ibid.,* 5-14 November 1913.
36. *Ibid.,* 17 March 1914.
37. Emil Edward Hurja, "Mining in the Far North: Operations of Canadian-Klondyke Gold Mining Company, Ltd," *Mining and Scientific Press* 109 (1914):769-771.
38. *Dawson News,* 7 November 1913.
39. *Ibid.,* 16 June 1914.
40. *Ibid.,* 29 July 1914.
41. *Ibid.,* 10 December 1917 and 13 June 1918.
42. The Yukon Consolidated Gold Corporation Limited, *Annual Report for 1966.*
43. *Dawson News,* 7 October 1914.
44. *Ibid.,* 12 October 1914.
45. *Ibid.,* 23 August 1919.
46. *Ibid.,* 7 and 21 July 1915.
47. *Mining Magazine* 15 (1916):125.
48. *Dawson News,* 15 July, 2 and 4 August 1915, 25 July and 12 September 1916.
49. Watt to Newhouse, October-November 1915, Papers of N. A. Watt, Yukon Archives, Whitehorse. *Dawson News,* October-November 1915.
50. Burrall and Baird, Balance Sheets 1905-1931, Records of YCGC, vol. 58.
51. *Dawson News,* 22 February 1916.
52. Watt to Newhouse, 11 February 1916, Watt Papers.
53. *Dawson News,* 27 May 1916.
54. *Ibid.,* 29 March 1916.
55. *Ibid.,* 1 June 1916.
56. *Ibid.,* 30 June 1916.
57. *Ibid.,* 9 June 1916.
58. Martha Louise Black, *My Ninety Years* (c1976), p. 118. Mrs. George Black, *My Seventy Years* (c1938), p. 260. Walter R. Hamilton, *The Yukon Story,* p. 242.
59. *Dawson News,* 17-18 July 1916.
60. *Vancouver Province,* 27 July 1916.
61. Harold Gordon Blankman. *First Annual Report of the Receiver and Manager of the Canadian Klondyke Mining Co., Ltd., and the Canadian Klondyke Power Co., Ltd., for the term ending December 31, 1918,* p. 25.
62. *Ibid.,* p. 2.
63. *Ibid.,* p. 25.
64. *Dawson News,* 19 November 1917.
65. *Victoria Times,* 26 January 1918.
66. *Ibid.*

Chapter Nine

1. Harold Gordon Blankman, *First Annual Report of the Receiver and Manager of the Canadian Klondyke Mining Co., Ltd., and the Canadian Klondyke Power Co., Ltd., for the term ending December 31, 1918,* p. 2.
2. *Dawson News,* 28 February 1918.
3. *Ibid.,* 14 March 1918.
4. *Ibid.,* 24 June 1918.
5. Blankman, pp. 22-23.
6. *Dawson News,* 1 May 1919.
7. *Ibid.,* 21 April 1919.
8. *Ibid.,* 15 July 1919.
9. *Ibid.,* 17 and 22 September 1919.
10. *Ibid.,* 11 November 1919.
11. Canadian Klondyke Mining Company, Reports, Liabilities, Letters, Foreclosures etc., 1921, Records of The Yukon Consolidated Gold Corporation Limited, vol. 60, Public Archives of Canada, Ottawa.
12. Canadian Klondyke Mining Company, Accounts and Company Records, 1917, Records of YCGC, vol. 60.
13. North West Corporation, Letters, Wires etc., 1917, part 2, Burrall to Dexter, 17 July 1917, Records of YCGC, vol. 55.
14. *Dawson News,* 1 May 1919.
15. Francis Cunynghame, *Lost Trail,* p. 75.
16. *Dawson News,* 8 September 1919.
17. *Ibid.,* 8 and 25 March 1920.

18. *Ibid.,* 29 November 1920.
19. *Ibid.,* 30 April 1920.
20. *Ibid.,* 7 June 1920.
21. *Ibid.,* 2 February and 2 and 22 July 1921.
22. *Ibid.,* 26 September 1921. Canadian Klondyke Mining Company, Reports, Liabilities, Letters, Foreclosures etc., 1921, Records of YCGC, vol. 60.
23. Canadian Klondyke Mining Company, Reports, Liabilities, Letters, Foreclosures etc., 1921, Records of YCGC, vol. 60. North West Corporation, Annual Accounts 1927-1933, Records of YCGC, vol. 53.
24. *Dawson News,* 24 January 1923.
25. Patton versus Yukon, Supreme Court, Toronto, 21-23 June 1933, Transcript, vol. 8, p. 2557, Records of YCGC, vol. 77.
26. *Dawson News,* 28 March and 9 April 1923.
27. Cunynghame, p. 79.
28. *Dawson News,* 13 March 1923.
29. *Ibid.,* 21 April 1924.
30. *Ibid.,* 21 May 1924.
31. *Ibid.,* 28 April 1925.
32. Andrew Baird, *Sixty Years on the Klondike,* p. 88.
33. North West Corporation, Letters, Wires etc., 1925-1926, Records of YCGC, vol. 55.

Chapter Ten

1. *Dawson News,* 12 June 1923.
2. *Ibid.,* 7 July 1925.
3. C. Gloslie, personal communication.
4. J. W. Hoggan, personal communication.
5. *Dawson News,* 10 and 29 September and 8 October 1925.
6. J. W. Hoggan, personal communication.
7. *Dawson News,* 24 November and 15 December 1925.
8. *Ibid.,* 15 December 1925.
9. Francis Cunynghame, *Lost Trail,* pp. 95-96.
10. *Dawson News,* 11 February 1926.
11. Cunynghame, pp. 102-103.
12. Clarkson Investigation, Exhibit 149, Records of The Yukon Consolidated Gold Corporation Limited, vol. 70,

Public Archives of Canada, Ottawa.
13. North West Corporation, *Annual Report 1925-1926,* Records of YCGC, vol. 53.
14. Burrall and Baird, Auditor's Report 1926, Records of YCGC, vol. 58.
15. Mrs. J. F. Sealey, personal communication.
16. Treadgold-Patton Litigation, Old Telegrams 1918-1932, Records of YCGC, vol. 82.
17. *Dawson News,* 16 and 26 April and 8 October 1927.
18. *Ibid.,* 24 March, 3 May and 17 November 1927.
19. Clarkson Investigation, Exhibit 149, Records of YCGC, vol. 70.
20. *Dawson News,* 2 August 1927.
21. J. W. Hoggan, personal communication.
22. *Ibid.*
23. *Dawson News,* 24, 26 and 29 November 1927.
24. *Ibid.,* 1 December 1928.
25. Treadgold-Patton Litigation, Old Telegrams 1918-1932, Records of YCGC, vol. 82.
26. Treadgold-Patton Litigation, Treadgold Circulars 1931-1933, Records of YCGC, vol. 82.
27. *Princess Louise* is now moored at Terminal Island, Los Angeles, where she is in use as a floating restaurant.
28. Andrew Baird, *Sixty Years on the Klondike,* p. 87.
29. J. W. Hoggan, personal communication.
30. Baird, p. 89.
31. *Dawson News,* 16 December 1929 and 28 January 1930.

Chapter Eleven

1. Francis Cunynghame, *Lost Trail,* pp. 77 and 105-111.
2. *Ibid.,* pp. 109-111.
3. Patton versus Yukon, Examination for Discovery of J. T. Patton, 5 March 1931, Records of The Yukon Consolidated Gold Corporation Limited, vol. 72, Public Archives of Canada, Ottawa. *Dawson News,* 5 and 26 September 1916.
4. J. T. Patton 1917-1919, Records of YCGC, vol. 51. Patton versus

Yukon, Examination for Discovery of J. T. Patton, 5 March 1931, Records of YCGC, vol. 72.

5. Patton versus Yukon, Supreme Court, Toronto, 12-14 June 1933, Transcript, vol. 5, pp. 1225-1266, Records of YCGC, vol. 76.
6. Cunynghame, pp. 88 and 109.
7. Patton versus Yukon, Examination of Witnesses, 24 June 1931, Records of YCGC, vol. 72.
8. Patton versus Yukon, Supreme Court, Toronto, 12-14 June 1933, Transcript, vol. 5, pp. 1225-1266, Records of YCGC, vol. 76.
9. Cunynghame, pp. 104 and 112-118.
10. *Ibid.*, p. 120.
11. Clarkson Investigation, Records of YCGC, vol. 69-70.
12. *Dawson News,* 26 April 1932.
13. Cunynghame, p. 122.
14. Treadgold-Patton Litigation, Treadgold Circulars, 1931-1933, Records of YCGC, vol. 82.
15. *Ibid.*
16. *Ibid.*
17. *Ibid.*
18. Clarkson Investigation, Exhibit 149, Records of YCGC, vol. 70.
19. YCGC letter to shareholders, 10 February 1932.
20. *Ibid.* Report of Annual General Meeting, 9 November 1932.
21. Andrew Baird, *Sixty Years on the Klondike,* p. 89.
22. H. S. Bostock, *Yukon Territory,* p. 633.
23. Cunynghame, pp. 124-126.
24. *Ibid.*, pp. 129-131.
25. *Ibid.*, pp. 127-128.
26. *Dawson News,* 22, 25 and 27 July 1933.
27. In his judgment, Mr. Justice Davis gave his interpretation of some of the more important facets of the consolidation, as reported in the *Dawson News* of 22, 25 and 27 July 1933:

First there were the transactions through which YCGC acquired four parcels: one, the Beatty interest; two, the Govett interest; three, the Gold Fields interest; and four, the Harrison and Patton interests which, taken altogether, gave almost full control of what had been the Burrall and Baird

and New North West companies. At a meeting of the YCGC Board of Directors held in the office of the Chrysler law firm in Ottawa on 11 February 1925, Treadgold recited an offer from North Fork Power Company to sell the four parcels to YCGC for 3,750,000 shares of YCGC.

At the time, the directors, three of them members of the Chrysler firm, each held one of the five issued shares of YCGC. North Fork, an old company dating back to 1911 with neither assets nor liabilities, was controlled by Treadgold; in the judge's opinion, it was Treadgold's *alias.* The four parcels, collected by the E. Y. Syndicate (a small company formed by Treadgold's backers for that purpose in late 1922) and also by individuals, had been transferred to North Fork through various powers of attorney held by Treadgold.

Davis was satisfied that the first three parcels represented at least seven-eighths of the value of the securities involved. Shares were set out against the Beatty and Govett parcels reflecting the agreements with those parties. The Gold Fields agreement had been for £60,000 cash but shares had also been alloted to it. Parcel four, the Harrison and Patton interests, had a much larger number of shares, both ordinary and preferred, set against it. Davis concluded that the Harrison interest was worth little or nothing but, despite this, felt bound to accept a previous court decision which had placed it at 6,667 preferred and 156,333 common shares. The Patton agreement, covering only the Anderson Concession, called for £15,000 cash and 75,000 preferred shares of YCGC.

At the 11 February 1925 Directors' meeting, Treadgold had recommended acceptance of the North Fork offer for the sale of the four parcels. Later the same day, at a meeting of the five YCGC shareholders (each with one share), Treadgold again recited the advantages of the proposed transaction with North Fork. A year later, in February 1926, the

YCGC meeting was told that the parcel four (Harrison and Patton) interests had been received but those of parcels one, two and three had not yet been delivered and would have to be dealt with differently. Subsequently, Treadgold had taken a million shares of YCGC in the name of Harrison and a further million in his own name. On his return to England the one million Harrison shares were returned to J. B. Watson, an Ottawa accountant who was Secretary-Treasurer of YCGC, with instructions to issue 750,000 shares in the name of E. M. Williamson, a New York stockbroker and a nominee of Treadgold, and 250,000 in Treadgold's name.

Other parcels were later passed through North Fork and conveyed to YCGC in return for shares of that company. These included the Granville Mining assets, exchanged in agreements of 9 and 12 July 1929 for 1,788,900 common shares, and, on 16 July 1929, a parcel that included Yukon Gold Company's assets in the Klondike for 2 million shares—although in the latter case the shares had never been issued. Davis was satisfied that the securities that had been passed through North Fork were in fact already the property of YCGC, paid for by its own money or by exchange of its own shares.

28. The Yukon Consolidated Gold Corporation Limited, *Annual Report for 1935.*
29. Clark Action, Reasons for Judgment, 26 September 1936, Records of YCGC vol. 68.
30. YCGC *Annual Report for 1938.*
31. *Dawson News,* 5 April 1934.
32. Cunynghame, p. 149.
33. *Ibid.,* p. 150.
34. *Ibid.,* pp. 156-159.
35. *Ibid.,* p. 80.
36. *Ibid.,* p. 147.
37. *Ibid.,* p. 165.
38. *Vancouver Sun,* 28 June 1950.
39. Cunynghame, p. 152.
40. *Ibid.,* p. 153.
41. *Ibid.,* p. 154.

Chapter Twelve

1. Clarkson Investigation, Report, p. 50, Records of The Yukon Consolidated Gold Corporation Limited, vol. 70, Public Archives of Canada, Ottawa.
2. H. S. Bostock, *Yukon Territory,* pp. 633-635.
3. *Dawson News,* 29 April 1933.
4. *Ibid.,* 17 July 1934.
5. *Ibid.,* 28 November 1933.
6. *Ibid.,* 6 January, 20 February and 19 April 1934.
7. Bostock, *Yukon Territory,* pp. 633 and 645.
8. YCGC, letter to shareholders, 19 May 1934.
9. YCGC, report of annual general meeting, 22 June 1934.
10. YCGC, letter to shareholders, 24 December 1934.
11. H. S. Bostock, *The Mining Industry of Yukon,* 1937 edition, pp. 5-6. Andrew Baird, *Sixty Years on the Klondike,* pp. 68-72.
12. W.H.S. McFarland, "Operations of The Yukon Consolidated Gold Corporation," *Transactions of the Canadian Institute of Mining and Metallurgy* 42 (1939):537-549.
13. Bostock, *Mining Industry, 1935,* pp. 2-3.
14. YCGC, *Annual Report for 1935,* and Report of Meeting of 24 July 1936.
15. Bostock, *Mining Industry, 1936,* pp. 1-3. YCGC, *Annual Report for 1936.*
16. Bostock, *Mining Industry, 1937,* pp. 3-7. YCGC, *Annual Report for 1937.*
17. Bostock, *Mining Industry, 1938,* pp. 4-7.
18. *The Financial News,* London, 15 August 1939.
19. Bostock, *Mining Industry, 1939 and 1940,* pp. 4-12. YCGC, *Annual Report for 1939.*
20. W.H.S. McFarland, "Operations of The Yukon Consolidated Gold Corporation," *Transactions of the Canadian Institute of Mining and Metallurgy* 42 (1939):537-549.
21. Bostock, *Mining Industry, 1939 and 1940.* YCGC, President's Address, 30

May 1941. YCGC, *Annual Report for 1940.*

22. *Dawson News,* 31 July, 5 and 9 August 1941.

23. YCGC annual reports and letters to shareholders.

24. *Dawson News,* 20 June 1936. Mrs. A. H. Lewis, personal communication.

25. W. A. Hutchings, personal communication.

26. Jim Lotz, *Northern Realities,* p. 59.

27. D. C. Findlay, *The Mineral Industry of Yukon Territory and Southwestern District of Mackenzie, 1966,* pp. 69-72.

28. Financial Post Survey of Mines, 1973.

29. W.H.S. McFarland, "Operations of The Yukon Consolidated Gold Corporation, Canada," *Proceedings of the Symposium of Opencast Mining, Quarrying and Alluvial Mining, London, 16-19, November 1964,* Paper 9, The Institution of Mining and Metallurgy, p. 14.

30. YCGC, *Annual Report for 1966.*

Bibliography

Archives Material

Ottawa. Public Archives of Canada. Papers of Sir Clifford Sifton.

————.Records of The Yukon Consolidated Gold Corporation Limited.

Vancouver. Vancouver Archives. Papers of F. C. Wade.

Whitehorse. Yukon Archives. Papers of N. A. Watt.

Personal Communications

Bostock, H. S., an expert on the mining history of the Yukon Territory, now retired from the Geological Survey of Canada.

Bredenberg, C., a son of Edward Bredenberg; he knew Treadgold, Boyle and Patton in England.

Faulkner, (Miss) Victoria, a Dawsonite who was secretary to the Commissioner of the Yukon for many years.

Gloslie, Mr. and Mrs. C. Mr. Gloslie was associated with the dredging companies from 1913 until his retirement as Acting Manager in 1960.

Hoggan, J. W., a former dredgemaster.

Hutchings, W. A., a banker in the Yukon Territory in the 1930s and early 1940s.

Parker, Mrs. Bert, a secretary with Canadian Klondyke Mining Company from 1916 to 1918.

Sealey, Mr. and Mrs. J. F. Both were associated with the dredging companies for many years. Mrs. Sealey was secretary in the Dawson office.

Published Works

NOTE: Complete information on the following somewhat specialised periodicals may be found in the *Union List of Serials*, available in most large libraries:

Bulletin of the Canadian Institute of Mining and Metallurgy
  Mining and Scientific Press, San Francisco
The Mining Magazine, London
Transactions of the Canadian Institute of Mining and Metallurgy
Transactions of the Canadian Mining Institute
Transactions of the Institution of Mining and Metallurgy, London
Transactions of the Institution of Mining Engineers, London.

Adney, Edwin Tappan. *The Klondike Stampede of 1897-1898*. New York and London: Harper and Brothers, 1900.

Armstrong, Major Nevill A. D. *Yukon Yesterdays: Thirty Years of Adventure on the Klondyke*. London: John Long, 1936.

Baird, Andrew. *Sixty Years on the Klondike*. Vancouver: Gordon Black, 1965.

Beattie, Kim. *Brother, Here's a Man! The Saga of Klondike Boyle*. New York: Macmillan, 1940.

Becker, Ethel Anderson. *Klondike '98*. Portland: Binfords and Mort, 1949.

Begg, Alexander. "Notes on the Yukon Country." *The Scottish Geographical Magazine* 12(1896):553-559.

Berton, Laura Beatrice. *I Married the Klondike*. London: Hutchinson, 1955.

Berton, Pierre. *Klondike*. Revised Edition. Toronto: McClelland and Stewart, 1972.

Black, Mrs. George. *My Seventy Years*. As told to Elizabeth Bailey Price. London: Thomas Nelson and Sons, 1938.

Black, Martha Louise. *My Ninety Years*. Edited and updated by Flo Whyard. Anchorage: Alaska Northwest Publishing Company, 1976.

Blankman, Harold Gordon. *First Annual Report of the Receiver and Manager of the Canadian Klondyke Mining Co., Ltd., and the Canadian Klondyke Power Co., Ltd., for the term ending December 31, 1918*. Dawson: published privately, 1919.

Bostock, H. S. *The Mining Industry of Yukon*. Annual editions. Memoirs of the Geological Survey of Canada. Ottawa: King's Printer.
1934: Memoir 178, published 1935
1935: Memoir 193, published 1936
1936: Memoir 209, published 1937
1937: Memoir 218, published 1938
1938: Memoir 220, published 1939
1939 and 1940: Memoir 234, published 1941.

————.Ogilvie, Yukon Territory. Map 711A, Geological Survey of Canada. Ottawa: King's Printer, 1942. This is a geological map of the Ogilvie map area, prepared by Bostock.

————. *Yukon Territory: Selected Field Reports of the Geological Survey of Canada 1898-1933*. Memoir 284, Geological Survey of Canada. Ottawa: Queen's Printer, 1957.

Cadell, H. M. "The Klondike and Yukon Goldfield in 1913." *The Scottish Geographical Magazine* 30(1914):337-356.

Canada. *Sessional Papers.*
Number 87 (1899), "Report of the Ogilvie Commission of Inquiry." Ottawa: Queen's Printer.
Number 63 (1903), "Correspondence, Orders in Council or Applications Relating to or Concerning the Grant or Concessions to A.N.C. Treadgold, or to the Hydraulic Mining Syndicate. . . ." Ottawa: King's Printer.
Number 142 (1904), "Report of the Britton Commission on an Inquiry Into the Treadgold and Other Concessions in the Yukon Territory." Ottawa: King's Printer.

Canada, Department of Interior. *The Yukon Territory: Its History and Resources.* Ottawa: Government Printing Bureau. Editions of 1907, 1909, 1916 and 1926.

Canada, House of Commons. *Debates.* 1902 through 1904.

Cunynghame, Francis. *Lost Trail.* London: Faber and Faber, 1953.

Dafoe, John W. *Clifford Sifton in Relation to His Times.* Toronto: Macmillan, 1931.

Dawson, George M. "Report on an Exploration in the Yukon District, N.W.T. [Northwest Territories] and Adjacent Northern Portion of British Columbia, 1887." *Geological Survey of Canada Annual Report 1887-1888.* New Series. Vol. 3 (1889) part 1, report B. Reprinted as Report 629, Geological Survey of Canada. Ottawa: Queen's Printer, 1898.

Dawson News, 5 August 1899 through 25 March 1954.

Dawson Record, 16 July through 31 October 1903.

Downs, Art. *Paddlewheels on the Frontier: The Story of B.C.-Yukon Sternwheel Steamers.* Vol. 2. Surrey, B.C.: Foremost, 1971.

Edwards, W. W. "The Construction of the Klondike Pipe Line." *Proceedings of the American Society of Civil Engineers* 40(1914):1271-1283.

Ferry, Eudora Bundy. *Yukon Gold: Pioneering Days in the Canadian North.* New York: Exposition, 1971.

Findlay, D. C. *The Mineral Industry of Yukon Territory and Southwestern District of Mackenzie, 1966.* Paper 67-40, Geological Survey of Canada. Ottawa: Queen's Printer, 1967.

Green, L. H. *Geology of Nash Creek, Larsen Creek, and Dawson Map-Areas, Yukon Territory.* Memoir 364, Geological Survey of Canada. Ottawa: Information Canada, 1972.

Hall, H. H. "The Water Supply for the Klondike Hydraulic Mines." *Mining and Scientific Press* 111(1915):321-323.

Hamilton, Walter R. *The Yukon Story.* Vancouver: Mitchell, 1964.

Hoover, Herbert. *The Memoirs of Herbert Hoover, 1874-1920: Years of Adventure.* New York: Macmillan, 1951.

Hoyt, Edwin P., Jr. *The Guggenheims and the American Dream.* New York: Funk and Wagnalls, 1967.

Hurja, Emil Edward. "Mining in the Far North: Operations of Yukon Gold Company." *Mining and Scientific Press* 109(1914):568-569.

————."Mining in the Far North: Operations of Canadian-Klondyke Gold Mining Company, Ltd." *Mining and Scientific Press* 109(1914):769-771.

Innis, Harold A. "Settlement and the Mining Frontier." In *Canadian Frontiers of Settlement.* Edited by W. A. Mackintosh and W.L.G. Joerg, vol. 9, part 2. Toronto: Macmillan, 1936.

Klondike Nugget, 16 June 1898 through 14 July 1903.

Lawrence, Guy. *40 Years on the Yukon Telegraph.* Vancouver: Mitchell, 1965.

Lotz, Jim. *Northern Realities: The Future of Northern Development in Canada.* Toronto: New Press, 1970.

Lotz, Jim and Innes-Taylor, Alan. "The Yukon Ditch." *Canadian Geographical Journal* 74(1967):124-131.

Lund, John. "Cold Water Thawing of Frozen Placer Gravel." *Bulletin of the Canadian Institute of Mining and Metallurgy* 44(1951):273-277.

Lung, Edward B. *Black Sand and Gold.* As told to Ella Lung Martinsen. New York: Vantage, 1956.

Lynch, Jeremiah. *Three Years in the Klondike.* London: Edward Arnold, 1904.

Martinsen, Ella Lung. See Lung, Edward.

Mathews, Richard. *The Yukon.* New York: Holt, Rinehart and Winston, 1968.

McCarthy, E. E. "Stripping Frozen Gravel." *The Mining Magazine* 10(1914):289-295.

McConnell, R. G. "Report on an Exploration in the Yukon and Mackenzie Basins 1887-1888." *Geological Survey of Canada Annual Report 1888-1889.* New Series. Vol. 4(1890) report D. Reprinted in part in *Report 629,* Geological Survey of Canada. Ottawa: Queen's Printer, 1898.

———.*Preliminary Report on the Klondike Gold Fields, Yukon District, Canada.* Report 687, Geological Survey of Canada. Ottawa: Queen's Printer, 1900.

———."Report on the Klondike Gold Fields." *Geological Survey of Canada Annual Report.* Vol. 14(1901) part B. Ottawa: King's Printer, 1905. Also in Bostock, 1957, pp. 64-113.

———.*Report on Gold Values in the Klondike High Level Gravels.* Report 979, Geological Survey of Canada. Ottawa: King's Printer, 1907. Also in Bostock, 1957, pp. 217-238.

McConnell, R. G., and Tyrrell, J. B. "Preliminary Note on the Gold Deposits and Gold Mining in the Klondike Region." *Geological Survey of Canada Annual Report.* Vol. 11(1898) part A. Ottawa: Queen's Printer, 1901. Also in Bostock, 1957, pp. 17-23.

McFarland, W.H.S. "Operations of The Yukon Consolidated Gold Corporation." *Transactions of the Canadian Institute of Mining and Metallurgy* 42(1939):537-549.

———."Operations of The Yukon Consolidated Gold Corporation, Canada." *Proceedings of the Symposium on Opencast Mining, Quarrying and Alluvial Mining, London, 16-19 November 1964.* Paper 9. The Institution of Mining and Metallurgy.

McQuesten, Leroy N. *Recollections of Leroy N. McQuesten of Life in the Yukon, 1871-1885.* Dawson: Yukon Order of Pioneers, 1952.

Morgan, Murray. *One Man's Gold Rush: A Klondike Album.* Seattle: University of Washington Press, 1967.

Morrison, David R. *The Politics of the Yukon Territory, 1898-1909.* Toronto: University of Toronto Press, 1968.

Ogilvie, William. *The Klondike Official Guide.* Toronto: Hunter Rose, 1898.

———.*Early Days on the Yukon and the Story of its Gold Finds.* London: John Lane, 1913.

Payne, Henry M. "The Development and Problem of the Yukon." *Transactions of the Canadian Mining Institute* 16(1913):228-240.

———."Further Notes on Yukon Mining Problems." *Transactions of the Canadian Mining Institute* 20(1917):188-206.

Perry, O. B. "Development of Dredging in the Yukon Territory." *Transactions of the Canadian Mining Institute* 18(1915):26-44.

Rickard, T. A. "Dredging in the Yukon." *Mining and Scientific Press* 97(1908):290-293, 354-357.

————."Alaska and the Yukon." *Mining and Scientific Press* 98(1909):15-22.

————."The Yukon Ditch." *Mining and Scientific Press* 98(1909):117-120, 148-152.

————."Mechanical Elevator." *Mining and Scientific Press* 98(1909):415-418.

————.*Through the Yukon and Alaska*. San Francisco: Mining and Scientific Press, 1909.

Rodney, William. *Joe Boyle: King of the Klondike*. Toronto: McGraw-Hill Ryerson, 1974.

Schwatka, Frederick. *A Summer in Alaska*. St. Louis: J. W. Henry, 1894.

Steele, Colonel S. B. *Forty Years in Canada*. Toronto: McClelland, Goodchild and Stewart, 1915.

Treadgold, A.N.C. *Report on the Goldfields of the Klondike*. Toronto: George N. Morang, 1899.

Troop, G.R.F. "Gold Dredging in the Klondike." In *Mining in Canada*. 6th Commonwealth Mining and Metallurgical Congress, Canada, 1957. Published on behalf of the Congress; available in some technical libraries.

Tyrrell, J. B. "Dalton Trail, from Haines, Alaska, to Carmacks, on Lewes River, and Exploration of Nisling River." *Geological Survey of Canada Annual Report*. Vol. 11(1898) part A. Ottawa: Queen's Printer, 1901. Also in Bostock, 1957, pp. 3-11.

————."The Gold-bearing Alluvial Deposits of the Klondike District." *Transactions of the Institution of Mining and Metallurgy* 8(1899-1900):217-229.

————."Development of Placer Gold-mining in the Klondike District, Canada." *Transactions of the Institution of Mining Engineers* 31(1905-1906):556-574.

————."The Yukon Territory." In *Canada and Its Provinces*. Edited by A. Short and A. C. Doughty, vol. 22, pp. 585-636. Toronto: Publishers' Association of Canada, 1914.

Weeks, Walter S. "Thawing Frozen Gravel with Cold Water." *Mining and Scientific Press* 120(1920):367-370.

Whitehorse Star, 1901-1916.

Winslow, Kathryn. *Big Pan-Out*. New York: W. W. Norton, 1951.

Wright, Allen A. *Prelude to Bonanza*. Sidney, B. C.: Gray's Publishing, 1976.

Yukon Consolidated Gold Corporation Limited, The. *Annual Reports* and letters to shareholders, 1932 to 1966. The author worked from a set of these letters and reports that was made available to him by a company official. A similar set may be included in the records of the YCGC at Public Archives of Canada, Ottawa, but there is no mention of it in the incomplete listing of the collection that the author has.

Yukon Gold Company. *Annual Reports.* 1907 to 1925. The author got a few of these from the company, some were printed in full in the *Dawson News,* and a few are in the Yukon Archives. There is probably not a full set anywhere.

Yukon Sun, 11 June 1898 to 31 March 1904. Some gaps and name changes; the name *Yukon Midnight Sun* was dropped early in 1899.

Yukon World, 29 February 1904 to 7 August 1909.

Zaslow, Morris. *The Opening of the Canadian North, 1870-1914.* Toronto: McClelland and Stewart, 1971.

Acknowledgments

The Dawson newspapers have given me the framework of my book, and I would like to acknowledge the part played by Dawsonites (including Fred Caley, Elmer Gaundroue and others who are unknown) in preserving copies of this unique record in the midst of their decaying town. I would like also to acknowledge the part played later by Public Archives of Canada and other institutions in microfilming the material, making it available for library use.

Much of my work was done in the Library of the University of British Columbia, and I consider myself a beneficiary of the policy that makes this excellent facility available to the public. Members of the staffs of both the Public Archives of Canada, Ottawa, and the Yukon Archives, Whitehorse, have taken a personal interest in the project and have always been willing to search for that additional piece of information needed to fill a gap in the story. National Historic Sites, a federal agency involved in preservation of a record of Dawson and the Klondike gold rush, allowed me to examine their photographic collection at Dawson. Mr. N. B. Ivory, President of The Yukon Consolidated Gold Corporation Limited, kindly permitted me to make use of that company's Klondike records, now in the Public Archives of Canada. The volume of these records is awesome (it includes material from predecessor companies), and, in the case of the legal actions, I have been forced to condense them to little more than the effect of the final judgment. In doing so, I have arbitrarily left out many names and ignored other legal actions that are of secondary importance to the story as a whole. Mr. Ivory also made available to me a complete set of annual reports and letters to shareholders from the period 10 February 1932 through 1966. Mr. O. L. Gray, President of Pacific Tin Consolidated Corporation, successor to Yukon Gold Company, provided material from the original company's reports.

All of those interviewed have taken a great interest in the project but, in particular, I appreciate the help of W. A. Hutchings. His sense of history and his close ties with the Vancouver Yukoners' Association, of which he is currently president, have proved invaluable; time and time again, he has known whom to contact for additional information on a specific incident.

Others also have provided assistance. R. J. Cathro brought to my attention a number of references on mining in the Klondike. C. W. Craig and Mrs. Bert Parker provided photographs. B. W. Hester, on the staff of YCGC from 1960 to 1963, has an ear for anecdotes of earlier days, and he was the first to tell me many of them. G. B. Leech selected photographs from the Geological Survey of Canada collection. William Rodney supplied material from his book on Joe Boyle prior to its publication. Mrs. W. W. Rystogi provided a portrait of her father, Warren H. S. McFarland. W. A. Hutchings, C. W. Craig, Mr. and Mrs. C. Gloslie, B. W. Hester, J. W. Hoggan and Mr. and Mrs. J. F. Sealey read the manuscript. Finally, there is the help and encouragement given by my wife in a project that at times seemed lost in a maze of poorly-connected details.

Permission to quote excerpts from Francis Cunynghame's *Lost Trail,* published by Faber and Faber, and Andrew Baird's *Sixty Years on the Klondike,* published by Western Miner Press, is gratefully acknowledged.

Index

A

Acklen Ditch, 91, 96, 100
Acklen Farm, 90, 91, 93
Acklen, Joseph A. and Ellen, 90, 91, 93
Agnew, J. A., 279
Anderson Concession. See Concessions, hydraulic
Anderson, Robert, 17-19, 79, 138
Austin, E. A., manager of YCGC, formerly engineer with Yukon Gold, 274, 275
Australia-Sulphur Ditch, 279

B

Baird, Andrew, 210, 225, 227, 235, 240, 241, **242**, 243-245, 252, 260, 262, 263
Barwell, C. S. W., 43, 151
Barwick, Walter, 27-30
Bear Creek, 36, 75, 133, 142, 150, 158, 197, 307
Bear Creek camp and shops, 148, 150, 199, 211, 219, 223, 224, 235, 238, 240, 248, 252, 253, 290
Beatty, A. Chester, 109, 170, 172, 180, 229, 241, 270, 319
Belcourt, Senator N. A., 256, 259, 260
Bell, B. T. A., 71, 79, 86
Big Creek Mining Company Limited, The, 174, 240
Black, George, 41, 51, 52, 176, 188, 189, 190, **192, 193**, 200, 201, 213
Black Hills Creek, 279
Black, Mrs. George (Martha Louise), 195
Blankman, H. G., 218, 221-227
Boardman, Harry, 169
Bonanza Basin Gold Dredging Company, 170, 303
Bonanza Creek, 2, 4, 7, 8, 11, 27, 28, 30, 34, 36, 44, 75, 77, 78, 89, 93, 95, 98, 99, 107, 109, 121, 130, 133, 271, 284, 304-307
  dam on, 96, 103, 107
Boyle, Charles, Jr. "Charlie," 191, 198, 203
Boyle Concession. See Concessions, hydraulic
Boyle Concessions, 188, 228
Boyle, Joseph Whiteside "Joe," xi, 78, 82, 131, 137-139, **140**, 141-148, 150-154, 158, 165, 172-174, 176-180, 187-190, **191**, 194-203, 207-213, 216, **217**, 219, 223, 225-227, 295
Boyle, Joseph Whiteside, Jr., "Joe

Jr.," 194, 216, **218**, 219, 224, 226
Boyle Yukon Detachment, 207-210, **214, 215**
Bredenberg, Edward, 128, **168**, 219, 239, 257, 269, 270, 271
Bredenberg, Gus, 168, 172, 187
Brener, Otto, 148, 150, 151
Brenner, Howard, 189, 227
Britton Commission of Inquiry, 71, 74-79, **80-81**, 82, 86, 87, 137, 138
Britton, Mr. Justice B. M., 71, 79, 80, 86
Brown, Stuart, 264, 265
Brown, Waterfront, 83
Burrall and Baird, 231-235, 237, 240, 243, 251, 303
Burrall, F. P., 183, 221, 225, 227-231, 234

C

Cableway, 245, 246, **247**
Calder Mining Company, 174, 240
Caley, Fred, 331
Canadian Klondyke Mining Company, 98, 137, 148, 150-154, 167, 172, 173, 178, 179, 183-185, 187-189, 196-198, 202, 207, 211, 212, 216, 218, 219, 221-227, 231, 295
  dredge, Canadian Number 1: 148, **149**, 154, 158, 187, 230, 231, **232, 233**, 304
  dredge, Canadian Number 2: **155-157**, 158, **159-163**, 187, **206**, 208, **209**, 210, 231, 277, 304
  dredge, Canadian Number 3: **189**, 194, 211, 222, 239, 252, 277, **292, 293**, 304
  dredge, Canadian Number 4: **189**, 195, 198, **204-206**, 235, 277, 304
Canadian Klondyke Power Company, 174, 179, 198, 212, 231
Carmack, George, 1, 2
Cassiar Bar, 11
Cathro, R. J., 332
Chrysler, F. H., 260, 265
Clark, L. C., 267
Clarke, Joseph, 57, 58, 66
Clarkson, G. T., investigation by, 256, 259
Coal Creek thermal plant, 158, 187, 191, 194, 200, 201, 207. See also Northern Light, Power and Coal Company
Coffey, George, 79, **134**, 135

235, 245, 246, **247**, **281**, 291
underground, **4**, 10, **12**, **14**
Moore, Captain William, 4
Moosehide Creek, water from, 91, 96, 100
Moquin, Vic, 240, 262

N

N. C. Co. (Northern Commercial Company), 50, 83, 211, 250-252
New Consolidated Gold Fields Limited. See Gold Fields group of companies
New North West Corporation, 232-235, 237, 273, 278
    dredges, 239, 241-242, 277, 278, 305
    See also North West Corporation
Newhouse, Oscar, 201
Newspapers, 7. See also *Dawson News, Dawson Record, Klondike Nugget, Yukon Sun, Yukon World*
North American Transportation and Trading Company, 26
North Fork hydroelectric power plant, 168-170, **171**, 202, 276, 278
North Fork Power Company, 265, note 27, Chapter 11
North West Corporation, 178-185, 221, 228-232, 273, 304
    dredges, 230-231, 277, 278, 305
    See also New North West Corporation
North-West Mounted Police, 4, 5
Northern Light, Power and Coal Company, 191, 198, 200, 201, 203, 207, 212, 241
Northwest Hydraulic Mining Company, 99, 109
Nugget. See Klondike Nugget

O

Ogilvie, William, 4, 7, 8, 24, 45, 77, 142
Oliver, Frank, Minister of Interior 1905-1911, 87, 93
Orr, Ewing, M. H., 29, 30, 70, 84-86, 172

P

Pacific Tin Consolidated Corporation, successor to Yukon Gold Company, 135
Parker, Mrs. Bert, 332

Patton, J. T. "Tom," 176, 231, 256, 257, 259-261, 264, 266, 279
Pattullo, Dufferin, 41
Perry, O. B., 109, 115, 165
Portland, steamship, 5
Princess Sophia, sinking of, 224, 225
Pringle, Rev. John, 65
Prohibition and People's Prohibition Movement, 212, 256, 257

Q, R

Quartz Creek, 170, 174, 235, 245, 246, 249, 278, 306
Rabbit (Bonanza) Creek, 2, 71
Raney, Hon. Mr. Justice W. E., 259
Rendell, William J. "Billy," 169, 240, 245, 250-252
Riddell, Hon. Mr. Justice R. M., 151-153
Risdon Iron Works, San Francisco, 11, 303
Rock Creek, water from, 75, 82, 91, 144
Rodney, William, 332
Ross, James H., **34**, **35**, 40, 42, 43, 50-52, 54, 57, 58, 64-66, 69, 71
Rost, Mr. and Mrs. Peter, 174-176
Rothschild, Fred, 150, 152
Rothschild, Sigmund R., 146, 150
Rystogi, Mrs. W. W., 332

S

Schmidt, Mrs. Lizzie, 100
Sealey, Mr. and Mrs. J. F., 332
Senkler, Edmund C., Gold Commissioner 1898-1907, 34-37, 44, 45, 63, 77
Shaw, Miss Flora, 23
Sifton, Clifford, Minister of the Interior 1896-1905, 7, 15, 17, 21, 24-28, 30, 36, 37, 43-46, 52, 55, **56**, 64, 69, 87, 144, 146, 147
Sixtymile gold field, 1, 2
Skookum Jim, 3
Slavin, Frank P., 44, 138, 139, 143, 145
Smart, James, Deputy Minister of the Interior, 23, 54, 55, 145
Smith, W. O., 196
South Fork Ditch, 189, 249, 251, 253, 278, note 8, Chapter 8
Stewart River, gold on, 2
Sugrue, J. F. "Barney," 43, 46, 50-53
Sulphur Creek, 170, 256, 278, 279, 306
Sulphur Mining Company, 240